British soldiers, patrolling in southern Burma in 1945, file across a dike as a Burmese farmer tills a flooded rice paddy with his oxen. Tropical heat, jungles, rivers and rugged mountains, combined with torrential rains and hordes of insects, made the China-Burma-India Theater one of World War II's most forbidding arenas.

CHINA-BURMA-INDIA

WORLD WAR II · TIME-LIFE BOOKS · ALEXANDRIA, VIRGINIA

BY DON MOSER
AND THE EDITORS OF TIME-LIFE BOOKS

CHINA-BURMA-INDIA

Time-Life Books Inc.
is a wholly owned subsidiary of
TIME INCORPORATED

Founder: Henry R. Luce 1898-1967

Editor-in-Chief: Hedley Donovan
Chairman of the Board: Andrew Heiskell
President: James R. Shepley
Vice Chairman: Roy E. Larsen
Corporate Editors: Ralph Graves, Henry Anatole Grunwald

TIME-LIFE BOOKS INC.

Managing Editor: Jerry Korn
Executive Editor: David Maness
Assistant Managing Editors: Dale M. Brown,
Martin Mann, John Paul Porter (acting)
Art Director: Tom Suzuki
Chief of Research: David L. Harrison
Director of Photography: Robert G. Mason
Planning Director: Philip W. Payne (acting)
Senior Text Editor: Diana Hirsh
Assistant Art Director: Arnold C. Holeywell
Assistant Chief of Research: Carolyn L. Sackett

Chairman: Joan D. Manley
President: John D. McSweeney
Executive Vice Presidents: Carl G. Jaeger (U.S. and
Canada), David J. Walsh (International)
Vice President and Secretary: Paul R. Stewart
Treasurer and General Manager: John Steven Maxwell
Business Manager: Peter G. Barnes
Sales Director: John L. Canova
Public Relations Director: Nicholas Benton
Personnel Director: Beatrice T. Dobie
Production Director: Herbert Sorkin
Consumer Affairs Director: Carol Flaumenhaft

WORLD WAR II

Editorial Staff for China-Burma-India
Editor: William K. Goolrick
Picture Editor/Designer: Raymond Ripper
Text Editor: Sterling Seagrave
Staff Writers: Dalton Delan, Richard W. Flanagan,
Tyler Mathisen
Chief Researcher: Frances G. Youssef
Researchers: Michael Blumenthal,
Marion F. Briggs, Josephine Burke,
Oobie Gleysteen, Catherine Gregory,
Karen L. Michell, Dolores Morrissy
Art Assistant: Daniel J. McSweeney
Editorial Assistant: Connie Strawbridge

Editorial Production
Production Editor: Douglas B. Graham
Operations Manager: Gennaro C. Esposito
Assistant Production Editor: Feliciano Madrid
Quality Control: Robert L. Young (director),
James J. Cox (assistant), Michael G. Wight (associate)
Art Coordinator: Anne B. Landry
Copy Staff: Susan B. Galloway (chief), Victoria Lee,
Barbara F. Quarmby, Florence Keith, Celia Beattie
Picture Department: Dolores A. Littles,
Alvin L. Ferrell

Correspondents: Elisabeth Kraemer (Bonn);
Margot Hapgood, Dorothy Bacon (London);
Susan Jonas, Lucy T. Voulgaris (New York);
Maria Vincenza Aloisi, Josephine du Brusle (Paris);
Ann Natanson (Rome). Valuable assistance was
also provided by: Judy Aspinall (London), Carolyn
T. Chubet, Miriam Hsia (New York), Lawrence
Chang (Taipei), Sungyung Chang (Tokyo).

The Author: DON MOSER is a journalist and a former assistant managing editor of LIFE. He also served as LIFE's bureau chief in the Far East in the late 1960s. In addition to writing articles for LIFE, he has written for National Geographic, Smithsonian and Audubon. The author of two volumes in TIME-LIFE BOOKS' The American Wilderness series, The Snake River Country and Central American Jungles, Moser has written a book on the Olympic National Park, The Peninsula, and a novel, A Heart to the Hawks. He is now on the staff of Smithsonian.

The Consultants: COL. JOHN R. ELTING, USA (Ret.), is a military historian, author of The Battle of Bunker's Hill, A Military History and Atlas of the Napoleonic Wars. He edited Military Uniforms in North America: The Revolutionary Era and was associate editor of The West Point Atlas of American Wars.

LIEUT. GENERAL WILLIAM R. PEERS, USA (Ret.), commanded the Office of Strategic Services (OSS) Detachment 101 in northern Burma under General Stilwell between April 1942 and November 1943, and later directed OSS operations south of the Yangtze River in China. He co-authored, with Dean Brelis, Behind the Burma Road. During the Vietnam War, he commanded the 4th Infantry Division and First Field Force Vietnam. In 1969 he conducted the U.S. Army inquiry into the My Lai incident.

O. EDMUND CLUBB is a retired U.S. Foreign Service Officer. After the attack on Pearl Harbor he was interned by the Japanese for eight months in Hanoi, French Indochina; following his release in an exchange with several diplomatic personnel, he volunteered to be reassigned to Asia and was sent to China, where he spent two years. He is the author of 20th Century China; China and Russia: The "Great Game"; Communism in China—As Reported from Hankow in 1932 and The Witness and I.

CONTENTS

A TORMENT OF RUMORS

Smoke from Japanese fire bombs fills the sky over Chungking, the Chinese Nationalists' wartime capital, after an attack by Japanese planes on June 15, 1941.

A DEFENSELESS CITY UNIFIED BY FIRE

The U.S. gunboat Tutuila sits at anchor across from Chungking in 1941. On the day this picture was taken five bombs narrowly missed the vessel.

In the early evening of May 4, 1939, Japanese bombers swooped out of the north in wing-to-wing formation over Chungking. Moments later, the city shook with the fury of an all-out air attack, the first big raid on the capital since the Sino-Japanese War began in 1937. Antiquated antiaircraft guns peppered the sky in vain reply. Through the smoke-darkened streets came the sounds of crackling, popping wood and the cries of trapped civilians, as bamboo shacks flared like tinderboxes. People in narrow back alleys, unable to escape, were roasted to death. Mothers screamed for their children, and old men sat on the curbs and rocked back and forth, numb with shock. All told, 5,000 were killed and thousands more injured in the fire storm unleashed by the bombers. Only the embassy area across the Yangtze River from the old city got by without major damage.

For two years, the Japanese had been pursuing Chiang Kai-shek's Nationalist government, which fled first from Nanking and then from Hankow. When, in the autumn of 1938, Chiang moved his government 500 miles up the Yangtze River to Chungking, he felt he had found a perfect haven from the attackers. The intervening mountain ranges, deep river gorges and long distance seemed to provide a safe degree of protection.

Through the winter, the city lay safe under a canopy of fog and rain as government workers and students streamed into the newly designated capital. Whole factories arrived piecemeal from the east. In six months the city's population swelled to nearly one million—five times its original size of 200,000. Then in May the weather cleared and the bombers struck. The Japanese began pummeling Chungking with what LIFE photographer Carl Mydans, who took many of the pictures on these pages, described as "the worst bombing a city has ever received." Over the next three years, 3,000 tons of bombs fell on Chungking—an area the size of Manhattan island—destroying almost a third of the houses and severely damaging another third. But as the raids intensified, they had an unintended effect. They strengthened the resolve of the city's people to resist the Japanese.

The German Ambassador displays a patched flag at his Chungking embassy to warn off Japanese bombers in the days before Germany and Japan were allies.

In the dark, cramped confines of a sandstone shelter—here illuminated by flashbulb—Chungking residents huddle together while Japanese bomb the city.

After a mass panic, bodies were dumped outside the city's largest shelter.

BENEATH CHUNGKING, SHELTER FROM THE STORM

As the bombing went on, Chungking developed its own civil defense program utilizing shelters blasted out of the sandstone underlying the city. To alert the populace to impending attack, Chinese spies would relay by telephone and radio word of the departure of the enemy aircraft from Hankow, and in the capital red paper lanterns would be run up poles to signal a raid. People would then retreat into one of the more than 1,000 shelters.

The crush for space resulted in tragedy on June 5, 1941. Following a heavy raid, a crowd was starting to leave Chungking's largest shelter, a mile-and-a-half-long tunnel under the heart of the city, when the signal for another raid was suddenly given. Guards slammed the gates shut, and in the ensuing panic 4,000 people were suffocated or trampled to death.

A brigade of fire fighters, fortunate to have one working hose, makes a futile attempt to contain a blaze in a bombed building.

PICKING UP THE PIECES IN A WASTELAND

The Japanese could scarcely have selected a more combustible target for their fire bombs than the old part of Chungking. Here half a million people lived in bamboo shacks huddled back to back on crowded slopes leading down to the river. There was virtually no fire-fighting equipment, and what there was could not get through many of the narrow lanes or up the steep steps of the old town. Complicating matters still more, bombs very often destroyed the city's water mains, and water had to be hauled by bucket from the river.

Chungking's inhabitants were completely unprepared for the first attacks. Many of those who had fled to the capital as refugees were homeless once again and were forced to move in with relatives or camp on fields outside the city. Some families moved back into their bombed-out homes so they could keep squatters out.

A visitor to Chungking who had known the city before the war would hardly have recognized it after the bombing raids began. "Rubble is everywhere," noted British writer Robert Payne in 1941, "and the shop fronts are little more than façades." Yet here and there amid the devastation buildings were going up. In the winter, when the weather kept the Japanese planes at bay, workers cleared and widened streets, and a new Chungking began taking shape.

Several weeks after Chungking was devastated by Japanese fire bombing in 1940, neatly swept streets provide pathways through the ruins for civilian traffic.

13

Rescue workers face the gruesome task of identifying a man mutilated when a bomb hit his dugout.

DEATH'S DAILY TOLL OF THE INNOCENT

The Japanese tried to wear down the inhabitants of Chungking by repeated "fatigue" bombings. Crammed into shelters without lights or water, people were subjected to terrible stress. Many who worked down by the river on ferries and sampans had to hurl themselves into riverbank dugouts when the bombers struck.

But as the war went on, Chungking's defense system was improved and the impact of the bombings reduced. Sirens were installed to beef up the paper-lantern air-raid warning system. Residents were assigned to shelters and issued entry passes.

In time, the number of casualties fell to around 50 people per raid. The population once again began to increase. For every individual who had been killed during the three years of bombing, two new ones were born.

Survivors look on as bodies are piled up in the riverfront area on June 15, 1941. The casualties occurred near the U.S. Embassy, which was damaged in the attack.

1

Early in May 1942, a band of men and women slogged through the shin-deep water of a small stream in western Burma. On both sides of the stream rose walls of dense jungle, and monkeys chattered at the human procession as it passed. At the head of the column marched a slight, skinny man with steel-rimmed spectacles and short-clipped gray hair. He was a lieutenant general in the United States Army, but one could not have told that by looking at him, for he wore no badges of rank and he carried a carbine slung over his shoulder; the World War I campaign hat on his head and the canvas puttees laced around his calves gave him the appearance of a holdover from another era.

A three-star general usually commands an army corps—tens of thousands of men with all their weapons and supporting tanks and artillery. But the column following this general consisted of a hundred or so souls, carrying their belongings on their backs and armed only with a few rifles, carbines and Tommy guns. There were about 20 American officers and enlisted men, many of them beginning to sag from heat exhaustion; some British soldiers, hollow-eyed and worn from months of constant combat in malarial jungles; a handful of Chinese soldiers; some Indian and Anglo-Indian civilians; an American correspondent; a couple of American missionaries; a contingent of British Quakers, conscientious objectors who had come to Burma as a Friends Ambulance Unit; and a group of young nurses from the hill tribes of Burma, tiny butterflies of girls who wore simple white blouses and bright-colored sarongs and had their hair entwined with blossoms of jungle jasmine. As they marched along, the nurses sang aloud, filling the jungle with the strains of "Onward Christian Soldiers."

After a while an exhausted colonel of engineers fell out of line, and a medical officer moved to the head of the column to confront the general. The men were in no condition to march at such a pace in the heat of the day, said the doctor; the colonel could not go on.

The general did not even pause or slow his pace. "He'll have to go on," he snapped. "This column will not stop for anything."

"Vinegar Joe" Stilwell, one of World War II's most determined and acerbic commanders, was leading a desperate retreat from Burma. With the Japanese in hot pursuit, he drove his group at a killing pace, determined to get all of

"A HELL OF A BEATING"

them out safely to India. But even in the worst moments of the grueling withdrawal, he was already considering how to fight his way back.

When Joseph Warren Stilwell was sent to the China-Burma-India Theater in February 1942, the war in Asia had been going on for a long, long time. Japan had annexed Manchuria in 1931 and in 1937 had begun a systematic gobbling up of China's major cities—Peking, Tientsin, Shanghai, Nanking and Hankow—until most of the country was effectively cut off from the outer world. To maintain its imports of strategic goods and relief materials, China had built a 681-mile road to Burma in 1937-1938. Virtually all supplies to China had to make their way by ship to the Burmese port of Rangoon, and then by rail north to Mandalay and into the mountains to the railhead at Lashio, where the Burma Road ✓ began its hairpin course through high passes to the western Chinese city of Kunming.

After the Pearl Harbor attack, the Japanese turned from regional aggression to a sweeping armed conquest of all of Asia. With bewildering speed, Japanese forces overran the Philippines, occupied French Indochina and Thailand, fought their way down through the jungle-clad Malay Peninsula to overwhelm the British bastion of Singapore, and seized the oil-rich Dutch East Indies.

From neighboring Thailand, Japanese armies then thrust into the southern tail of British Burma at a score of points and smashed north, trapping the British defenders at the Sittang River, where they suffered heavy casualties.

Before the British could rally more than a few scattered units from India and the Middle East to defend the busy port of Rangoon, Japanese planes and troops pounced upon it. The battle of Rangoon began with an air raid on December 23, 1941, and raged for 75 days. Before it was over, the Allied defense of Asia turned from disorder to chaos.

In the grim days of December, the Americans, British, Dutch and Australians met in Washington and formed an alliance, under the acronym "ABDA Command," charged with the defense of the entire region except China. Britain's Prime Minister Winston Churchill wanted China to receive enough supplies to keep it in the War, but the prospect of a resurgent China worried him, and he did not want to equip and train Chinese troops that might later threaten British Far Eastern colonial possessions. Britain's primary goal was simply to secure India, the anchor of its Asian empire.

The American goal, on the other hand, was to keep the Chinese fighting and to help them build a more effective army, with the ultimate aim of using China as a springboard for an attack on the Japanese home islands. By December 29, Washington had its way and China was made a full-fledged Ally with Generalissimo Chiang Kai-shek named Supreme Allied Commander for China.

A former protégé of the great Nationalist revolutionary, Sun Yat-sen, Chiang was an ambitious soldier of peasant stock who had risen to the top of the Nationalist military establishment and assumed control of the Kuomintang, as the Nationalist Party was called. When the party's founder, Sun Yat-sen, died in 1925, Chiang came to power. This was a time of great upheaval for China: it was riven by internal divisions and the Chinese people were discouraged, humiliated and conditioned to survive by outlasting the enemy—whether foreigners, Manchu emperors or warlords.

The warlords had been a particular problem for Chiang; they had ruled the country for almost a decade when he took over. There were hundreds of them, and each one was backed by his own private army. Some warlords controlled a district or two, and others exercised their authority over two or three provinces. Chiang sent his armies sweeping through the interior, defeating many of the warlords and striking up alliances with others. In the meantime he was keeping a wary eye on another contender for power in China: the Communists.

The Communist Party in China had originated as a movement of intellectuals and students who were pressing for a social revolution after the Soviet Russian model. In 1923, the Communists made a marriage of convenience with Sun Yat-sen, and after his death, they joined Chiang in the campaign against the warlords. But a confrontation was inevitable, and in 1927 Chiang sought to deal his erstwhile partners a crippling blow. More than 300 key Communist organizers were massacred in Shanghai, and from then on Chiang concentrated on trying to annihilate the Communists. He did not succeed, but in 1934 he did force them into the famous Long March—a 6,000-mile, year-long fighting retreat to the mountain redoubts in wild Shensi Province. There they remained, 30,000 strong, a pervasive threat that

Chiang could keep bottled up only by keeping part of his army in the area.

Thus Chiang now exercised a tenuous control over most of China. As the war clouds gathered, he was consolidating his power—and setting a new example for the Chinese people. He applied strict Confucian discipline to his own daily life, rising early and spending an hour in silent contemplation, and he was impatient with laggards and the self-indulgent. It was this quality of rectitude and righteousness, as much as his military enterprise, that in the 1930s earned him widespread support in China. The same quality was to win him many admirers in the West—and to lead directly to his becoming an ally of the U.S. and Britain after the Japanese attack on Pearl Harbor.

At the end of December 1941, a China-Burma-India Theater was set up, with Allied headquarters split between the British command in Delhi and the Chinese in Chungking, the wartime capital of Chiang's Nationalist government.

The area encompassed by CBI, as the theater quickly came to be called, included all of China not in Japanese hands, ranging from the barren steppes of Mongolia in the northeast across the rice bowl of central China to the snow-swept mountain passes of Tibet. On the other side of the great Himalayas, it took in all of India from the tea plantations of Assam and Manipur to the dusty plains along the Ganges River and down to the steaming jungles of Ceylon. Lying like a keystone between India and China, Burma was cut off from both its giant neighbors by rugged mountain ranges, great rivers and dense jungles.

Stilwell was sent to Asia as the senior American military representative for CBI. In that capacity he was given several nearly impossible assignments, any one of which would have taxed the patience and ability of a paragon. He was to oversee the movement and allocation of Lend-Lease matériel to China. Little was now reaching troops in the field, as the meager supplies that arrived in CBI often disappeared in a web of corruption and official incompetence. He was also to serve as head of Chiang's Allied staff, although the Generalissimo in fact had no Allied staff of his own in Chungking and no Allied troops were earmarked to fight in China. Stilwell was to attempt to train Chinese troops and get them into battle, although the Generalissimo preferred to use the

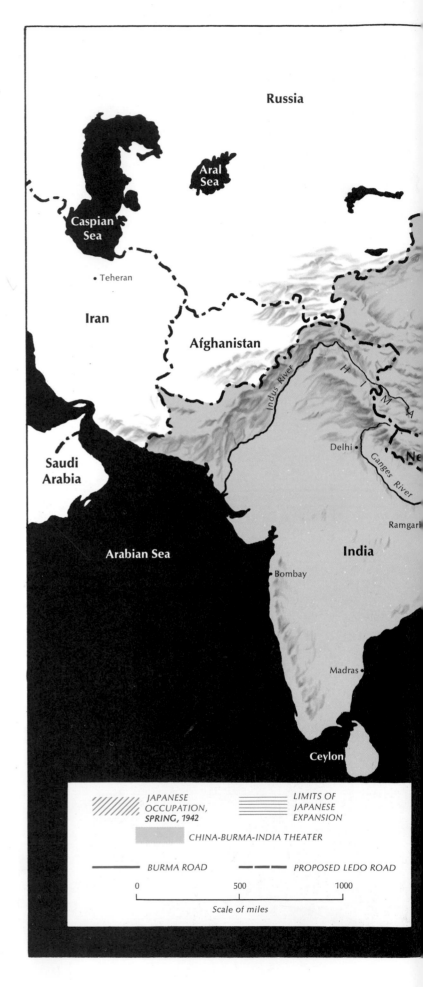

The China-Burma-India Theater, shown in pink, stretched more than 4,000 miles from Manchuria in China down through Burma and India to Ceylon. By late spring of 1942, the Allied withdrawal from Burma was under way; elsewhere the Japanese held territory designated by red diagonal lines. Subsequent conquests, including all of Burma, are indicated by horizontal lines. By spring 1945, the Allies forced the Japanese out of Burma, where some of the heaviest fighting of the theater had taken place, and opened a land route to China, the Ledo-Burma Road (red lines).

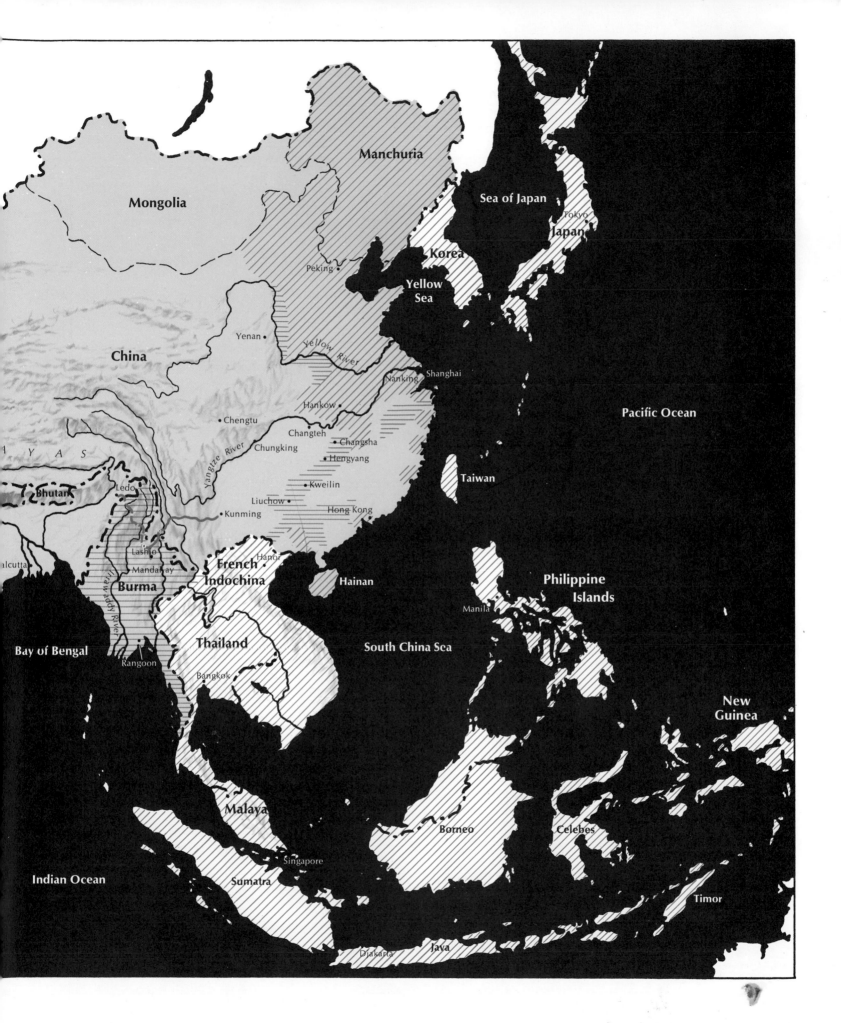

Mongolia

Manchuria

Sea of Japan

Tokyo

Japan

Korea

Peking

Yellow Sea

China

Yenan

Yellow River

Nanking

Shanghai

Hankow

Pacific Ocean

Chengtu

Changteh

Chungking

Changsha

Yangtze River

Hengyang

Taiwan

Kweilin

Liuchow

Kunming

Hong Kong

Bhutan

Ledo

Lashio

Hanoi

alcutta

Mandalay

French Indochina

Hainan

Philippine Islands

Burma

Manila

Bay of Bengal

Thailand

South China Sea

Rangoon

Bangkok

New Guinea

Malaya

Borneo

Celebes

Singapore

Indian Ocean

Sumatra

Timor

Djakarta

Java

sheer expanse of China as a natural defense and was reluctant to commit his forces to combat for fear of weakening his grip on the central government—a reasonable concern, under the circumstances. Nationalist China's intent, in fact, was to wait for its new allies to win the War, while hoarding Lend-Lease military equipment for a future resumption of the deadly long-running civil war with the Communists.

Stilwell was in many ways admirably suited for the CBI assignment. A tough, no-nonsense soldier, he was regarded as an outstanding tactician and one of the most effective trainers of troops in the U.S. Army. He had spent 13 years of his career in China, as a military attaché and in other capacities—indeed, he had traveled over much of the country—and he was so fluent in the language that he sometimes made his diary entries in Chinese rather than English. Moreover, he had enormous faith in the courage and endurance of the Chinese peasants, and he believed that with proper training and leadership they could be the equal of any soldiers in the world.

But in other equally important ways Stilwell could hardly have been more ill equipped for his new post. The job of chief of staff to Chiang was one that required infinite tact and patience, and Stilwell was singularly lacking in both qualities. In personal contact with Chiang, he was tolerant, but then he would return to his quarters and vent his spleen against the Generalissimo, and his outbursts would be duly conveyed, with embellishments, to Chiang by eavesdropping servants. On other occasions, he was so outspoken about the shortcomings of the Nationalist regime that he caused the Chinese leader an intolerable loss of face.

Ironically, Stilwell's strengths and weaknesses were perhaps most effectively assessed by Colonel Claire Lee Chennault, commander of the Flying Tigers, the colorful volunteer American flying group in China, and ultimately an archenemy of the doughty ground commander. "Stilwell's mission to China was certainly the toughest diplomatic job thrust upon a professional soldier during the war," Chennault wrote. "He was a rugged field soldier, a man of great personal bravery, who seemed most at ease and most capable when commanding troops under enemy fire." Chennault, however, added a fatal qualification: "All my experience with Stilwell led me to believe that he always thought of himself primarily as a simple field soldier and had little understanding of or patience with his primary duty as a military diplomat."

Even the U.S. Army Chief of Staff, General George C. Marshall, an old friend and admirer of Stilwell's, admitted that Vinegar Joe was "his own worst enemy," and that he poisoned his relations with the Chinese—and the British—by making little effort to conceal his contempt for what he considered their "do-nothing" attitudes.

Stilwell's unenviable task in CBI was complicated by the fact that Western strategists, preoccupied with the fighting in Europe and the Pacific, accorded CBI a low priority. Troops in CBI thought of their piece of the world conflict as a forgotten war. If it was not exactly forgotten, it was certainly remote; the supply line from America to India was more than 12,000 miles long, and freighters took two months to make the voyage. (Stilwell himself had to spend two weeks flying from Washington to the Far East by way of Brazil and Africa.)

To make matters worse, the American public had a wildly romantic, unrealistic conception of China and its military capabilities. Instinctively sympathetic to China to begin with, Americans had for years been subjected to a diet of Nationalist Chinese propaganda about magnificent but almost totally imaginary victories over the Japanese Army. Official visitors to China were mesmerized by the Generalissimo—known to Westerners simply as the Gimo. He was a man of considerable presence and his Wellesley-educated wife, Mei-ling Soong, had tremendous charm, which could melt the most coldhearted skeptic.

In America, Chiang's cause was championed by the so-called China Lobby, a term loosely applied to a broad

Equipped with saws for cutting their way through the dense north Burma jungles and wearing branches on their hats for camouflage, Japanese soldiers line up for inspection before setting out. In the China-Burma-India Theater the Japanese proved to be effective—though limited—jungle fighters. Britain's Lieut. General William J. Slim described them as being "ruthless and bold as ants while their designs went well," but added that when their plans went wrong "they fell into confusion, were slow to adjust themselves, and invariably clung to their original schemes."

spectrum of supporters of the Nationalist government. Included in their ranks were many Americans motivated by a sincere concern for China's plight, as well as paid Chinese agents and economic interests that stood to profit from continued American aid to the Nationalist regime. The China Lobby was helped by many Americans who were disturbed by the real prospect of a Communist take-over in China. President Franklin D. Roosevelt extolled the Chinese "who have withstood bombs and starvation and have whipped the invaders time and time again."

Stilwell thus had to cope with a widely held emotional feeling as well as the harsh military realities. Although Chiang Kai-shek had almost four million Nationalist troops organized into 346 divisions, they were poorly supplied, badly trained and often abysmally led. Indeed, many divisions were only nominally controlled by Chiang; they were commanded by generals who were autonomous warlords and whose loyalty to the central government was questionable. These commanders thought of their military divisions as personal property, useful for keeping the peasants in line and squeezing taxes out of them—35 years in advance in the case of Szechwan Province—but not to be risked against enemies as fierce and determined as the Japanese.

The warlords had good reason to be cautious in the use of their troops. Few of them were professional soldiers; the majority were either men who could find no other means of survival or conscripts who had been seized in pillaging raids through the countryside and were too frightened to escape. Pay was so low that even junior officers could not afford adequate food, and enlisted men existed on little more than rice. Most of the men had no boots, just straw sandals, and their bedding consisted of one blanket for every five soldiers. Dysentery, smallpox and typhus were rampant, and some units lost as much as 40 per cent of their strength in a year without ever entering combat. Since division commanders handled their own payrolls—calculated on the basis of a unit's strength on paper—they frequently kept their units drastically understrength so they could pocket the pay of the phantom soldiers.

So uncertain was the Generalissimo of the loyalty of many of his commanders—and of the ability of their soldiers to fight the Japanese—that he frequently withheld equipment and supplies from all but a few trusted subordinates. Thus most Chinese divisions had no artillery or motor transport, and mortars and machine guns were almost as scarce.

The Generalissimo flabbergasted Stilwell shortly after his arrival with a two-hour lecture on how Chinese forces should be used. According to Chiang, in a static situation it took three Chinese divisions to defend against one Japanese division, and if the Japanese were attacking, the ratio was increased to 5 to 1. Chiang ordered Stilwell to play it safe and let the Japanese take the initiative. Only if the Japanese stopped attacking and withdrew from captured territory, should the Chinese take the offensive. Chiang warned Stilwell not to concentrate his forces under any circumstances, since if the Chinese armies were massed they could be destroyed all at once. Stilwell was instead to use "defense in depth," meaning a column of divisions strung out one behind another, about 50 miles apart.

Chiang probably was right about his forces' ability to fight. But his views ran counter to U.S. military doctrine, which stressed aggressiveness and forbade piecemeal commitment of forces. As a tactical expert, Stilwell was particularly offended by Chiang's deliberate sacrifice of initiative. Chiang's lecture was the first of a long series of frustrating and disillusioning experiences for both Stilwell and the Generalissimo. "What a directive," wrote Stilwell in his diary. "What a mess." It was Stilwell's habit to bestow disparaging nicknames on people he did not respect, and he selected a special one for the Supreme Allied Commander in China: Peanut.

Stilwell had scarcely begun to face up to the nearly impossible task of creating an effective fighting force out of this military rabble when an even more impossible mission was thrust on him. When he arrived in Chungking on March 4, the long battle of Rangoon was nearing its end, and the British were preparing to abandon the city. The defense of Burma was collapsing, and British forces were soon fighting a desperate retreat northward that was rapidly assuming the proportions of a rout. Chinese troops were being rushed to Burma to help block the Japanese advance, and no sooner had Stilwell reported to the Generalissimo than Chiang confirmed that he was to command all the Chinese forces on the Burma front. It was an assignment that Stilwell, a fighting soldier, welcomed.

After conferring with Chiang, Stilwell flew into Burma to the British headquarters at Maymyo, a cool, pleasant hill town above Mandalay, bright with tidy British colonial gardens and streets lined with orange-flowered flame trees. There he met the man who had presided over the fall of Rangoon and who was to be his superior in the field, Lieut. General Sir Harold R. L. G. Alexander, the new British commander in Burma. Alexander, an impeccably moustachioed Guards officer and the third son of an earl, had served with great gallantry in World War I and had become a national hero in the early part of World War II by successfully commanding the British rear guard during the evacuation of Dunkirk. Nevertheless, Stilwell was not impressed. Nor did Alexander seem impressed with Stilwell. Wrote Stilwell in his diary: "Astonished to find ME—mere me, a goddam American—in command of Chinese troops. 'Extrawdinery!' Looked me over as if I had just crawled out from under a rock."

With the port of Rangoon now in Japanese hands, effectively cutting off Burma as well as China from the outside world, the crucial issue was whether a new defensive line could be established north of Rangoon with the help of Stilwell's Chinese troops; if not, the Allies would be pushed completely out of Burma into India.

The loss of Burma would pose grave consequences for the Allies. It would mean closing the Burma Road, which despite the fall of Rangoon was still serving as China's supply route. Not only would China be in danger of final defeat; India would be faced with the imminent threat of Japanese invasion from Burma. Anticipating this prospect, the Japanese had already trained an army of Indian dissidents—the Indian National Army—intended to gain support from Indians eager to cast off British rule, and give the Japanese invaders the image of liberators. In India at the time, Mohandas K. Gandhi and his Congress Party were already shaking the foundations of British power.

Burma, which thus became the key to the defense of the entire theater, was a remote outpost of the British Empire whose name conjured up in the minds of many abroad visions of a tropical paradise of gold-spired pagodas and almond-eyed maidens, elephants and teak forests. In fact it was a rich prize eagerly sought by Japan both as a means of severing the Allied link between India and China and be-

cause of its bountiful natural resources. Burma had abundant oil, tungsten, manganese and other minerals, and it was the world's largest exporter of rice.

When the Japanese invaded the country, the British were unprepared for the speed of their advance. The Japanese were aided by Burma's difficult terrain. Troops had to operate in trackless rain forests or parched, dusty plains, ford great rivers that became all but impassable during monsoon seasons, and claw their way up steep jungle ridges in temperatures that reached 115° F. in the shade, and in rainfall that ran to more than 200 inches per year. To these hazards was added a long list of tropical illnesses caused by parasites, bacteria and viruses.

The Japanese were jungle-wise, the British were not. The tough invaders pummeled the defenders again and again. The Japanese were well equipped with light machine guns, trench mortars and light armor, which they used to great effect. The British troops were roadbound, reluctant to strike off into the jungle and overly dependent on their motor transport. The Japanese exploited this weakness masterfully with a tactic they were developing to perfection— the roadblock. Small Japanese vanguard units bypassed British units by moving quickly through the jungle, then used felled trees or gutted vehicles to create a roadblock in the British rear, emplacing machine guns, mortars and mobile artillery around the roadblock to cut off the British as they attempted to retreat from Japanese frontal assaults. The Japanese first used roadblocks against small units; later they used them with devastating effect against regiments and finally against whole divisions.

The Japanese found it easy to infiltrate British lines and bypass British positions because so many of the lowland Burmese who inhabited the areas around Burma's major cities regarded them as liberators. British officers and colonial officials in Burma had long led the kind of comfortable life associated with the British raj. In the process they had stirred deep resentment among many Burmese. The Japanese, arriving with the slogan "Asia for the Asiatics," and the promise of ultimate independence, were welcomed into Burmese villages that British troops could safely enter only by virtue of superior arms.

The Burmese independence movement was supported by students and the Buddhist hierarchy, which had been a major political force under the old Burmese monarchy of precolonial days. Agents of the independence movement, who were often disguised as *pongyis*, the orange-robed Buddhist monks, carried out sabotage and espionage for the Japanese. Allied soldiers soon came to believe that all monks were spies, and priests were sometimes shot on sight. The movement was led by a hard core of paramilitary officers, called the Thirty Comrades, who had slipped out of Burma before the invasion for training in Japan, Taiwan and Hainan Island. The Comrades then had taken part in the invasion at the head of a ragtag Burma Independence Army. Unlike ordinary Burmese, the Comrades had no illusions about exchanging one form of colonialism for another. As soon as the British administration began to collapse, the Comrades began working against the Japanese as well.

Adding to the chaos were countless brigands and renegades. The Burmese had always been more prone to violence than most other Southeast Asians. Indeed, their rate of murder and assault was one of the highest in the world. The countryside was alive with bloodthirsty bandits known as dacoits, and now dacoits and all manner of village thugs and petty criminals joined in harrying the British; they even strung wire across the jungle roads in the hope of decapitating British jeep drivers.

All of Burma's lines of communication ran north and south along three great river valleys that separated the country's rugged mountain ridges. When General Alexander took command there he reasoned that if the Allies could dominate the valleys—the Chindwin on the northwest, the Irrawaddy in the center and the Sittang-Salween on the east—they might be able to hold onto at least a piece of northern Burma. Conferring with Stilwell, Alexander decided to form a defensive line about 150 miles north of Rangoon running west to east from Prome to the ancient capital of Toungoo, across the Pegu Yoma Mountains.

Stilwell and the Chinese would hold the east flank, centering on Toungoo, which dominated the Sittang valley and the Mandalay-Rangoon Railway. The British I Burma Corps, under Lieut. General William J. Slim, would hold the west flank at Prome, astride the broad Irrawaddy River, thereby blocking access as well to the Chindwin valley.

Slim, who had just arrived in the theater from the Middle East, was a good man in a tight spot. A plain-spoken soldier who had spent most of his career in the Indian Army, he was so free of affectation that even Stilwell admired him. His corps consisted of two divisions, the 17th Indian (Black Cat) Division and the 1st Burma Division, which included only four battalions of British troops.

The bulk of the 17th Indian Division consisted of Gurkhas, as well as Sikhs, Rajputs and other peoples of India. All first-rate soldiers, they were at a disadvantage in Burma because they had been trained for highly mobile mechanized desert warfare in North Africa and the Middle East. The bulk of the 1st Burma Division, on the other hand, numbered three brigades consisting largely of lowland Burmese and representatives of the tough, independent hill tribes of Burma—Karens, Kachins and Chins. These individualistic mountaineers had great endurance and courage and were well disposed toward their British officers. This was due in part to the realization that only so long as the British stayed in Burma would the hill tribes continue to be free of the age-old domination of the lowland Burmese. As for the lowlanders, as the Japanese seized more and more of their hometowns and villages, more and more of these Burmese soldiers slipped away to look after the safety of their families and rescue what they could of their own lives.

No sooner had the new defensive line been established and as many troops as possible pulled into position than Slim realized its many fundamental weaknesses. Rather than let the attacking Japanese test the line at whim, Slim and Stilwell—both very aggressive commanders—determined to mount a counteroffensive back toward Rangoon. But

Wearing German helmets, Chinese artillerymen line up beside a German-made antiaircraft gun in 1941. Germany's influence on Chiang's army began in 1928 when the Generalissimo invited a German military mission to train his troops. The mission remained in China until 1938 when Japan, Hitler's new ally and China's enemy, insisted it be withdrawn.

before such an operation could begin, Stilwell had to marshal his Chinese troops. Chiang had promised him three Chinese armies—each in effect about the size of an American division—the Fifth Army, the Sixth Army and the Sixty-sixth. One of these, the Sixty-sixth, was to remain in reserve in China near the Burmese frontier where the Burma Road crossed the Salween River gorge.

Of the other two armies, only the 200th Division of the Fifth Army was actually in place facing the Japanese on the eastern end of the defensive line at Toungoo—and it was already in danger of encirclement. The Fifth Army's two remaining divisions, the 22nd and the 96th, still had not left China; Chungking's explanation was that they had to wait until supplies were ready for their arrival. Even then they were to advance only as far as Mandalay, in central Burma. When Stilwell asked permission to move these two divisions immediately from China to Burma to rescue the 200th at Toungoo, the Generalissimo refused. As for the last of the promised Chinese armies, the Sixth Army with its three divisions had indeed entered Burma but had moved along the Burma Road only to the northeastern Shan States.

It was under orders from Chiang to remain in position there to block an expected Japanese advance across the border from northern Thailand.

Finally, after considerable wrangling, Stilwell got permission on March 19—or at least thought he got it—to move the 22nd Division into Burma in support of the imperiled 200th at Toungoo. He gave the appropriate orders to the commander of the Chinese Fifth Army, Lieut. General Tu Yu-ming. But Tu and the commander of the 22nd, the French-educated, intellectual Major General Liao Yao-hsiang, proved to be masters of delay. Day after day they found excuses to keep the 22nd out of battle. There were too many problems with the railroad, or the trip was too dangerous, or the Japanese had too many tanks, or Liao wanted to wait for additional reinforcements, or a regiment could not move because there was a Japanese detachment in the area. When Stilwell leaned on him, Tu was apt to take to his room and hide, or explode into fits of screaming at his subordinates. "The pusillanimous bastards," wrote Stilwell of Tu and Liao later. "I can't shoot them; I can't relieve them; and just talking to them does no good."

General Alexander learned something of the problems Stilwell faced when he visited General Tu at the front and asked him where his field guns were. Tu said they had been withdrawn. "But then what use are they?" Alexander asked.

"General," Tu replied, "the Fifth Army is our best army because it is the only one that has any field guns, and I cannot afford to risk those guns. If I lose them the Fifth Army will no longer be our best."

In all likelihood, Tu was procrastinating on orders from Chiang, who in keeping with his theory of defense in depth had first resisted Stilwell's plan to reinforce the 200th Division. While Stilwell had been told by the Generalissimo that he was in command in Burma, his written orders did not make his position as commander explicit, and his subordinate generals were not likely to carry out his directives without checking first with Chungking.

Throughout the Burma campaign Chiang continued to address orders to Tu and the other Chinese generals, often bypassing Stilwell. From 1,600 miles away Chiang tried to exercise tactical command right down to the regimental level. His orders, wrote Stilwell, "direct all sorts of action and preparation with radical changes based on minor changes in the situation." Occasionally, given Chiang's distance from the front, the timing of his orders made them seem downright silly. At a crucial point in the campaign when the Chinese troops were fighting desperately, Stilwell received this message from the Generalissimo: "Watermelons are good for the morale of thirsty troops. Stilwell will provide one watermelon for every four Chinese soldiers."

In the end, the 22nd Division never did enter the battle at Toungoo, the 200th had to fight its way out alone, and the only Allied counteroffensive in Burma—the drive on Rangoon—collapsed in confusion and recrimination before it even got started.

Meanwhile, to the west in the Irrawaddy Valley, the Japanese were pushing Slim's I Burma Corps north toward the great oil fields at the town of Yenangyaung. The British troops were stunned and demoralized by the calculated ferocity of the Japanese. The invaders stripped their British captives, tied them to trees and used them for bayonet practice. They soaked captured ambulances with gasoline and set them afire, wounded soldiers and all. They tied a captured officer to a roadblock that was under British artillery bombardment. (Somehow the officer struggled free

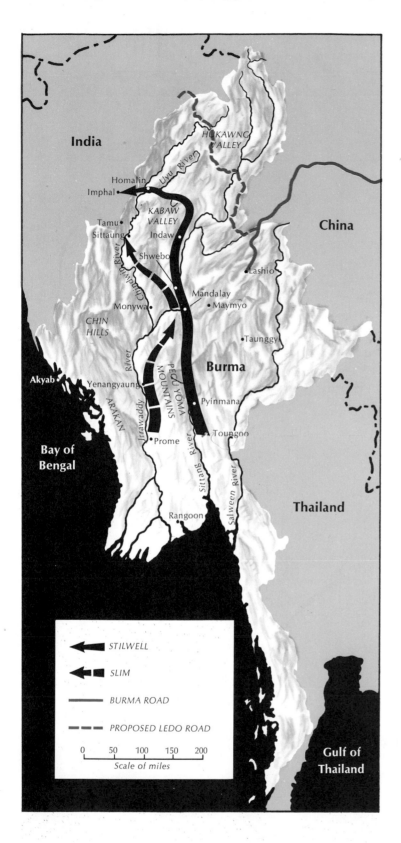

India

HUKAWNG VALLEY

Homalin
Imphal
Uyu River

KABAW VALLEY

Tamu
Sittaung
Indaw

China

Shwebo

Lashio

Mandalay
Monywa
Maymyo

CHIN HILLS

Taunggy

Burma

Akyab

Yenangyaung

PEGU YOMA MOUNTAINS

Pyinmana

Bay of Bengal

ARAKAN
Irrawaddy
Prome

Toungoo

Chindwin River

Sittang River

Salween River

Thailand

Rangoon

STILWELL

SLIM

BURMA ROAD

PROPOSED LEDO ROAD

0   50   100   150   200
Scale of miles

Gulf of Thailand

The desperate Allied retreat from Burma in 1942 involved British forces under Lieut. General William J. Slim (broken arrow) and the Chinese Fifth Army commanded by U.S. Lieut. General Joseph W. Stilwell (solid arrow). From Prome on the Irrawaddy River, Slim's I Burma Corps had to withdraw north and west some 900 miles before reaching the Indian border south of Tamu. The Fifth Army, after being routed at Toungoo, began its withdrawal with Stilwell, but scattered along the Sittang and Irrawaddy rivers. Stilwell went on with a party of 114 and finally reached Imphal in India on May 20, 1942—two months after the retreat began.

and raced back to his own lines, where he told the gunners that their rounds were falling 50 yards off target. The artillery corrected its fire, and the British broke through.)

Their supply lines severed with the fall of Rangoon, Slim's troops were now living on bully beef and tooth-breaking biscuits fortified (they said) with "vitamin W"—weevils. April is the hottest month of the year in Burma, and the men suffered terribly from heat and thirst. Most of Southeast Asia, with its monsoons and rain forests, has an abundant water supply, but the British had been pushed back into the hot, dry zone of central Burma, where the rainfall averages only 30 inches a year. Water, or the lack of it, became the kind of problem usually associated with desert warfare. Men urinated on their hands, then passed them over their cracked lips just for a touch of moisture. At one point a small British detachment waged a fierce battle for possession of a water tank that contained only a few inches of water. When the Japanese were finally driven away, the British fired bullets into the pipes and gulped down the rusty water. Japanese planes strafed the British constantly. Jack Belden, a U.S. correspondent, recalled that the worst thing about the planes was not the strafing, but the fact that under the air attacks the men had to run for cover in the pitiless sun, intensifying their terrible thirst.

With his defenses collapsing, Slim ordered the destruction of the greatest prize in Burma, the vast oil fields at Yenangyaung. On the 15th of April, 5,000 oil wells and the largest power station in the country went up in flames. So thorough was the demolition job that it was six months before the Japanese could get the wells flowing again.

Slim's order was given just in time, for the Japanese, in another of their enveloping moves, not only had reached the fields but also had set up one of their dreaded roadblocks and cut off the entire 1st Burma Division. The division's tanks and infantry repeatedly attacked the roadblock, with no success. General Alexander already had permission from Chiang Kai-shek to move another Chinese division—the 38th, which was part of the Sixty-sixth Army and had just arrived from China—to the British sector of the front, and he sent it now in relief of the trapped 1st Burma Division.

The commander of the 38th, Lieut. General Sun Li-jen, was to distinguish himself as far and away the ablest Chinese general in CBI. A graduate of the Virginia Military Institute, the old school of General Marshall, he spoke good but stilted English, freely intermixed with current American slang. Sun had no trace of the defensive attitude that infected most Chinese commanders. Indeed, he was aggressive and cool under fire. At Yenangyaung his troops broke through in fierce fighting and saved the 1st Burma Division—or what was left of it—and the 17th Indian Division farther to the east. Overall the British thought the Chinese worthless as allies, but for his action at Yenangyaung, General Sun received the Order of the British Empire.

Back to the east, Stilwell's own predicament was becoming graver by the hour. By now he had established a new defensive line at Pyinmana about 60 miles north of Toungoo. A key road junction in this line was held by the Chinese 55th Division of the Sixth Army, which had finally become engaged in combat as the Japanese swept into the Shan States. The 55th's commander, General Chen Li-wu, had acquired the nickname "Dynamite" in earlier battles in China, but Stilwell considered him incompetent and had tried unsuccessfully to relieve him of command. When one of Stilwell's liaison officers, Colonel Frederick McCabe,

went to visit Chen's position he was stunned by what he found. Chen's division was deployed for miles along a road, with the lead elements so constricted that they could have been enveloped by a platoon. Trucks and troops were jammed up on the narrow road, and machine guns were placed in heavy brush where they had no fields of fire. To make matters worse, Chen's command post was 30 miles behind the front, and McCabe found the general himself 15 miles behind that. McCabe suggested that Chen move his units out into the surrounding hills so that they could dominate the road, but that advice was never taken.

The next day, a Japanese reinforced regiment attacked the strung-out division and quickly severed unit from unit. What followed has rarely occurred in modern warfare. The 55th Division vanished into thin air as the men took to the hills. "There's not a trace of it," Stilwell told correspondent Belden. "It's the god-damnedest thing I ever saw. Last night I had a division, and today there isn't any." Indeed, the 55th vanished so completely that it was removed from the rolls of the Chinese Army.

The collapse of the 55th left a hole through which the Japanese could race northward toward Lashio, the western

terminus of the Burma Road. From there, they could speed northeastward toward China. Desperate to plug the gap, Stilwell tried to rush the 200th Division to block the Japanese advance at the pretty hill resort town of Taunggyi, but he was frustrated by General Yu Fei-p'eng, a relative of Chiang's who was in charge of supply and logistics. The corpulent Yu was notorious for using his position to supply the black markets of Kunming with whatever could be brought out of Burma. His reputation for corruption was so substantial that the Chinese, in a pun on his name, called him "T'u Fei-p'ang"—"fat bandit." Yu had more than 700 trucks under his command at Lashio, but most of them were engaged in black-market operations, and when Stilwell requested 150 trucks to move the 200th Division, Yu sent only 22. As a result, the 200th arrived at Taunggyi 24 hours too late; the Japanese already held the town.

Hoping to recapture it, Stilwell rushed to the front, where he wound up in the middle of the advance company's forward position, with bullets snapping overhead and mortar rounds falling on all sides. The Chinese captain in charge was losing courage. Stilwell dressed him down and ordered him to lead a charge. Then, right in front of Stilwell, a mortar fragment tore off part of the captain's face. Pointing to the next Chinese officer in line, Stilwell shouted to his aide, Colonel Frank Dorn: "Grab that lieutenant! Boot him in the tail! For Christ's sake get him moving!" With a three-star general in command and the lieutenant leading the way, the Chinese company began a counterattack.

Nothing if not a pragmatist, Stilwell then offered the division's troops a reward of 50,000 rupees if they could retake the town by five in the afternoon. They took it with an hour to spare.

Stilwell had shown, as had General Sun at Yenangyaung, that, if properly motivated, Chinese troops could successfully stand up to the Japanese. But the retaking of Taunggyi was too little, too late. The Japanese bypassed the town with motor transport and raced northward toward Lashio. The Allied east flank had now been turned, and the Allied defense was collapsing all along the front.

In the British sector, Slim had only about 13,000 men left in his I Burma Corps. One 700-man battalion of Gloucesters had been reduced to 50 effectives. Slim's tanks were running out of gasoline and spare parts, and had only about 100 miles left on their tracks. Lines of communication had been shattered by members of the Burmese independence movement, and by now the Allies had not a single plane left in Burma for reconnaissance. Railway personnel had fled, and it was impossible to move troops by train. After a grim conference, Stilwell recorded in his diary that Alexander had told him he could no longer control his troops—they were afraid of the Japanese.

Most of the eyewitness accounts of the final days of that first campaign in Burma have a kind of surreal quality—they describe a scene of horror, even madness, especially for the more than a million Indians in Burma. The Indians had come to Burma to serve the colonial administration as civil servants or simply to make their fortune. More thrifty than most Burmese, who loved to gamble and generally enjoy themselves, the Indians soon controlled much of the economy that was not already in the hands of canny Chinese merchants who had migrated to Burma earlier, and much of the arable land as well. As the Indians tried to flee the country, Burmese villagers attacked them and almost casually decapitated some of them with sharp, square-tipped swords called dahs. Bitterly resenting the ruthless, high-handed treatment they felt they had received for many years from the Chinese merchants in Burma, villagers attacked the Chinese soldiers too; if they caught them looting they sometimes cut off their hands. In turn, the Chinese took to shooting Burmese on sight.

Refugees were raped, robbed and beaten, dacoits were everywhere, and an epidemic of looting and arson swept the countryside. Every major town for 200 miles along the approaches to Mandalay was burned to the ground. In Mandalay, the country's capital in the days before the British arrived, fires started by Japanese bombs were spread by Burmese agents. The abandoned city burned for 27 days and nights; in the moat that surrounded the old Royal Palace corpses floated among the white lotuses and the pink hyacinths, and in the streets dogs, pigs and kite hawks fed on bloated bodies.

The Japanese were pouring up the Shan plateau toward Lashio on the northeast, pressing up the Chindwin on the northwest, threatening to surround what remained of the Allied armies. On April 25 a tired Stilwell met with General

As black smoke billows from a deliberately sabotaged storage tank, British soldiers (foreground) prepare to destroy machinery collected in a pit at Burma's Yenangyaung oil fields in April 1942. The pit was flooded with oil, which was then ignited. Thousands of wells were also set on fire as part of British efforts to prevent the advancing Japanese from using the fields.

Alexander at Kyaukse, 25 miles south of Mandalay. They agreed that a general retreat was the only hope of escape before they were enveloped by the Japanese pincer. It was a depressing meeting. Said Stilwell, "As our Chinese friends would put it, we are all 'eating bitterness.'"

Even as the meeting was going on, Japanese bombers attacked Kyaukse. Bombs fell within 100 yards of the conference site, and the officers fled for shelter—all but Alexander and Stilwell, who stood defiantly in the garden during the raid, Stilwell leaning quietly against the porch railing and smoking a cigarette in a well-chewed black holder.

According to Alexander's plan, Slim's troops would head northwestward over mountain trails through the Chin Hills to India, in hope of escaping before the Japanese advance up the Chindwin cut them off. But Stilwell's Chinese armies—or what disorganized divisions were left of them—were scattered all across northeastern Burma. He wanted to withdraw them to the country's far north and there establish a base for a future counteroffensive that he would supply by building a new road from India. At the very least, he hoped to supervise their orderly retreat to sanctuary. Thus as the British began withdrawing toward the west, Stilwell moved his own headquarters north to Shwebo, a rail junction five miles above Mandalay, where his men began assembling an engine and as many railway cars as they could commandeer for the journey to Myitkyina.

The events that followed were a nightmare for the British troops and Stilwell's men that had no parallel in military history. For the British, it was the longest and perhaps most ignominious retreat in more than a century. Hounded every step of the way by the Japanese, bedeviled by snipers and parched for water, they withdrew from Mandalay on the Irrawaddy to Monywa on the Chindwin, then north to Ye-u, stopping again and again to fight. Units were cut off and nearly destroyed before they could battle their way free and rejoin the main force. The British were trying to escape on roads that did not exist except on maps; gradually they abandoned their transportation and heavy equipment, salvaging only four-wheel-drive vehicles. Enemy "jitter parties," as the British soldiers referred to them, kept Slim's command posts awake all night by lobbing in grenades and even harmless fireworks. Men's nerves grew frayed and Slim

remarked: "If somebody brings me a bit of good news, I shall burst into tears."

The route—really no more than a cart track—ran from Ye-u west through jungle to the Chindwin at Shwegyin, where it abruptly stopped. If there was to be any escape at all, the British force had to commandeer ferry boats to carry men, artillery and trucks six miles upstream to Kalewa. Six ferries were available for the purpose, but the boarding area, called "the Basin," was a natural site for ambush. It was an open, horseshoe-shaped depression, a thousand yards wide, surrounded on three sides by sheer 200-foot cliffs surmounted by dense jungle. Packed with civilian and military refugees, mules, soldiers, trucks, tanks and artillery all jammed up to board the ferries, the Basin was a potential death trap. Slim deployed a Gurkha commando group to give advance warning of approaching Japanese. To block the passage of any Japanese naval craft on the Chindwin, Slim had a floating boom built across the river with a small Marine flotilla and an Indian battalion deployed to cover both banks. A pathetic array of antiaircraft artillery was raised to guard against air attack, and all men still able to fight were positioned in the jungle beyond the exposed cliffs.

While the defense perimeter was being set up, vehicles were maneuvered carefully onto ferries, heavy guns were manhandled aboard and the wounded were packed into all available spaces. Men still able to walk were sent to cut wood for ferryboat fuel, and as they filed onto the deck each man handed over one log in return for his passage. On the 7th and 9th of May, air attacks panicked the

Indian refugees strain to pull an oxcart loaded with family and belongings on a road in southern Burma. Of the 900,000 Indians who fled toward India before the Japanese advance, almost 90 per cent perished—victims of disease, exhaustion, famine and Burmese who preyed on them.

Burmese boat crews, and most of them slipped overboard and disappeared.

On May 10, Japanese troops struck so suddenly that Slim's first warning came only when a stream of red tracer bullets flew over his head as he stood on the deck of a ferryboat. A great din of rifle, machine-gun, mortar and artillery fire broke out. The Japanese had run into the rear guard of the Gurkha commando group, but the Gurkhas' radio had failed to work and their commander had for some reason chosen to withdraw rather than fight. Taken wholly by surprise, the Basin's defenders poured everything they had at the enemy; at one stage an Indian Bofors antiaircraft gun dueled point-blank with a small Japanese field piece until the Bofors hit it squarely and turned it over, wiping out its crew.

Slim, trying to maintain some semblance of poise, walked erect through a battalion of Gurkhas who were crouching behind scrub brush. A Gurkha officer got up from behind a bush, grinned and laughed heartily at Slim, who demanded to know what was so funny. The Gurkha replied that it was very funny to see the General Sahib wandering along there by himself not knowing what to do! "And, by Jove," Slim observed dourly, "he was right; I did not!"

After the Gurkhas counterattacked, Slim returned to the jetty and found among the civilian refugees an Indian woman dying of smallpox while her four-year-old son tried desperately to feed her a tin of milk given him by a soldier. The woman died. Slim ordered a doctor to give the boy a vaccination, then bribed another Indian family with a blanket and passage on the steamer to take the boy to safety.

As the Japanese attack grew more fierce, it became impossible to get other boats to the landing. Slim let the rest of the refugees herd themselves onto the last ferry, and it slowly chugged away to safety upriver. Ordering all remaining artillery shells expended in a last deafening salvo, Slim abandoned the rest of his matériel and led his men in a fighting withdrawal northward up the jungle-clad riverbank to safety. The Japanese did not follow. It was, in fact, the last contact the British had with the enemy during their retreat from Burma.

Ahead lay only jungle, monsoon rains, leeches and a 90-mile march through the malaria-infested Kabaw Valley—which the British renamed the Valley of Death. At night they slept in the mud without blankets or cover while rain beat down on them. Their clothes had turned to rags and many had no shoes; they were gaunt with hunger. Like his men, Slim let his beard grow—then discovered to his dismay that it was coming out completely white, and cut it off to spare his troops the shock.

On May 16, the last day of the 900-mile retreat, the ragged scarecrows of the British Army in Burma hobbled into India. Twelve thousand made it to India. More than 13,000 were lost through casualties and desertions during the withdrawal. The 1st Burma Division was reduced to little more than a brigade. A battalion of the King's Own Yorkshire Light Infantry counted only 84 survivors. But battered, sick and beaten as they were, most of the survivors still carried their weapons. Just south of Tamu, the men were met by an Indian transport company. So fearsome was the sight of the tattered armed force that emerged from the jungle that the Indian drivers fled. Slim had the Indians seized, and his tank drivers held guns on them to force them to transport the wounded into Indian base hospitals. The Indian Army was completely unprepared to receive the survivors; in disgust Slim compared their reception unfavorably with that given the survivors of Dunkirk. There were no dry clothes, blankets or tents awaiting them, nor the slightest word of encouragement after defeat. Men who had managed to hang on only by the prospect of eventual relief from the terrible strain, the promise of welcome and rest, found none. Disappointed and dispirited, many lost the will to continue and died of malaria, dysentery and exhaustion.

For Stilwell, the ordeal was to be quite different. From Shwebo he planned to withdraw by train, heading toward the terminus at Myitkyina, some 250 miles to the north. This plan quickly went awry when General Lo Cho-ying, Stilwell's deputy and liaison with the Chinese armies, commandeered an engine and 17 cars at gunpoint and tried to escape north with his staff. Lo's train collided with a southbound one, 25 miles up the line, completely blocking the track. "That fat turtle egg," raged Stilwell in Chinese.

The next day a C-47 arrived in Shwebo on a special mission from U.S. Army Air Forces chief Henry H. "Hap" Arnold. It was flown by Colonel Caleb V. Haynes, a big, bluff pilot who resembled actor Wallace Beery, and by Colonel Robert L. Scott, who was to become a hot-shot pursuit pilot and the author of a best-selling memoir, *God Is My Copilot*. Haynes and Scott had hedgehopped in from India, dodging rain, sleetstorms and Japanese fighters. They found Stilwell in his headquarters, wearing his old campaign hat and writing at his desk in longhand. "General Arnold sent us to rescue you, sir," they said. When Stilwell made it clear that he had no intention of being rescued, the fliers were dumbfounded. "Let's knock the old fool in the head and take him anyway," said Haynes to Scott.

Needless to say, the fliers did no such thing. Stilwell sent most of his staff out to India on the plane—it was the last plane to leave Burma—but remained behind himself with a few picked men.

With the railway blocked by General Lo's train wreck, Stilwell's party started north in a convoy of jeeps, trucks and sedans, hoping to get around the block by road and then regain the railway at a junction farther to the north. The task was complicated by the fact that up-to-date maps were nonexistent. Belden, who had chosen to cover Stilwell's retreat, recalled watching the general's intelligence chief, Colonel Frank Roberts, kneeling on the headquarters floor,

trying to plot an escape route by piecing together a single map of Burma out of many different local maps—but there was always a section missing.

With Stilwell were about a hundred people: 26 American officers, enlisted men and civilians, 16 Chinese soldiers, the seven-man British Friends Ambulance Unit, correspondent Belden, assorted Malay, Burmese and Indian helpers and cooks, and a contingent of 19 Burmese nurses. These were led by Dr. Gordon S. Seagrave, an American Baptist medical missionary born in Rangoon who would become famous as "the Burma Surgeon." First as a civilian and later as a lieutenant colonel in the medical corps, Seagrave had provided most of the meager medical care that was available to the Chinese armies in Burma. Frequently performing two operations simultaneously, he spoke to his multitribal Burmese nurses and Chinese orderlies in six languages, and worked in blood-spattered shorts under conditions so primitive that he once had to use the sawed-off wing of a wrecked fighter plane as his operating table.

Still determined to reach Myitkyina by rail, the convoy detoured north on a bullock-cart track clogged with refu-

gees. The human flood of panic-stricken civilians fleeing the advancing Japanese kept the speed of the convoy down to a walking pace, and the rutted road began to take a heavy toll of vehicles. On May 2 a scout car blew its tires. "Burn the damned thing," said Stilwell. "Keep moving." An axle went on another vehicle. "Burn the son-of-a-bitch," said Stilwell. A sedan broke a crankcase. "Burn it." Finally a supply truck caught fire. "Turn 'em over. Get moving. Forward."

On the next day Stilwell's party came upon a better stretch of road and was able to move a little faster, but then the general received some bad news. A string of railway cars had got loose on the tracks far ahead—perhaps the result of sabotage—wrecking a bridge and blocking the line. It would now be impossible to reach Myitkyina by rail. But Stilwell stubbornly retained hope of organizing and leading at least some of his Chinese troops northward, although he was uncertain at this point exactly where each unit was in the disorderly retreat. The party pressed on toward Myitkyina by road. Cars bogged down in the sand, trucks were abandoned in rivers. The whole party got lost one night in a labyrinth of elephant trails.

In Indaw on May 5, Stilwell learned that even the cart roads north were impassable and, moreover, that the Japanese were now nearer to Myitkyina than he was.

There was no longer any prospect of organizing an orderly retreat. The remnants of the Chinese Fifth and Sixth armies had lost contact with Stilwell and with each other, and were now making their way as best they could either toward India or back toward China. In fact, of all the Chinese forces in Burma, only the highly effective 38th Division of the Sixty-sixth Army, under General Sun, managed to fight its way to India intact. The Japanese net was closing around Stilwell, and a single possibility remained—to try to break out to the west and India, almost 200 miles away across some of the worst jungle, wildest rivers and steepest mountains in Burma. The Stilwell caravan started moving, but on the next day the road ended.

Stilwell assembled his motley command in a circle. Some British soldiers, a few Eurasian women and assorted stragglers of different races had attached themselves to the group, which now numbered 114. Stilwell gave them the news: they were going to walk to India. They might encounter the Japanese at any moment, the monsoon was due

to begin, making every river and stream impassable, and their rations were nearly gone. But Stilwell was determined. If they could reach the town of Homalin on the Chindwin River before the Japanese, they could cross the broad river and escape into the mountains of India.

That night Stilwell sent a final message before ordering his burdensome radio smashed and abandoned. Dorn, Stilwell's aide, later recalled the ominous words of the message. "We abandon all transportation here. . . . We are running low on food with none in sight. Alert British in India to send food and bearers to Homalin. Tens of thousands of refugees and troops are headed for India on trails from Sittaung to Hukawng Valley. It is urgent repeat urgent to stock trails with food and medicines soon as possible. Urgent or thousands will die. . . . This is our last message repeat our last message. Stilwell."

The message did not exaggerate the plight of those who took to the trails for India. An estimated 900,000 frantic civilian refugees, many of them Indians, tried to escape over trails inadequately and carelessly stocked with food and medicine by the fleeing British colonial administration. Instead of finding help, the refugees discovered that wells had been poisoned and ferryboats burned by the Burmese. Some refugees wandered for months over ancient caravan routes to China, while others, heading north, got lost in giant mountains thrusting down from Tibet. Malaria, cholera and smallpox flamed through the refugee bands. Bodies of every age marked the trails. In the end, it was estimated that the death toll ran to the hundreds of thousands.

On the morning of May 7, with the aid of 20 mules hired from a trader, Stilwell's party set out from a village on foot for India. They soon reached a small river, the Chaunggyi, and there the trail disappeared. Without missing a step Stilwell strode into the water and led his column downstream. At the general's fast pace, men soon began to collapse from heat exhaustion. Major Frank Merrill—who later would command Merrill's Marauders—collapsed beside the stream. But Stilwell refused to stop, and the British Friends towed the victims downstream on inflated air mattresses, keeping up as best they could.

Pinched with hunger—they were on half rations supplemented by jungle roots and herbs—the party continued

The fall of Rangoon, Burma's colonial capital, is celebrated by jubilant Japanese soldiers raising their swords in front of Government House. The Japanese occupation of the port city severed the last access route for seaborne supplies to blockaded China, effectively isolating the country.

marching downstream for three days. Once they came upon an elephant, a rogue bull that, they learned, had trampled two local villagers to death. Stilwell and others kept guns trained on the animal until the party got safely past.

One morning Stilwell found a huge bedroll packed on one of the mules. When he learned it belonged to a junior officer, fury consumed him. He had the roll spread out on the ground and assembled the whole party to look at what it contained—sheets, blankets, a mattress and pillow, shoes and clothing. "I had you all line up here," Stilwell said bitingly, "so you could see how little one member of this party cares about the rest of you so long as he has his own comforts. I'm not mentioning his name because some of you might hurt him, and that would slow up the column. . . . I'll take care of this matter after we get to India. When we take off in a few minutes, the owner will leave these things here. I hope he feels properly ashamed."

As the fuming Stilwell turned away, one of the men said, "Jeez! Even his old hat looks mad."

At first, the men in the party assumed that Dr. Seagrave's nurses would be a hindrance, not only because they were women but because they were tiny; few of them weighed more than 100 pounds. But the men were quickly proved wrong. The young Karen and Kachin girls were made of stern stuff. Some were barefoot, others wore oversized army boots that fit like galoshes, but they bore up under the rigors of the march better than most of the men—and cared for the sick and the lame while they were doing it.

They infused the party, which had cause enough to be depressed, with their high spirits. At rest stops they twined jungle flowers into their hair, splashed gaily in streams, helped kill fish with hand grenades or taught the men such tricks of jungle survival as a way to purify water by filtering it through leaves. On the march they giggled, chattered and sang songs—old Karen love songs, American jazz tunes, Baptist hymns and even their own slightly scrambled version of "She'll Be Comin' round the Mountain," which went: "We'll follow General Stilwell when he comes, singing ki yi yeepi yeepi yi." As for Seagrave, the missionary doctor, his legs were crippled with running sores from having minor cuts and scratches infected at combat operating tables, but he kept stumping along and caring for the sick at the all-too-brief rest stops Stilwell allowed.

When the party reached a larger river, the Uyu, they managed to obtain bamboo rafts from local villagers at Maingkaing. While the pack train continued by land, the main party set off downriver in a flotilla to meet at the Chindwin. The raft trip was supposed to provide some

respite for the weary, but it turned out to be as strenuous as walking. The flimsy rafts kept coming apart, swinging broadside in the current or running aground and forcing all hands overboard to help out. A British airplane came over and dropped some welcome supplies, but no message.

On May 12, 1942, Stilwell's battered little navy finally reached Homalin, where the general hoped to get some answer to his last radio message. But on arrival he found that the telegraph was out and the telephone lines cut. There was no food, there were no boats for crossing the Chindwin, and the British commissioner had taken the only launch and headed upriver. In an ill temper, Stilwell ordered an arms inspection and was furious when he found weapons dirty and in no condition to fire.

That night the party slept in a Buddhist temple. There was only enough food left for three more meals, and everyone was depressed. They might just make it, Stilwell mused to Dorn, *"If we can find boats and cross the river before the Japs beat us to it; if they"*—he meant the pack train—*"can negotiate the steep trails in their beat up condition; if the sick can keep up, with their malaria, dysentery, bad feet, jungle sores and infections; if we don't get bogged down in the monsoon rains; if we can find food where I'm damned sure there is none."*

The next morning they left Homalin—they were unaware of it but they were only 36 hours ahead of the Japanese— and marched to the wide, swift Chindwin. After some delay they found a group of Kachins with five dugouts and a raft to ferry the party across the river. The pack train crossed downstream and then rejoined the column. When they reached the far shore, they were probably safe at last from the Japanese, but they still had a long march ahead of them through steep, wild mountains.

Stilwell drove the column mercilessly. He was about to turn 60 years old and he had lost 20 pounds on the trail, but he was in the best physical condition by far of all the men in the group, and entries in his own diary for the period show that "Walking Joe" had little patience with those who could not keep up. "Limeys' feet all shot," he wrote. "Our people tired. Damn poor show of physique." And later: "The sissies are pooped out. They can't take it." And again, "The cream-

puffs are doing better." Anyone who fell behind felt the lash of his tongue, ranking officers not excepted. When Major General Frank Sibert, one of Stilwell's staff officers, could not maintain the pace, Stilwell snapped: "You'll have to do better. You're a general officer. An infantryman. You ought to be setting an example."

"I'm sorry, sir. But I can't help it."

"Dammit, Sibert, I'm telling you to keep up with this column. And that's what I mean."

It began to rain, turning the trail to muck and indicating that the monsoon was beginning. That evening—May 14— the party came to a small cluster of huts in the mountains at Kawlum, in Burma, which was the main border-crossing point in that sector. Entering India, they were met by a tall British district officer with a grin on his face. Stilwell's radio message *had* been received, and the Englishman had come to Kawlum to meet him, followed by 500 porters with pack animals, food, cigarettes and whiskey. At their meeting Stilwell was characteristically unemotional, but he confided to his diary, "Quite a relief."

They had been rescued, but they still had a long way to go to Imphal, the British corps headquarters in India, and Stilwell never let the pressure off. They walked for six more days, Stilwell driving the party as much as 21 miles a day.

On the 19th of May, some British officers in a government station outside Imphal looked up to see a ragtag column of emaciated men and women come marching out of the mountains through a steady rain. At the head of the column walked a wiry little man in a battered campaign hat; near the end of the column were a score of young Burmese girls. One of the officers greeted Stilwell and asked him how many people he had lost on his march out of Burma.

"Not a one," said Stilwell. "Not a single one."

A few days later, in Delhi on May 25, Vinegar Joe Stilwell held a press conference, for he was famous now, a hero. Till then, the world had viewed the Allied flight from Burma as a kind of glorious strategic retreat. With customary vigor, Stilwell told a different story.

"I claim we got a hell of a beating," he said. "We got run out of Burma and it is humiliating as hell. I think we ought to find out what caused it, go back and retake it."

A pair of blindfolded Burmese farmers are escorted into a British Army headquarters at Yenangyaung by Gurkha soldiers. The two men came to the headquarters to sell eggs, but because spies were active among the local population, the Gurkhas took the precaution of blindfolding the farmers in order to keep them from picking up information.

THE MAN CALLED VINEGAR JOE

On his celebrated escape from Burma in May of 1942, Lieut. General Joseph W. Stilwell (far right) confers about a supply problem with members of his party.

AN IRON RESOLVE FOR AN IMPOSSIBLE JOB

"Vinegar Joe" Stilwell, the senior American commander in the China-Burma-India Theater, once described himself as being "unreasonable, impatient, sour-balled, sullen, mad, hard, profane, vulgar." The cantankerous Stilwell might well have added another more felicitous adjective to his list: iron-willed.

For nothing was more characteristic of Stilwell than the strength of his determination to accomplish his objective —no matter what it might be. As a high school senior trying to make the height requirement for West Point, Stilwell once stayed in bed for a week, on the theory that he would thus be able to stretch himself and add a quarter of an inch to his length.

Stilwell's resolve was matched by his tactical ability, giving him the reputation of being one of the War's outstanding field commanders. His talent first came to light in the 1930s at Fort Benning, Georgia, where he taught tactics for four years and did so well that the Assistant Commandant of the Infantry School, Colonel George C. Marshall, termed him "qualified for any command in peace or war." By January of 1942, when Stilwell was dispatched to CBI, he had risen to the rank of major general and had come to be regarded as the best corps commander in the entire United States Army.

In his CBI assignment Stilwell was faced with what his old friend Marshall—now Chief of Staff of the U.S. Army—called the "most impossible job" in World War II. His duties included no fewer than eight different tasks—from serving as head of Generalissimo Chiang Kai-shek's Allied staff to commanding Chinese troops in battle and supervising the flow of Lend-Lease supplies in CBI.

His first assignment was to lead Chinese troops in Burma. Within weeks the Japanese swept through the country, and Stilwell was forced to flee. Even in some of the worst moments, he never lost his assurance that victory would come, although he thought it might take a long time. In a letter to his wife, he wrote, "Someday I'll be back home . . . With a long white beard and a bent back!!"

Stilwell sits on the right of George C. Marshall (front row, center) at Fort Benning in the early 1930s. Standing directly behind them is Omar Bradley.

At a conference in Maymyo, Burma, in April 1942, General Stilwell and a beaming Generalissimo Chiang Kai-shek are linked by the arms of Madame Chiang.

Fire sweeps through a section of Maymyo after Japanese planes plastered the town with 150 bombs—many of them captured from the Allies at Rangoon.

Chinese artillerymen go into action at Toungoo. Moments later three of them were shot by snipers.

A PACK OF TROUBLES FOR A NEW COMMANDER

Almost from the moment that he arrived in Burma on the 11th of March, 1942, Stilwell was beset by troubles. The lines of communication were appalling, medicine and medical facilities were lacking and ammunition was in short supply. When the Japanese attacked his Chinese forces at Toungoo, Stilwell made an attempt to dispatch reinforcements to the front by rail. The railroad crews, however, threatened to desert their trains rather than go into the battle zone, and they had to be ordered at gunpoint to continue.

By this time the whole Allied front was falling apart. Maymyo, where Stilwell had established his headquarters, was bombed. When he tried to make a stand farther north at Pyinmana, Japanese planes struck again. As the enemy shoved north, Stilwell relocated his headquarters to Shwebo. But by the 29th of April, Japanese troops were only 60 miles away, and Stilwell was left with no alternative but to keep moving with his command.

Wearing glasses and his legendary campaign hat, Stilwell discusses plans for an attack against the Japanese with Chinese generals at the Toungoo front.

Against a backdrop of giant pagodas, Chinese soldiers beat out brush fires started by Japanese incendiary bombs that were dropped on Pyinmana in Burma.

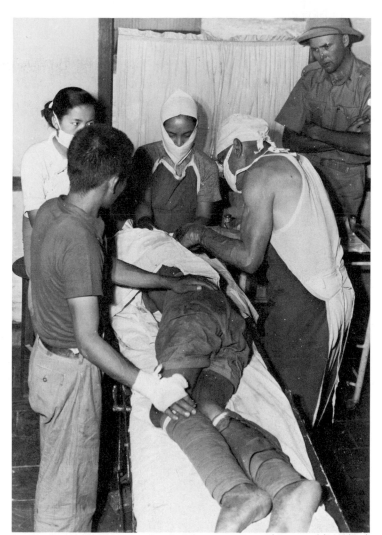

Dr. Gordon Seagrave probes for shell fragments in a Chinese soldier's back.

Surgeon Seagrave and nurses travel to the north in their camouflaged jeep.

Members of Stilwell's group abandon their vehicles after reaching the end of the road in northern Burma and prepare to travel the rest of the way out of the

A LONG WALK OVER GRIM OBSTACLES

With the enemy advancing on Shwebo, Stilwell decided to strike out for the airfield at Myitkyina. Traveling with him by jeep, truck and sedan was a polyglot group that would ultimately number 114 people from no fewer than nine nations. When the roads gave out 50 miles west of Indaw, Stilwell abandoned his trucks and ordered the members of his party to keep only what they could carry. He hoped to commandeer a train farther up the line, but the tracks were blocked by a wreck.

Stilwell was left now with a single option—walk to India. He was undaunted by the prospect. "By the time we get out of

A raft ferrying the command is guided past a sand bar on the Uyu River.

country on foot. Their discarded excess baggage litters the foreground.

Stilwell and a Burmese native retrieve supplies air-dropped on a sand bar.

here," he told his charges, "many of you will hate my guts but I'll tell you one thing: you'll all get out."

True to his word, Vinegar Joe drove his scraggly column relentlessly through the forbidding countryside of northern Burma. Hiking for as many as 11 hours in a single day, the marchers stumbled over rooted jungle trails and sloshed along graveled river bottoms. Shoes filled with sand, causing painful blisters and rubbing feet so raw that they bled. Even when the party took to rafts on the Uyu River, there was no respite: the bamboo poles used for propelling the craft gashed and scratched hands.

On land again, the party accelerated its pace. The monsoon was coming. Stilwell managed to cover 15, 17 and eventually 21 miles in a day. Only when he was over the last hurdle, the rugged Chin hills at the Burma-India border, did he let up.

Puffing on a cigarette, Stilwell cleans his Tommy gun during a break.

THE TRIUMPH AND ORDEAL OF A TIRELESS LEADER

On May 20, Stilwell finally reached Imphal in India, "looking like the wrath of God and cursing like a fallen angel," one observer said. During the 14-day hike, he had covered 140 miles, and had endured physical handicaps that few other men his age could have survived.

At 59, he was much older than most of the people in his expedition—and not in good health. Jaundice plagued him constantly, and his eyes were a continuing source of trouble. A World War I injury had rendered his left eye useless, and he needed glasses for his weak right eye.

Although hundreds of thousands of soldiers and refugees fled the Japanese at the same time, no group had fared better than Stilwell's. All of his party made it to India—thanks to the tenacious general who kept his promise to bring them out alive.

An indefatigable Stilwell leads his men along a jungle trail in Burma. The thought of what might happen to them, he said, made his "guts turn to water."

CHINA'S GENERALISSIMO

Student officers are reviewed by Chiang Kai-shek at a new American-run training center in Kweilin in 1944. The center specialized in infantry and artillery tactics.

A SELF-WILLED RISE TO POWER

The close relationship between China's revolutionary leader Sun Yat-sen (seated) and Chiang Kai-shek is suggested in this portrait, made in 1924.

"Politics makes man lead a dog's life," Chiang Kai-shek confided to his diary in March 1926. But he excelled at politics—and politics, coupled with patriotism and burning ambition, drew Chiang into a life of turmoil and danger.

Born the son of a modest salt merchant in China's Chekiang Province in 1887, Chiang was left fatherless at an early age and was reared by his stalwart mother. When, as a teenager, he was unjustly arrested by Manchu authorities for not paying a rice tax, he felt "the first spark that kindled my revolutionary fire." At 18, he cut off his pigtail, symbol of subservience to the Manchus, and went to Japan for military training. There he met Dr. Sun Yat-sen, the Chinese Nationalist leader, who was in Japan raising money to overthrow the Manchus. Inspired by Sun Yat-sen, Chiang cast his lot with the revolutionaries. Chiang returned to China in 1911 to help the rebels. He led a strike force—the "dare-to-dies"—organized uprisings, and over the next decade rose in the ranks of Sun's Nationalist Party, or Kuomintang.

Chiang had an undeniable flair for leadership, but Sun saw another side of his character. "Whenever you are disappointed at some trifle, you let your anger go unchecked," he said. In a rage, Chiang would pound the table and hurl dishes. Once during the war, after he saw a movie he disliked, he had the projectionist thrashed.

When Sun died in 1925, Chiang set out to lead the Nationalists. He began a campaign to eliminate his warlord rivals, and launched an offensive against his political opponents that resulted in the massacre of 300 Communists and other "radical" leaders. He assumed control of the Nationalist Party's right wing in 1927, and the next year was named Generalissimo and then chairman of the central government at Nanking. In 1938 he was officially designated head of the party with veto power over all its decisions.

During the war, Chiang's regime was threatened on one side by Communists, and beset on the other by the Japanese. To many Westerners he symbolized China's will to survive. But as events proved, not even his own stubborn determination was enough to preserve his hard-won power.

Chiang stands behind his mother in a 1920 photo. A stern disciplinarian, she made him mop floors and wash dishes to build character.

Engaged in 1927, Chiang takes tea with his
fiancée, Mei-ling Soong, in Shanghai. Mei-ling
won the hearts of countless admirers with
her charm and her vivacious good looks.

In Peking, Chiang (above, center) joins other generals—with whom he had combined forces in order to gain power—for ceremonies held at the tomb of Sun Yat-sen in 1928.

At the reburial of Sun Yat-sen in Nanking in 1929 (below), Madame Sun is accompanied by Chiang (center) and her brothers; banker T. V. Soong is wearing glasses at left center.

A POLITICAL JEWEL OF A WIFE

When Chiang Kai-shek met lovely Mei-ling Soong at the home of Dr. Sun Yat-sen in 1922, he sensed that her patriotism and ambition matched his. Charming, intelligent, wealthy—her father, Charles Soong, had made a fortune printing and selling Bibles in China—she seemed the perfect partner for a man bent on rising to the top of the military and political power structure. Mei-ling's two sisters were already married to influential men, the eldest to banker H. H. Kung, a direct descendant of

Confucius, the other to Dr. Sun. Her brother T. V. Soong was a financier who would become an internationally known China lobbyist during the war. Marriage to Mei-ling would ally Chiang with one of China's leading families.

On the morning of his wedding, Chiang wrote: "We two are determined to exert our utmost to the cause of the Chinese Revolution." He wasted no time. In early 1928 he led a military expedition that toppled the powerful warlord government in Peking, and by the end of the year he was chairman of a Nationalist regime whose flag flew over all of China.

Planning strategy in Hankow, Chiang holds a conference with his Supreme War Council in 1938.

PLAYING THE GAME OF SURVIVAL

Although Chiang Kai-shek had united his country under the Nationalist flag, powerful military leaders and opponents within the party continued to challenge his rule, as did the Communists, based in Kiangsi Province in southern China. But beyond these persistent problems, Chiang faced another threat.

In September 1931, the Japanese invaded Manchuria. Chiang—holding to the traditional Chinese maxim: "to expel foreign aggression, one must first pacify internal insubordination"—was reluctant to commit his armies to resisting the invaders. Obsessed with defeating the Communists, he was engaged in a series of "campaigns of extermination" against them. The fifth and last drive in 1934 forced the Communists to retreat on the "Long March" from Kiangsi to the remote mountainous Shensi Province in the northwest, where they remained throughout the war.

Chiang's strict policy of subduing the Communists before turning on the Japanese aroused intense opposition in China. In 1936, while on a trip, the Generalissimo was ignominiously kidnapped in the early morning clad only in a robe and nightshirt and without his dentures. His captors—members of his own Nationalist Party—demanded that he form a united front with the Communists against the Japanese. After 13 days of extensive negotiations—in which Madame Chiang and her brother T. V. Soong took part—Chiang was released. Though his pride would never let him admit that he had accepted the terms of his abductors, an uneasy alliance between the Nationalists and Communists was formed during the following year.

When the Japanese invaded China a second time, in 1937, Chiang fell back on a plan of trading space for time. By the end of 1938 his armies had yielded more than 550,000 square miles, with a population of 170 million.

Chiang had an ace up his sleeve. In 1939 he approached the U.S. government for aid and was granted $45 million. In 1940, T. V. Soong visited the U.S. and received an additional $25 million. Then, in 1943, with America now at war, Madame Chiang went to Washington to plead for further assistance. She stayed at the White House, addressed both houses of Congress and later appeared at a huge rally in the Hollywood Bowl. Her eloquence and the efforts of other China lobbyists garnered more than $1.5 billion in Lend-Lease aid and financial credits.

In civilian clothes, the Generalissimo arrives at Chungking headquarters to be named party head.

The first ladies of the U.S. and China, Mrs. Eleanor Roosevelt and Madame Chiang, take time out from their talks for a picture break at the White House.

Under orders from President Roosevelt, Chiang's bitter critic, Lieut. General Joseph Stilwell, pins America's Legion of Merit on the Generalissimo.

THE TOP TIER AT LAST

By the summer of 1943, Chiang Kai-shek was at the peak of his international prestige. In July, at the direction of President Roosevelt, Chiang received the U.S. Legion of Merit, the highest award conferred by the U.S. on a foreigner. Four months later the Generalissimo and Madame Chiang were invited by Roosevelt to join him and Prime Minister Winston Churchill at the Cairo Conference.

As the meetings got under way, Chiang and the President became involved in discussions about the war in CBI. Churchill, who had wanted to talk to Roosevelt about the invasion of Europe, found the China talks "lengthy, complicated and minor."

As for Chiang, he was delighted with the meetings. "The President will refuse me nothing," he crowed. Among other things, F.D.R. promised Chiang a massive Allied operation in the Bay of Bengal and Burma in 1944. But after the Teheran Conference two days later, at which the President and the Prime Minister met with the Soviet Premier, Roosevelt, swayed by Churchill and Stalin, withdrew his pledge.

When he heard about the President's change of mind, the Generalissimo was furious; nothing but a billion-dollar loan, he said, would "assure the Chinese people and army of your serious concern." The loan was never made. But the determined salt seller's son had one consolation: he had at least gained the status on which his stiff pride insisted—membership in the Allies' highest war councils.

In a moment of conviviality at the Cairo Conference, Chiang and his wife sit as wartime equals of President Roosevelt and Prime Minister Winston Churchill.

2

On the morning of December 20, 1941, ten twin-engined Mitsubishi bombers, each loaded with incendiaries and 500-pound bombs, took off from the Japanese-held airfield at Hanoi and began a 300-mile flight to Kunming, the China terminus of the Burma Road. The Japanese pilots anticipated a routine mission; they had been bombing Kunming on every clear day for a year. The bombers had no fighter escort and had never needed one—the Chinese had neither fighters nor antiaircraft fire to oppose them. Today, as before, the Japanese planes would fly over the Chinese city at 6,000 feet, in a stately, lethal procession.

But on this morning, approximately 30 miles southeast of Kunming, the pilots saw something unexpected—four fast fighter planes bearing down on them. Taking no chances, the Japanese jettisoned their bombs for greater speed and headed back for Hanoi. For a while they seemed to be losing their pursuers, but suddenly 10 more appeared. The fighters, garish, fearsome-looking aircraft with their noses painted to resemble the toothy grins of giant sharks, raked past the Japanese formation with machine guns blazing. One by one, the bombers exploded or fell smoking to the ground. Soon only one Mitsubishi was left to limp toward Hanoi. The shark-snouted fighters returned to Kunming, where they did triumphant slow rolls over the airfield.

The attackers belonged to a colorful new American fighter group known as the Flying Tigers, and they had just flown their first combat mission in China.

Though the Tigers were to exist as a fighting unit for only seven months, from December 1941 to July 1942, and though they would never have more than 55 planes and 70 pilots in service on any given day, they would compile an extraordinary record of victories over the Japanese. Flamboyant on the ground, daring in the air, they filled not only a military vacuum but an aching psychological need on the part of the American public. They were portrayed in the press as nearly superhuman and achieved a kind of fame rarely granted to such a small unit. Indeed, so exalted was the reputation of the Tigers and their successor organizations that many people, including Generalissimo Chiang Kai-shek, began to think that perhaps American air power could defeat Japan.

But for all the headlines they made, the Tigers could hardly begin to compensate for the losses being inflicted on

STILWELL VS. CHENNAULT

the Allies by the Japanese in the China-Burma-India Theater as a whole. The fall of Burma was just one more crushing blow, and it left the two major parts of the theater cut off from each other except by air. After his harrowing 20-day trek through the jungles and mountains to India, Stilwell had returned to Chungking determined to raise new ground forces for the campaign to retake Burma. But such a campaign would require extensive preparation. In the meantime, the Flying Tigers appeared to be the only Americans able to best the Japanese in combat.

In the months ahead, China was to become the scene of an intense struggle almost as old as the airplane itself: the argument between those who believed that a war could be won by the application of air power and those who held that victory could be achieved only through a conventional ground strategy. The argument would be echoed in Washington and London, where Allied planners were trying to devise a way to stop the seemingly invincible Japanese, and the controversy that it stirred was to have repercussions that would last as long as the War itself.

In China the argument achieved a special force. Arrayed against each other in the contest were two strong-willed men who carried themselves like porcupines with their quills erect. On one side was Stilwell, an infantryman by trade, who deeply believed that a ground war could be won only on the ground and that an air force could not do much more than "knock down a few Jap planes." On the other side was the leader of the Flying Tigers, Colonel Claire Lee Chennault, who felt that he was confronting a man who did not understand aerial warfare. Though Chennault was Stilwell's subordinate in China, he was an international hero by virtue of his airmen's accomplishments, and he communicated directly with heads of state via personal channels. He was to have an extraordinary influence on the conduct of the war in CBI.

Chennault was one of those engaging, egocentric characters in which CBI abounded. A Louisianian of Huguenot descent, he was a distant relative of Sam Houston's and Robert E. Lee's; as a young man he had been a country schoolteacher and a dedicated hunter and fisherman—indeed, his skin became so weathered by exposure to the elements that in China he was called "Old Leatherface" by his pilots. In

1917 he had joined the Army Air Corps; he spent much of his early career as a flying instructor, but his star did not rise. A prickly, cross-grained maverick, he was an outspoken critic of Air Corps doctrine.

During the years between the world wars, the Air Corps was dominated by generals who believed that technology had made the heavy bomber an invincible instrument. They were influenced by men like Billy Mitchell and Sir Hugh Trenchard, father of the Royal Air Force, and later by a book called *The War of 19—* by the Italian General Giulio Douhet, which advanced the idea that great fleets of unescorted and invulnerable bombers would decide the outcome of future wars. The Air Corps' "bomber generals" were reinforced in this belief by the development of the Martin B-10 bomber, a kind of aerial pillbox that was not only more heavily armed than standard pursuit planes of the time, but also much faster. With planes like this, the bombing advocates saw no need for fighter aircraft. Colonel Clayton Bissell, a World War I ace, suggested that the only way a fighter could knock down a modern bomber would be to drop a ball and chain into its propeller. An Air Corps general claimed that "due to increased speeds and limitless space it is impossible for fighters to intercept bombers and therefore it is inconsistent with the employment of air force to develop fighters."

In spite of the opposition of the bomber generals, Chennault remained an insistent, vocal proponent of the fighter. In his view, the pursuit plane's ineffectiveness in combat stemmed not from inherent limitations in the plane, but from the dogfight tactics devised during World War I. "There was too much," he wrote, "of an air of medieval jousting in the dogfights and not enough of the calculated massing of overwhelming force so necessary in the cold, cruel business of war." Chennault was convinced that dogfighting involved too much dispersion of fire power; he believed that planes, like infantrymen, did not win engagements individually, but by joining together to fight as teams and achieving superior fire power over the enemy.

The idea was not original with Chennault—the German ace Baron Manfred von Richthofen had employed such tactics successfully with his Flying Circus during the First World War, before the flamboyant Luftwaffe ace Hermann Göring took over the unit and led it back into tail-chasing dogfights. But Chennault clung tenaciously to his belief at a

OL' DUMBO, CONQUEROR OF THE HUMP

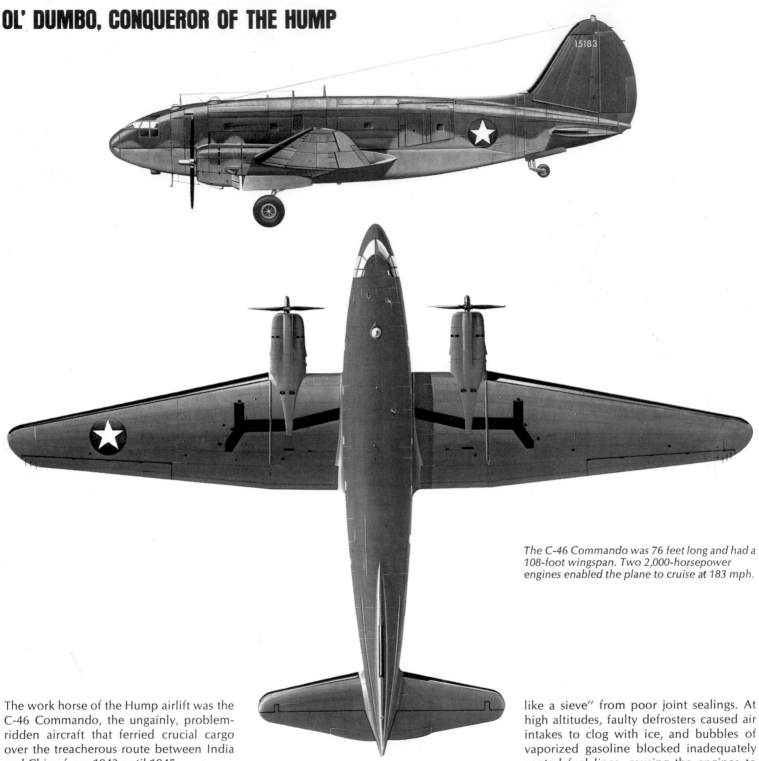

The C-46 Commando was 76 feet long and had a 108-foot wingspan. Two 2,000-horsepower engines enabled the plane to cruise at 183 mph.

The work horse of the Hump airlift was the C-46 Commando, the ungainly, problem-ridden aircraft that ferried crucial cargo over the treacherous route between India and China from 1943 until 1945.

Originally a 36-passenger luxury plane designed by Curtiss-Wright in 1937, the C-46 was the largest, heaviest twin-engine transport used by the Army Air Forces in the War. Its 2,300-cubic-foot cargo hold could be crammed with four tons of supplies—nearly twice the capacity of its predecessor, the C-47. Moreover, the plane could operate at altitudes of more than 24,000 feet—and often had to fly that high to get over the highest peaks in bad weather. Pilots nicknamed it Ol' Dumbo, after Walt Disney's flying elephant.

But whatever its virtues as a cargo carrier, the C-46 was not without serious defects. In heavy rains, the fuselage "leaked like a sieve" from poor joint sealings. At high altitudes, faulty defrosters caused air intakes to clog with ice, and bubbles of vaporized gasoline blocked inadequately vented fuel lines, causing the engines to lose power or quit. Even more hazardous were fuel-line breaks, which spewed gasoline onto hot engine compartments, causing fires and mid-air explosions. Scores of C-46s went down over the Hump; there were so many wrecked planes over one stretch of rugged country that pilots referred to it as the "aluminum trail."

time when the Air Corps was still teaching dogfight tactics.

To prove that a group of planes could operate as a tightly knit team during the violent maneuvers of combat, Chennault and two other pilots formed a precision-flying team known as "Three Men on a Flying Trapeze." They performed breath-taking acrobatics—loops, spins and turns—in formation and executed a spectacular "squirrel-cage" maneuver in which the planes did slow rolls while barrel-rolling around each other. To cap their performance, the pilots tied their wing tips together with 20-foot lengths of rope and executed more loops and spins. Appearing at air shows around the country, Chennault won public acclaim, but his displays had little influence on the hierarchy of the Air Corps—indeed, in 1936 the tactical school at Maxwell Field, Alabama, where he was an instructor, stopped teaching fighter tactics altogether. In 1937, when he was a 47-year-old captain, Chennault retired from the service for medical reasons—partial deafness and chronic bronchitis—and many of his superiors were happy to see him go.

But the Chinese had heard of Chennault and his expertise with pursuit planes, and they asked him to advise their government. Upon arriving in China in May 1937, Chennault met Madame Chiang Kai-shek, who had been assigned by her husband to vitalize the tottering Chinese Air Force. Chennault was captivated by her, and the day they met he wrote in his diary, "She will always be a princess to me." In the years ahead Madame Chiang was to be Chennault's patron and steadfast champion.

At the time, the Chinese Air Force existed mostly on paper, with 500 planes on the books but only 91 fit for combat. The rest either were not in flying condition or did not exist. Funds to purchase aircraft were raised by subscriptions in different Chinese cities. A rally would be held in one city and a new plane flown in. At the climax of the rally the name of the city would be painted on the fuselage. In reality, the same plane was flown from city to city, its name being changed for each new rally. As often as not the money raised vanished into government coffers, and the Chinese Air Force remained ineffectual.

Within weeks of Chennault's arrival, the Sino-Japanese War broke out and he soon found himself overseeing a rag-tag air force composed of Chinese pilots and international mercenaries—a kind of aerial foreign legion. Some of the mercenaries were skilled, but others were distinguished chiefly by their uncanny ability to crack up planes on landings and takeoffs. Most of the Chinese pilots were the scions of influential families. They had learned to fly at an Italian-staffed school at Loyang in north-central China, which operated on the principle that wealthy young men were not to be washed out. As a result, Chinese pilots who supposedly were combat-ready left airfields strewn with the wreckage of their planes. On a single infuriating day, in perfect weather, Chennault watched them destroy six out of 13 pursuit planes in landing and takeoff accidents.

Chennault set about making the Chinese Air Force into an effective fighting unit. He revised training procedures, taught new tactics and established a vast radio and telephone network to signal the approach of Japanese bombers. To overcome Chungking's inertia and accomplish his objectives, he adopted the trick of periodically offering his resignation to Madame Chiang. She never accepted.

In the months that followed, Chennault's pilots put up a spirited defense, but they were no match for the superior numbers of the Japanese and the high performance of their planes. By the summer of 1940 a hundred enemy planes a day were bombing Chungking and the Chiangs decided to exert every effort to get American planes and well-trained American pilots into the war.

However, this was not an easy plan to realize, for the United States was not yet a belligerent. But China had a skillful and persuasive advocate in T. V. Soong, Madame Chiang's brother and China's chief lobbyist in the U.S. With help from influential American friends of China, Soong got President Roosevelt's reluctant permission for Chennault to hire American military pilots for China's Air Force. Since all of those concerned were anxious to keep the operation quiet, Chennault used an aircraft maintenance company as a cover employer.

Chennault recruited 112 pilots from the Army, Navy and Marine Corps with Roosevelt's approval—they were permitted to resign with the unspoken understanding that they could return to their branches of service when their work was done. Chennault also managed to buy 100 P-40 fighters that had been earmarked for the British but had been rejected by them as obsolete. In the late summer of 1941 the mercenaries—now officially known as the American Volunteer Group, or AVG—were sent to China, where Chennault put them through intensive training at Loiwing on the Burma border.

Chennault was a man of vast ambition and pride, but he understood fighter planes, and even General Marshall, the Army Chief of Staff, who neither liked nor trusted him, was moved to comment that Chennault was probably "a tactical genius." Now Chennault put that genius to work. His basic aircraft, the P-40 Tomahawk, had been used by the British with a notable lack of success against German fighters. But with their own Spitfires and Hurricanes, RAF pilots had confirmed the worth and versatility of fighter aircraft in the defensive war of the Battle of Britain. The P-40 was a heavy, durable airplane with thick armor to protect the pilot. It was relatively fast in straightaway flight and could achieve great speed in a dive, but its excessive weight made it sluggish in climbing and clumsy to maneuver by comparison with the lightweight, agile Japanese fighters.

Chennault devised offensive tactics that were geared to the P-40's strengths and weaknesses. The pilots were to fight in pairs, diving, shooting and breaking away, and then, if possible, returning for another diving pass—but they were not to engage the light-footed Japanese Zeroes or Kate fighters in one-on-one duels. He cautioned his men: "Never, never, in a P-40, try to outmaneuver and perform acro-

batics with a Jap Kate or Zero. Such tactics, take it from me, are strictly nonhabit-forming."

From the start, the AVG was anything but a spit-and-polish outfit. Military formalities were dispensed with, and discipline was lax to the point of being nonexistent. The pilots often wore high-heeled cowboy boots as part of their uniform, and they took pleasure in high living and in performing daredevil acts. Many scandalized the British by turning up at the Silver Grill in Rangoon with native girls on their arms and carousing into the night. On one occasion at a bar in Rangoon, Chennault's men talked the pilot of a C-47 cargo plane into making a night raid on Hanoi. They loaded the fuselage with old French, Russian and Chinese bombs, and fueled themselves with a hefty store of liquor. When the plane reached the target, the well-lubricated fliers simply kicked the bombs out the open door.

Inspired by a British squadron in Africa, the pilots painted the noses of their planes to make them look like sharks. This, they felt, would have a psychological effect on the Japanese. The AVG pilots adopted the nickname Flying Tigers and a Walt Disney artist contributed a whimsical AVG mascot in the form of a Bengal tiger with tiny wings leaping through a V for victory. The symbol was painted on the tails of the planes.

The Tigers were ready to begin active operations at the time of Pearl Harbor. Chennault split his forces between Burma, where one unit joined the British in the defense of

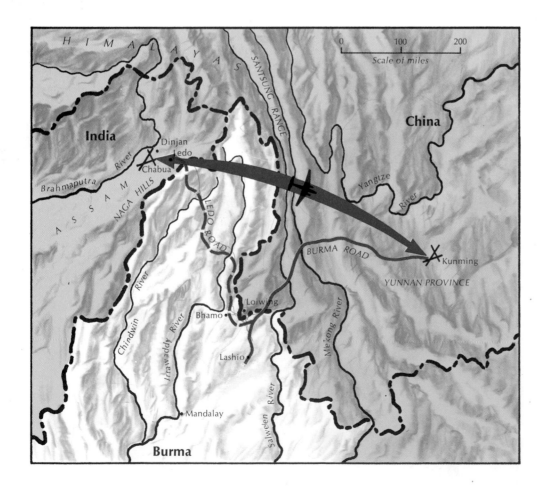

Taking off from bases near Chabua in Assam, India, U.S. Air Transport Command planes flew military cargo via the so-called Hump route (red arrow) over the Himalayas to Kunming and other points in China's Yunnan Province. For nearly three years after the Japanese conquered Burma early in March of 1942, the treacherous 500-mile sky route was the sole means of supplying Allied forces in China.

Rangoon, and Kunming, where the other unit set up a protective air screen for western China. From the outset, theirs was a makeshift operation. In daily combat against superior forces and without replacement planes or spare parts, the Tigers plugged bullet holes in their gas tanks with chewing gum and patched up riddled fuselages with adhesive tape. Since their airplanes had neither bombs nor bomb racks, they experimented with incendiaries made of gasoline-filled whiskey bottles and dropped homemade pipe bombs down chutes normally used for flares.

Yet for all their improvised operations, the Tigers raised such hob with the Japanese over Burma that Tokyo radio broadcast: "The American pilots in Chinese planes are unprincipled bandits. Unless they cease their unorthodox tactics, they will be treated as guerrillas"—that is, they risked being executed if captured. After the fall of Rangoon on March 7, 1942, Chennault finally withdrew his last few planes from Burma to China. There they provided air defense for the bomb-battered cities of western China and also continued to run raids over Burma, primarily to protect convoys on the Burma Road.

Japanese ground forces had rushed through the gap left when the Chinese 55th Division melted away at Toungoo and were now moving up the Burma Road, across the Chinese border and toward the Salween River, whose mighty gorges posed a major obstacle to any further advance. Chennault sent a pitifully small force to bomb and strafe the road, and only a handful of Japanese crossed the river. Chennault, not unreasonably, assumed that his few airplanes had stopped the offensive. Actually, the Japanese had no intention of pressing on across the Salween and deeper into China at the time. It was a misconception that was to have important ramifications in months to come.

By their own count, in seven months of combat in CBI, the AVG destroyed a total of 299 planes, plus 153 probables. It is possible that the mercenaries, who got a bonus for every plane they shot down, exaggerated their claims, but the fact is indisputable that the Tigers had dealt the Japanese a stunning blow. Most surprising of all, only four Tigers had been killed in aerial combat—far more died in accidents or as a result of ground fire.

It was an extraordinary record, but now that the United States was in the War, it had no interest in supporting a private air force that functioned outside military channels. On July 4, 1942, the American Volunteer Group was disbanded and re-formed into a regular Army Air Forces unit known as the China Air Task Force, with Chennault—who was now a brigadier general—in command. Chennault felt that he had earned the right to run his own show. But his maverick reputation still worked against him back in Washington, and he was made subordinate to Clayton Bissell, his old adversary in the fighter-versus-bomber dispute and now the commander of the Tenth Air Force, which was based in India. Chennault was also subordinate to the American theater commander, Stilwell, now actively planning the new ground campaign in Burma.

A showdown between Stilwell and Chennault and their opposing strategies for winning the war in CBI was inevitable. In Stilwell, Chennault would encounter a determination as unyielding as his own. But in a contest of conflicting theories, Stilwell lacked finesse. As a diplomat and salesman he was no match for Chennault.

Upon his arrival in Chungking from India in June, Stilwell had given the Generalissimo a no-punches-pulled critique of the Chinese Army's performance in Burma. In general, Chinese manners—and a long tradition of circumspection—preclude the blunt expression of disagreeable truths. Chiang, who was accustomed to being spoken to deferentially, reacted so sharply to what Stilwell had to say that Stilwell noted later in his diary that "it was like kicking an old lady in the stomach."

The Generalissimo was disturbed by Stilwell's aggressive insistence on an early offensive to recapture Burma. In Stilwell's view, however, and that of his superiors in Washington, the Allies needed to move as quickly as possible to reopen a supply line to China—for China loomed large in the eyes of American planners. With Allied forces moving slowly in the southwest Pacific, China seemed a logical place from which to launch the ultimate offensive against Japan. If a land line of communication could be established and military supplies delivered to China in quantity, and if the Chinese Army could be built into an effective fighting force, then China could become a base for bombing Japan and launching an amphibious assault against the enemy's home islands. This hooking blow, in combination with the drive up the Pacific islands, could destroy the enemy.

Stilwell hoped to reenter Burma in the fall of 1942 to take advantage of the winter dry season, but it was not until November of that year that the British and the Chinese tentatively agreed to a plan code-named *Anakim*. In *Anakim*, the British would thrust from India back into central and southern Burma, establish naval superiority in the Bay of Bengal and mount an amphibious assault against Rangoon. Meanwhile, in north Burma, Chinese troops would attempt to close a great pincer.

Approximately 9,000 Chinese soldiers had fled into India when Burma collapsed, and this force would be augmented with thousands of soldiers airlifted from China to provide two full-strength divisions plus supporting units. Trained by newly arrived Americans at an Indian base called Ramgarh and outfitted with modern equipment, this X Force, as it was called, would plunge into Upper Burma from the west. Back in China proper, the Chinese Sixth Army would be reorganized, trained and equipped in Yunnan Province. This force, known as the Y Force, would attack westward across the Salween from China. Once the X and Y forces completed their pincer, they would turn south to link with British troops thrusting north from newly recaptured Rangoon. If the entire operation could be completed successfully the old Burma Road would be reopened and China once again could be supplied via the port of Rangoon.

There was a backup provision, too. As the Chinese infantrymen fought their way across north Burma, engineers would follow in their tracks and build a new road from Ledo, in Assam in India, across monstrously difficult country to link up with the old Burma Road near Bhamo. Thus, even if the British failed to retake Rangoon, a successful campaign by the Chinese in the north would allow the completion of the new Ledo Road and end China's long blockade. From India, goods could then flow by land directly across north Burma for the first time, join the Burma Road at the border of China, then make their way up its twisting, precipitous path the last 600 miles to Kunming.

The *Anakim* plan had one great weakness—neither the British nor the Chinese were wholeheartedly behind it. For the British, with their resources stretched thin by the war against Germany, *Anakim's* demands for men and matériel would be extremely difficult to meet. The road and rail network in India, which would be the base for any Burma campaign, was in such disarray that the logistical problems seemed almost insuperable to General Sir Archibald Wavell, who had succeeded General Alexander as the British commander in Southeast Asia. (Alexander had been reassigned as commander in chief in the Middle East.) There were other factors that contributed to British reluctance. The British remained cool to the idea of China emerging from the War as a great world power. And they had no great enthusiasm for fighting again in the jungles; at one point Churchill likened the recapture of Burma to "munching a porcupine, quill by quill."

The Generalissimo had his own reservations about *Anakim*. He felt that Stilwell's aggressive tactics in the first Burma campaign had resulted in the destruction of his Fifth Army. He still had about 400,000 well-trained troops, but he was using these in northwest China to contain his archenemies, Mao Tse-tung's Communist forces; if the Communists brought down the Nationalists the result might be disastrous for the Allies. Chiang was therefore unwilling to commit any of these troops to a Burma campaign. Furthermore, with his well-founded mistrust of his generals, he felt wary about letting Stilwell train an elite force, which could add to his woes by creating a powerful rival out of the man who commanded it. Finally, Chiang did not want to send his armies to battle in Burma unless the British first took Rangoon and established control of the Bay of Bengal, thus eliminating the possibility that the Japanese could reinforce their land troops there by sea. Chiang had little confidence that the British would keep their part of the bargain.

Frustrated but determined, Stilwell labored to make the ground campaign in Burma a reality. He commuted between Chungking and the British headquarters in Delhi, badgering Chiang on one hand and Wavell on the other, using what he called his "sleeve-jerking" technique. "Hell," he said, "I'm nothing but an errand boy. I run up to Chungking and jerk the Gimo's sleeve. I tell him he better get ready to move down the Salween because the British are planning to move into Burma from the south. I tell him that the Chinese are going to lose a lot of face if the British do it alone. Then I fly down to India and jerk Archie Wavell's sleeve. The Gimo is going to move down the Salween, I tell

Archie, and you better get going too. You limeys are going to have a hell of a time with the white man's burden if the Chinese have nerve enough to fight and you haven't."

In response to Stilwell's importuning, Wavell seemed to the American "mumbly and indefinite" and a "tired old man." Time and again he expressed a reluctance to start a campaign in early 1943, citing logistical problems, the imminence of the next monsoon and numerous other obstacles. With his problems in China to distract him, the Generalissimo was also on-again, off-again. He would promise cooperation, then make that cooperation contingent on receiving increased Lend-Lease supplies.

The growing animosity between Stilwell and Chiang was becoming a major obstacle to effective cooperation in CBI. The Generalissimo believed that Stilwell had overstepped his authority and had repeatedly shown contempt for the Chinese head of staff by talking behind his back and harping on the shortcomings of his army. In an *aide-mémoire* the exasperated Chiang expressed the conviction that Stilwell "had no intention of cooperating with me but believed that he was in fact appointed to command me."

On Stilwell's part he began to show an increasingly sharper edge with Chiang in his letters and diaries. He referred to him as a "stupid little ass" or the "little jackass," or as a "stubborn, ignorant, prejudiced, conceited despot who never hears the truth except from me and finds it hard to believe." He compared the Chinese Nationalists to the Nazis and raged that Americans had been "manuevered into the position of having to support this rotten regime and glorify its figurehead, the all-wise great patriot and soldier—Peanut. My God." While Stilwell was generally discreet with his more sulfuric observations, his own household staff in Chungking included informers, and there is little question that the gist, if not the specifics, of his views got back to the Generalissimo and exacerbated the deteriorating relations between the two men.

Stilwell wanted to use Lend-Lease as a lever to move Chiang. He felt that action should be required in return for continued U.S. support. He asked Washington for authority to administer Lend-Lease on a *quid pro quo* basis. Roosevelt was adamantly opposed, for he felt it would be demeaning to treat a fellow chief of state and commander in chief in such a fashion. The President warned Marshall and Stilwell:

"One cannot speak sternly to a man like that or exact commitments from him the way we might do from the Sultan of Morocco."

Despite the squabbling among the Allies, planning for a Burma campaign continued. The Generalissimo designated the units to be organized into the Y Force on the Salween. The British—worried that old Chinese claims to parts of India and Burma would be reactivated by a large Chinese presence in India—reluctantly agreed to allow additional Chinese troops to move to Ramgarh to beef up the X Force.

At the beginning, the quality of troops sent to Ramgarh was so poor that the Americans setting up the training camps all but despaired. American doctors—accustomed to U.S. standards—rejected 40 per cent of the men because of their poor physical condition; in one group the rejection rate reached 89 per cent. In order to cram more men onto the planes to India, the Chinese commander, General Lo Cho-ying, made them strip naked. "It's only three hours!" he said. In the frigid flight over the mountains, several men froze to death, and others became ill. To the American fliers the troop airlift became known as "Operation Vomit." Once in India, though, the Chinese soldiers encountered conditions unlike any they had ever known. With good medical attention and all the food they could eat, they soon gained an average of 20 pounds a man. They were paid directly by the Americans, without losing the customary rake-off to their commanders, and they learned how to handle mortars, 75mm howitzers and field telephones—at the time, telephones were still a novelty in much of China—with a speed that impressed the American teachers.

The competition between Stilwell and Chennault was to be intensified by the supply situation in CBI. In Europe, which had first priority on U.S. war matériel, supplies were so abundant that a massive air strategy and major ground campaigns could be conducted against Germany simultaneously. But in CBI, which was receiving only limited supplies, it was an either-or proposition. A priority had to be given to the air or ground strategies, and even then nobody—on the ground or in the air—got what he really needed. In China, Stilwell's Y Force faced a critical supply problem. With the Japanese holding all of Burma, every bean and bullet had to be flown from air bases in Assam 500 miles to Kunming in China. During the flight, cargo planes of the Air Transport Command (ATC) had to cross the 15,000-foot Santsung Range, a Himalayan spur that became famous as "the Hump." Violent storms and high winds made every trip a nightmare, and monsoon rains reduced visibility to zero. Pilots began calling one peak in the Hump the "aluminum-plated mountain" because so many planes were splattered on it.

War matériel entering China amounted to a mere trickle. Neither Stilwell nor Chennault ever had enough of anything. For Chennault in particular the logistical problem was mind boggling. "It was as though," he wrote, "an air force based in Kansas was supplied from San Francisco to bomb targets from Maine to Florida."

In fact, the situation was worse. Chennault's planes operated at the end of the world's longest and most complicated supply line. After the 12,000-mile sea trip from the U.S. to Karachi or Bombay, his supplies had to cross India by rail for 1,500 miles, then transfer to an ancient railway between Bengal and Assam known to Americans as the "Toonerville Trolley." Built to carry tea down from the Assam highlands, the railway changed gauge three times, and its freight had to cross the unbridged Brahmaputra—one of Asia's great rivers—by barge. From Assam the ATC then had to fly the matériel 500 miles across the Hump to Kunming.

After Chennault established forward air bases in China in 1942 from which to attack Japanese lines of communication, his supplies had to be transported from Kunming over horrible roads by truck and donkey cart for another 400 to 700 miles. Sometimes coolies rolled drums of aviation gasoline as much as 100 miles to fuel Chennault's aircraft. Under ideal conditions, supplies from Kunming took eight weeks to reach the forward bases. To airlift gasoline from Kunming to these fields, cargo planes burned three gallons of fuel for every two gallons they delivered. One of Chennault's units, the 308th Bomber Squadron, tried to become self-supporting by flying its own fuel and ordnance over the Hump. For every combat mission that the 308th flew in China, it had to make three round trips to Assam to keep itself adequately supplied. Chennault calculated that for him to drop one ton of bombs on Japanese-held Shanghai, 18 tons of supplies had to be delivered to an Indian port. As a result, Chennault's entire command

was once grounded for 33 days because of lack of fuel.

To keep planes operating in spite of shortages, engine oil was filtered and used over and over again, worn tail wheel casings were stuffed with old rags, and auxiliary fuel tanks were manufactured from bamboo and fish glue.

For all its problems, Chennault's China Air Task Force managed—as had the Flying Tigers before it—to perform with remarkable effectiveness against the numerically superior Japanese. To avoid being caught on the ground, Chennault's pilots hopscotched about from one small airstrip to another. They were helped by the extensive radio- and telephone-warning net that Chennault had established; not only did it allow the Americans to keep one step ahead of the Japanese, but it frequently enabled them to take the enemy by surprise in the air. Chennault continued to work out new tricks and tactics, and—although he now had eight B-25 bombers—his men continued to improvise with the work-horse P-40s, converting them into photoreconnaissance planes, night fighters and even dive bombers.

As time passed, and air operations improved, the argument over the strategy for winning the war in CBI intensified. Chennault became more and more convinced that, given a modest-sized air force and a priority on supplies, he could destroy the Japanese Air Force, interdict the enemy's sea-lanes and ultimately launch bombing attacks against the home islands—a combination of blows that he thought would quickly bring Japan to its knees. Given his own accomplishments in Burma with a tiny force, he felt that Stilwell's advocacy of a ground offensive there was absurd. To the airman, Stilwell was a myopic, hidebound old infantryman who had "a strong prejudice against air power coupled with a faint suspicion of any weapon more complicated than a rifle and bayonet." As Chennault saw it, Stilwell's desire to fight his way back into Burma simply reflected a determination to avenge his earlier defeat, a kind of "I shall return" obsession.

Stilwell, meanwhile, was becoming all the more convinced that Chennault's air strategy was a prescription for disaster. He felt that Chennault's proposals, if followed, would produce the same grim results as the dramatic but widely misunderstood Doolittle raid of early 1942. In an attempt to deliver a blow to the Japanese homeland and boost sagging American morale, Colonel James Doolittle had led a flight of carrier-based B-25 bombers on an attack against Tokyo on April 18, 1942. After striking the city, the planes flew on to China, where many of them crash-landed in Chekiang Province. Japan retaliated by sending 53 battalions of infantry raging through Chekiang, where they annihilated entire villages suspected of having aided Doolittle's pilots, killed 250,000 Chinese and plowed up every airfield in an area of 20,000 square miles.

Stilwell felt that Chennault's plan would produce similar terrible results. Until the Chinese Army as a whole was trained to a higher standard, any serious attempt by Chennault to hurt Japan would result in swift, effective retaliation. Stilwell's view was summed up in an exchange with an engineering officer he encountered at a new airstrip. "What the hell are you building this airfield for?" the general demanded.

"Well, Chennault says he needs it."

"How's he going to defend it?"

But if Stilwell was not impressed with Chennault's plan, Chiang was. If American air power could win the war, it would eliminate the need for the Burma campaign, it would make unnecessary the reorganization of the Chinese Army, and eventually it would leave Chiang in possession of large numbers of soldiers and large quantities of unexpended matériel for use against the Communists after the war.

Chiang was also growing increasingly unhappy with Stilwell. The Generalissimo wanted more Lend-Lease supplies than he was getting and he believed that Stilwell, in his capacity as Lend-Lease administrator, was holding out on him. At one point, Chiang went so far as to suggest that if the United States did not increase its support he would seek "other arrangements"—a veiled threat that he might make a separate peace agreement with Japan. Regarding Stilwell an intolerable obstacle, he preferred to deal with Roosevelt directly or by special emissary, and he was soon to reach the point where he would ask for Stilwell's recall and his replacement by Chennault.

Chennault gained another ally in October of 1942, when Wendell Willkie visited China. Having beaten Willkie in the 1940 election, Roosevelt had sent his former rival on a round-the-world trip as a good-will ambassador. Regarding Willkie as an envoy of great stature—and mindful of the possibility that he might run for President again in 1944—Chiang laid out the red carpet.

In his diary Stilwell forecast that Willkie would be "thoroughly immersed in soft soap, adulation and flattery," and that the Chinese would "keep him so torpid with food and drink that his faculties will be dulled and he'll be stuffed with the right doctrines." Indeed, Willkie was wined, dined and feted, and even given a tour of the "front"—a long-somnolent area along the Yellow River near Sian where Chinese and Japanese soldiers peacefully traded goods with each other. During the visit Willkie was exposed to the Chiangs' strong backing for Chennault.

With Stilwell as his guide, Willkie then went to Chennault's Kunming headquarters, where he had a private two-hour conversation with the aviator. During the conversation Chennault presented his plan for defeating Japan through air power, and Willkie must have been impressed, for on his trip back to Chungking he found nothing at all to discuss with Stilwell. "Willkie off, thank God," wrote Stilwell in his diary. "He hardly spoke to me. Utterly indifferent."

During their meeting Willkie asked Chennault to explain his plan in a letter, which could be passed on to Roosevelt on Willkie's return to the United States. Chennault did so. In his letter he claimed that "given full authority as the

Bespectacled T. V. Soong, meeting here with Chinese generals, was one of Nationalist China's most effective advocates. As Minister of Foreign Affairs and head of the Bank of China, he frequently visited Washington to lobby for aid. Through his friendship with fellow Harvard alumnus Franklin Roosevelt, he persuaded the U.S. to grant China $100 million.

American military commander in China," he could "bring about the downfall of Japan." To accomplish this feat Chennault needed an air force of 105 modern fighters, 30 medium bombers and 12 heavy bombers, plus replacements. With such a force Chennault would "guarantee to destroy the principal industrial centers of Japan," save the lives "of hundreds of thousands of American soldiers and sailors," and leave nothing but a minor mopping-up operation for MacArthur. The defense of the lifeline over the Hump—a task that Stilwell had made Chennault's top priority—was unnecessary, an idea produced by an "orthodox, rigid military mind." Chennault would defend the Hump as Scipio Africanus had defended Rome against Hannibal—that is, by attacking the enemy's homeland.

Upon reaching Washington the letter came to the attention of the War Department, where it caused an uproar. Chennault was not only claiming that he could defeat Japan with a tiny air force, but demanding that he replace his own superior, Stilwell. Marshall, always a staunch backer of Stilwell, was infuriated, and said later that Chennault's plan was "just nonsense; not bad strategy, just nonsense."

But the Chennault proposal had a far different impact on Roosevelt. Madame Chiang came to the United States for an extended visit in November of 1942, stayed as a guest in the White House and took advantage of the occasion to bring her famous charm to bear. Although Roosevelt treated her gingerly for fear she might vamp him, Madame Chiang had the opportunity to make clear the Generalissimo's preference for Chennault and his strategy. Other emissaries from China brought Roosevelt the same word, and Chennault's public-relations aide, the peacetime newspaper columnist Joseph Alsop, made articulate pleas on Chennault's behalf to Roosevelt's close adviser, Harry Hopkins.

Despite Marshall's support for Stilwell and the War Department's continuing distrust of Chennault, Roosevelt began to lean toward the aviator's point of view. For one thing, Chennault's proposal seemed to offer a cheap way of winning the war against Japan. There were political considerations, too. Roosevelt was determined to see China emerge from the War a major power, a free nation that would fill the Asian vacuum created by the fall of Japan. Chiang was the only man who appeared to have any chance of holding the country together, and if he wanted to follow

an air-power strategy, Roosevelt felt disposed to go along.

Thus, in the fall of 1942 enthusiasm for a ground offensive in Burma was collapsing on all sides. The Allies were deeply involved in the landings and subsequent build-up of forces in North Africa, and Marshall sent Stilwell a letter saying that for *Anakim* he could depend on little more than Lend-Lease supplies already on hand or in the pipeline. An exasperated Stilwell noted in his diary: "Peanut and I are on a raft, with one sandwich between us, and the rescue ship is heading away from the scene."

Soon after, in December, Wavell began to pull back from *Anakim* on the ground that the British were not yet prepared for such a major undertaking. On January 8, Chiang announced that he, too, was pulling out—and wrote to Roosevelt of the "remarkable potentialities of an air offensive" as recommended by Chennault. In his diary Stilwell noted down the day as "Black Friday" and wrote: "Peanut says he won't fight. . . . What a break for the Limeys. Now they will quit, and the Chinese will quit, and the goddam Americans can go ahead and fight. Chennault's blatting has put us in a spot; he's talked so much about what he can do that now they're going to let him do it."

From time to time Stilwell indulged himself in the writing of doggerel verse, often rich in scatological references, and not long after Black Friday he vented his spleen in a poem, "Lyric to Spring," which he sent to his wife back home in Carmel, California. The last stanza read:

Take me back to the Coast, to the place I love most,
Get me out of this odorous sewer.
I'm in . . . to my neck, but I'm quitting, by heck!
And I'll nevermore shovel manure.

At the Casablanca Conference in January 1943, however, Marshall and Admiral Ernest J. King, the U.S. Chief of Naval Operations, argued forcefully on behalf of continuing *Anakim*. When the British objected that the campaign would draw off many of the landing craft needed for the planned cross-Channel invasion of Europe, King offered to release landing craft from the Pacific for Burma operations. The British then agreed, and the combined chiefs decided to launch the Burma offensive in November 1943. But Roosevelt was still thinking of Chennault's proposals. In March he dissolved the old China Air Task Force and placed Chennault in charge of a new, China-based Fourteenth Air Force. Chennault was given a second star and made independent of Bissell's Tenth Air Force command in India; he was now subordinate only to Stilwell, and only marginally subordinate at that.

In late April, 1943, at the urging of the Generalissimo, Roosevelt decided to call Chennault back to Washington for conferences—climaxing in the Trident Conference attended by Churchill himself. Marshall, angered by this bypassing of the chain of command, insisted that Stilwell return too, and it was determined that both commanders would attend the conference to be held in May.

Stilwell undoubtedly felt that his subordinate was undermining him, and was dismayed that Roosevelt was seriously considering Chennault's "six-months-to-drive-the-Japs-out-of-China plan." When the two generals met in Kunming for their flight back to America, Stilwell simply growled "Where are your bags?" and made no attempt to be cordial.

In Washington, Stilwell and Chennault each met privately with Roosevelt. In his own audience Stilwell, ordinarily an articulate man, was so embarrassed at having to press his case before the President that he seemed tongue-tied, and Roosevelt thought he might be sick. Chennault, on the other hand, radiated confidence. At one stage in the discussion Chennault said that his planes could sink a million tons of Japanese shipping; the statement so excited the President that he pounded his desk and exclaimed: "If you can sink a million tons, we'll break their backs."

For Roosevelt, the difference between the two generals may have become most pronounced during a joint meeting when he asked each one in turn to give a personal appraisal of Chiang Kai-shek. According to Chennault, Stilwell responded: "He's a vacillating, tricky, undependable old scoundrel who never keeps his word." Chennault replied: "Sir, I think the Generalissimo is one of the two or three greatest military and political leaders in the world today. He has never broken a commitment or promise made to me." Roosevelt was persuaded by Chennault's position and he invited the airman to communicate with him personally in the future.

At the Trident Conference, Stilwell, as the U.S. commander in CBI, was called upon to present his views on strategy, and he found himself in the uncomfortable position of then being rebutted by his subordinate, Chennault, who spoke up in opposition from a corner of the room. Stilwell was surly and ill-tempered, and repeatedly objected to Chennault's plan on the ground that as soon as the Fourteenth Air Force stung the Japanese enough, Japan would march on Chennault's airfields and easily capture them. He reminded everyone of the grisly aftermath of the Doolittle raid and warned that Chennault's air offensive would fail unless a Chinese army was trained and equipped to repel the Japanese on the ground. And training and equipping such an army meant that *Anakim* had to go forward.

The American Chiefs of Staff were planted firmly behind Stilwell, but the countervailing forces were too great. The British Chiefs claimed that full-scale operations to recapture Burma could not be started in the 1943-1944 combat season, and Wavell advanced a host of arguments about the difficulties of fighting in the jungle. Churchill proposed that Burma be bypassed entirely. He favored operations against the island of Sumatra as a stepping stone toward the recapture of Singapore. After having taken a positive position toward *Anakim* at the Casablanca Conference four months earlier, the British now felt that operations on the Asian mainland should be limited to those supporting Chennault's air offensive against Japan. Roosevelt agreed, and told the conference that he wanted immediate action in China and that only Chennault could offer it.

The result of Trident was a compromise favoring the Chennault plan. *Anakim* was discarded and replaced by *Saucy,* a much more modest operation, which involved advances by Stilwell's Chinese troops into north Burma and a limited offensive by the British into central Burma. *Saucy* left out the blow toward Rangoon, and as Stilwell complained to Churchill, it offered many loopholes to an unaggressive commander. Chennault was to press ahead with his air offensive, and to this end he was to receive a priority on supplies over the Hump until the end of October. The decision in favor of air power meant that at a critical point Stilwell's attempts to prepare the Y Force and build an effective Chinese army would be seriously impaired.

Chagrined and bested by his subordinate, Stilwell recorded his frustration in his diary during the return flight to Asia: "What's the use when the World's Greatest Strategist is against you?"

THE FLAMBOYANT TIGERS

A rakish P-40, mainstay of the Flying Tigers, re-created in full detail by an artist, is adorned with a shapely nude, winged tiger and Chinese Nationalist star.

AN OUTFIT THAT BEAT THE ODDS

Chinese Air Force wings (top) and a patch bearing the Chinese Nationalist flag and flier identification (below) were worn by the Flying Tigers.

While Allied ground forces were suffering humiliating defeats in Burma in 1942, Claire L. Chennault's sharpshooting Flying Tigers were racking up impressive victories over the Japanese in the air. Flying durable but obsolete P-40s, emblazoned with the chilling eyes and jagged teeth of a shark, the Tigers were one of the most colorful and deadly fighting units of World War II.

Recruited from the U.S. armed services to fight for the Chinese before the United States itself was at war, the Flying Tigers originally were a ragtag band of 112 mercenary pilots called the American Volunteer Group (AVG). Their bogus passports for the trip to the Orient listed them as salesmen, teachers, tourists, musicians, vaudeville artists, bankers and baseball players. They fought as the AVG for just over six months, then were disbanded after the U.S. went to war; they thereafter provided the nucleus for the U.S. China Air Task Force's 23rd Fighter Group, which was made part of the U.S. Fourteenth Air Force in March 1943.

The Flying Tigers had to brave overwhelming numbers of Japanese planes—including darting Zeroes that could turn and climb more than twice as fast as P-40s. On February 25, 1942, the Japanese dispatched 166 planes to bomb and strafe Rangoon. The Tigers met the attack with nine P-40s, bagged 24 aircraft and lost only three. The next day some 200 Japanese planes raided the city. This time, 18 enemy planes went down; all six AVG craft landed safely. Each kill meant another miniature Japanese flag painted beneath the canopy of a P-40.

The major reason for the Tigers' success lay in the unorthodox tactics taught by Chennault. "Use your speed and diving power to make a pass, shoot and break away," he told his men. To emphasize his point, he diagramed tactics on a chalkboard like a football coach and scrutinized flying skills through binoculars from a rickety bamboo tower.

By the war's end, the Flying Tigers had made a key contribution to Allied victory in CBI; they were credited with destroying more than 1,200 Japanese planes, plus up to 700 probables. Their own losses came to 573 planes.

Commander of the U.S. Fourteenth Air Force and founder of the Flying Tigers, Major General Claire L. Chennault—"Old Leatherface"—stands beside a P-40.

Original pilots of the AVG's Hell's Angels Squadron line up before a P-40 in 1942. The plane bears the unit's insignia—a nude angel—and five "kill" flags.

Gregory "Pappy" Boyington shot down six Japanese planes in CBI; later he won the Medal of Honor in the Central Solomons.

A GUNG HO BREED OF DAREDEVIL PILOTS

The original Flying Tigers were a rough-and-tumble band of ex-Army, Navy and Marine pilots who had itched for combat and leaped at the chance to join the AVG. "Here's an opportunity for real experience, combat experience," said an AVG recruiter in 1941. "And besides, there's good dough in it." Although the financial rewards for the Tigers were great for the time—between $600 and $750 per month (almost the price of a small car) and a $500 bonus for each enemy plane that they destroyed—a quarter of the thrill-seeking fliers did not even bother to ask about the pay when they joined up.

Organized into three squadrons—Hell's Angels, Panda Bears and the Adam and Eves—the pilots always were eager for a fight. To trick the Japanese into treating them respectfully, pilots changed the numbers on the fuselages and repainted the noses of their P-40s in different colors at frequent intervals; the idea was to make the enemy think more planes were opposing them. Such ploys were so effective that, in the fall of 1942, Tokyo radio broadcast a pledge to destroy all 200 fighter planes of the Flying Tigers. In reality, there were only 29 in commission at the time.

On the ground, the Tigers led a close-to-normal life. Military discipline was minimal; only during formal celebrations and at funerals did they don their full uniforms. In off-duty hours, some of them hunted ducks on the shores of Lake Kunming in China or tigers in Burma. Others lounged in the ready room, catching up on their sleep, reading month-old magazines, playing darts and cards. They caroused in Rangoon's bars, crooned bawdy ballads and played poker with Chennault, who usually managed to beat them.

Frank Lawlor of Winston-Salem, North Carolina, a Navy dive-bomber pilot before joining the AVG, climbs out of his P-40 after a 1942 mission over China.

Perched on a fuel drum, a mechanic works on a P-40's 1,040-horsepower engine at a maintenance area in Loiwing, China, as a curious Chinese looks on.

Flying Tiger Colonel Robert L. Scott, with .50-caliber ammunition slung around his neck, helps armorers load the guns of his P-40 at a Chinese airfield.

KEEPING THE PLANES FIT FOR COMBAT

The success of the Flying Tigers depended heavily on resourceful ground crews who minimized the enemy's numerical advantage in the air by keeping battered, bullet-riddled P-40s in flying shape. The men who serviced the planes—mechanics, armorers, propeller specialists, parachute riggers and radio technicians—operated like a precision pit crew at an auto track. They often made repairs during enemy bombing raids, thus ensuring that planes that had been damaged fighting off the attackers could return to the air.

Spare parts were in such short supply that ground crews scavenged jungles and rice paddies where planes had crashed for usable engine parts, ammunition and tires. Even parachute silk was recycled.

The ground crews used their ingenuity to improve the P-40's fighting capacity. Fuselages were rubbed down with wax to increase speed by as much as 10 miles an hour. Mechanics fitted two fighters with makeshift air scoops to allow higher ceilings, and added improvised belly bomb racks to others to make the planes effective dive bombers. So versatile were the souped-up fighters that one Tiger joked: "If we only had a periscope, we could use the P-40 as a submarine."

The men labored in sub-zero temperatures on the Kunming Plateau in China and in 115° F. steaming heat in the nonmountainous areas of Burma. All the while, they were under constant threat of Japanese bombings and strafings. To deceive the enemy, mechanics at some fields fashioned fake P-40s from wood and canvas, then placed them on runways to draw fire away from the real planes hidden under trees. Many of the ground crews armed themselves with Tommy guns and fired at low-flying enemy aircraft. One mechanic even heaved a wrench at a swooping Japanese plane. (He missed.)

The large debt the Flying Tigers owed to the men who serviced their planes was readily acknowledged by the fliers. "Save some big words for our ground crews," one of the grateful pilots told a newsman. "They have gone through strafings, dodged bombs, and have always been out there working on our planes at all hours."

PUTTING MACHINES AND MEN TO THE ULTIMATE TEST

The Flying Tigers had to be ready to take to the air on the double. When air-raid sirens sounded or red cloth balls were hoisted up warning masts to signal the approach of enemy planes, the men grabbed the nearest parachutes and sprinted to their P-40s.

Once they were airborne, they could expect to be outnumbered by the Japanese planes by a ratio of as much as 6 to 1. The American pilots, who sometimes took the battle-scarred P-40s into action eight times a day, would alter their voices over the radio and give orders to imaginary squadrons to create the impression of superior force and to fool any Japanese who might be listening in on AVG frequencies.

The Tigers' most effective tactics, however, were those they learned from Chennault. Using their leader's precepts, pilots took their planes high above enemy formations, then zoomed down to achieve a diving speed of more than 400 miles per hour. Attacking in pairs or groups, they swooped so close to enemy planes that they could see the pilots' teeth.

When the Tigers had scattered the Japanese or fired their last bullet, they returned to base as unruffled as when they took off. "How many this time?" mechanics asked "Duke" Hedman after one mission. "Don't know," he said. "Bad luck to count 'em."

Flying Tigers at the Chengkung base in China scramble for their P-40s (top), then wing off (bottom) to tangle with the Japanese.

VAULTING THE HIMALAYAS

A C-46 Commando flies over a portion of the Hump, the Himalayan route used by U.S. pilots delivering supplies to China. C-46s could carry four tons of cargo.

A PERILOUS ROUTE THROUGH THE SKY

For nearly three years after the Japanese completed the conquest of Burma in the spring of 1942, the sole means of getting supplies to U.S. and Chinese forces in China was to fly them over the Himalayas from India. The hair-raising 500-mile route from bases in Assam in northeastern India to Kunming in China, nicknamed "the Hump" by pilots, passed over some of the most inhospitable terrain in the world. Below were the Naga Hills, up to 10,000 feet high, named for the head-hunting tribe that lived among them; the jungle-covered gorges of the Irrawaddy, Salween and Mekong rivers; and—backbone of the Hump—the 15,000-foot crags of the Santsung Range. Enemy planes and weather conditions—freak winds up to 248 mph, monsoons from May to October, turbulence that caused planes to flip over or suddenly rise or plummet 3,000 feet a minute—made the Hump the most treacherous air route of World War II.

Only men of special caliber could live up to the demands placed upon them by the Hump. They were the swashbuckling pilots of the India-China Wing, Air Transport Command (ATC). Before measures were taken to relieve some of the pressures on them in 1944, they worked 16-hour shifts routinely and sometimes flew three round trips a day. They took off and landed on crude, quickly constructed airstrips. They used a variety of planes, but the work horse was the balky C-46, prone to engine failure, plagued by carburetor icing and often flown overloaded at far above maximum ceilings. Journalist Eric Sevareid, who once had to bail out over Naga country, visited a base at Chabua, India, and wrote of living conditions in 1943: "There were at this time absolutely no amenities of life—no lounging places, no Red Cross girls, nothing cool and refreshing to eat and drink, no nearby rest resort to visit on leave. It was a dread and dismal place."

The Hump took a heavy toll: more than 1,000 men killed, nearly 600 planes lost. Yet by the war's end, the airlift was operating with business-like precision—accident rates had decreased while tonnage increased. All told, 650,000 tons of cargo crossed the Hump to China.

A trained elephant named Elmer hoists a 55-gallon drum of fuel aboard a C-46. One elephant could do the work of a dozen Indian laborers.

Jagged "W" Pass above the Salween River was a landmark for pilots negotiating the Hump. Planes navigated to either side of "Gunsight Peak" at the center.

Laborers, balancing baskets of crushed stone on their heads, pause to watch a B-24 land at an airfield under construction in India in 1943.

SCRATCHING RUNWAYS FROM THE EARTH BY HAND

At the start of the Hump airlift in the spring of 1942, there was one airfield at Dinjan, the India end of the run, and one at Kunming in China. By the end of the war, ATC pilots were using 13 bases in India and six in China. Many of the new fields were built largely by civilian workers, frequently women, who chipped large rocks into gravel with hammers and carried it to the site in baskets on their heads. Whole families were drafted from tea plantations and rice paddies for the task. Some lived in grass huts they built beside the runways. At one airfield on the Yangtze in China, more than 100,000 coolies labored on a strip.

Construction equipment was scarce, especially in China. After an area was cleared and graded—often by hand—heavy rocks for the foundation were moved into place on oxcarts, wagons and trucks. The rocks were covered with smaller stones, then the strip was topped with tar and strewn with gravel. Steam rollers, if available, leveled the surface; otherwise, hand-operated rollers were used—200 men to a roller.

The end product was a bumpy airfield, usually some 6,000 feet long. But to the men of the Air Transport Command even the most primitive landing area was a welcome sight after the hazardous three-to-four-hour flight over the Hump.

Men and machines surface a ramp with tar and gravel, as American officers supervise. The airplane hangars at the rear were brought over from the U.S.

Shooting craps in the officers' mess, Hump fliers whoop it up on a Saturday night in India. Entertainment was rare, and liquor could cost $75 to $100 a bottle.

THE FIENDS WHO FLEW THE HUMP

ATC pilots were described as "living like dogs and flying like fiends." They took off day and night, year round, halting only for weather so bad that—as the saying went—even the birds were grounded.

Until late 1944, some pilots flew up to 165 hours a month to fulfill as quickly as possible the quota of 650 to qualify for rotation home. Many never made it: in January 1944, three men died for every 1,000 tons of cargo reaching China. Others went "Hump-happy" under the strain. Hundreds had to bail out over the jungle, facing capture by hostile tribes or the Japanese, or a perilous trek to safety. Many ATC personnel were stricken with malaria, and most suffered from chronic dysentery.

Despite hardships, the Hump crews developed a unique style and spirit. Units vied to see which could carry more cargo to China. The men formed betting pools, handicapping bases according to the number and kinds of planes on hand and their distance from China, and followed the daily tonnage charts as they would a racing form at home. Subject to sporadic Japanese attacks, ATC pilots had a cocky sense of superiority over fighter pilots. "What the hell?" said one. "A pursuit pilot has six .50-caliber guns in front of him and 400 mph in his engine. We fly the same country with a pistol and a Tommy gun."

A Hump pilot (left) points to a close call, a bullet hole in the wing of his C-46. At right, a crewman wears a hat and scarf Tibetans gave him after he bailed out.

Pilots wore heavy jackets (left) and sucked oxygen from hoses (right); cockpit temperatures dropped to 40° below, and the air was thin above 10,000 feet.

A Hump flier plays with a pet leopard. At right, another pilot displays the crushed cap and .45-caliber pistol in shoulder holster that were pilot hallmarks.

Major overhauls are performed on a group of C-46s at a maintenance revetment in Assam, India.

THE STRUGGLE TO STAY AIRBORNE

The strain of flying the Hump took its toll not only of the flight crews, but also of the planes they flew. "An airplane doesn't need to sleep," said General Edward H. Alexander, commander of the India-China Wing of the ATC in 1943. But the planes used on the Hump run required round-the-clock maintenance of a quality that was hard to provide at remote airstrips in India and China. At times, fewer than half the planes at a base were flyable.

Maintenance crews faced some of the same problems that bedeviled Chennault's Flying Tigers: spare parts were scarce. Although some replacements arrived in India via the "Fireball Express," a cargo route direct from the United States, more often than not they were insufficient in number and variety. Mechanics had to cannibalize wrecked planes for usable parts.

Not all the problems could be traced to wear and tear. Some of the planes were faulty to begin with, particularly the new C-46, which was rushed into action before its bugs were ironed out. The first 30 C-46s received by the ATC had to be returned to the factory. Even after the plane was modified, hundreds of extra man-hours were required for its maintenance. But once the bugs had been eliminated, the C-46 became a reliable performer and transported thousands of tons of freight—including fuel, guns, ammunition, and medical and PX supplies—over the Hump to China.

A sergeant salvages an undamaged part from the wing of a scrapped C-47 to use as a replacement.

Mechanics repair the damaged tail section of a C-46. Nighttime maintenance was required because the sun made metal too hot to touch during the day.

The remains of cargo planes that crashed upon takeoff or landing or plummeted into jungles and mountainsides dramatize the myriad dangers of the Hump. The

miniature camels painted on a fuselage (bottom row, second from right) record the number of successful Hump missions flown before the plane cracked up.

After ferrying cargo over the Hump, Captain "Bamboo Joe" Barube, of Woonsocket, Rhode Island, and Lieutenant Ernest Lajoie leave the ATC operations office in China. During stopovers, pilots were fed fried eggs and coffee, and were often dispatched for the return trip to India in an hour.

While coming in for a landing, a C-46 skims over the tile roofs of a village near the Kunming airstrip at the China end of the Hump run. During the final months of the airlift operation, 650 planes landed in China every day.

3

The 18-month period from the late spring of 1942 until late autumn of 1943 was the lowest ebb of the war in the China-Burma-India Theater for the Allies. They not only had been driven ignominiously out of Burma by the Japanese; they could not agree on a plan for regaining the initiative.

During this interlude the Allies struggled to achieve a common strategy for reconquering Burma. At Trident and other conferences, plans were discussed and shelved, postponed or rejected. Aggressive-sounding code names for offensives—*Toreador* and *Buccaneer*, *Tarzan* and *Champion*, *Gripfast* and *Pigstick*—drifted like autumn leaves in and out of the Allied vernacular. A British assault on Rangoon, a move by the Chinese Y Force across the Salween and into Burma, an advance by the British from the Indian base at Imphal back across the Chindwin—these and other schemes came and went in various forms. One operation, however, did remain firmly fixed in the minds of Allied leaders—the plan for Stilwell's India-based Chinese divisions to thrust eastward into north Burma to open the way for the new land route to China, the Ledo-Burma Road. But the date for this and other Allied operations slipped from November 1942 to February 1943, then to November 1943.

In fact, the Allies were hardly in a position to mount a major offensive. First they had to develop a logistical base and train and equip an army that could face the Japanese on equal terms, and since CBI had the lowest priority and was the most difficult to supply of any theater, this was a formidable task. The two divisions of Stilwell's X Force from Ramgarh—General Sun's 38th and the remnants of General Liao's 22nd—had become very proficient. But little progress had been made with the much larger Y Force, the other arm of the Chinese pincer that was to swing into north Burma.

Like Stilwell, the British in India confronted imposing problems. The country lacked the logistical base necessary to mount and sustain a large offensive operation. The Indian railway system had been bled of locomotives, equipment and technical personnel for support of other theaters. Of the remaining employees, many were ill educated or even illiterate, and they responded with difficulty to the increased demands placed on them by the war.

The front along the India-Burma border was 700 miles long, and General Slim once described it as "some of the world's worst country, breeding the world's worst diseases,

HIGH STAKES AND HEAVY ODDS

and having for half the year at least the world's worst climate.'' Because they regarded the terrain itself as a sufficient barrier to any invasion, the British had never prepared the roads and railways that would be needed to fight a war on the frontier. To reach the southern part of the front near the Bay of Bengal, cargo had to be transferred first from broad- to narrow-gauge railway lines, then to river steamer. To reach the central front around Imphal, supplies had to travel 600 miles, shifting back and forth between slow barges and the two different railway gauges. At each transfer point, coolies had to unload and reload every item by hand. The northern front, based on the town of Ledo in Assam, was 800 miles from Calcutta via the old tea railway. On that line, trains could pass each other only at stations, and the track was frequently washed away by floods, buried by landslides or fractured by earthquakes.

Food for the troops along the India-Burma front was in critically short supply. British troops subsisted largely on bully beef, biscuits (of the type that Americans called hardtack) and a much-despised item known as soya link, a processed-meat product composed primarily of soybean meal. Since Indian troops came from a variety of castes and religions that sometimes had strict dietary regulations, it was impossible for the British to standardize their rations. The food problem was greatly intensified by the fact that India was in the grip of an economic crisis. Hoarding was widespread and inflation was spiraling ever higher. After the rice crop failed in 1943, famine swept the land, killing more than a million people. Attempts to relieve the famine by shipping food from one area to another further congested the already-overloaded transportation system.

Every conceivable kind of military equipment was in short supply—radios, vehicles, guns, medicine. Slim, in command of the newly created XV Corps, calculated that shortages of the various types of ammunition he required ran anywhere from 26 to 86 per cent. Morale was poor throughout the army, the desertion rate was high, and disease took such a toll that Slim found his corps disappearing before his eyes. A lethal and incurable malady called mite typhus, previously unknown in Burma, had begun to take a heavy toll, and the annual malaria rate was up to 84 per cent of the strength of the army. Some of the soldiers refused to take the mepacrine pills that were given them to prevent malaria, because they believed that the medicine would make them impotent; other men were more than happy to exchange a case of malaria for relief from duty at the front.

The British had yet another problem: they were preparing for an offensive in an atmosphere poisoned by civil dissent and even outright revolt. India seethed with rebellion in 1942. Mohandas Gandhi, the Indian nationalist leader, demanded that the British quit India and urged the followers of his Congress Party to practice civil disobedience. The resulting ugly mood of the populace hampered the recruiting of troops. When Gandhi and his lieutenants were jailed, riots erupted in Calcutta and eastern India along the Burmese border. Mobs assaulted key lines of communication, tearing up railroad tracks, destroying signal devices, cutting telephone and telegraph wires and killing Europeans.

Fearing that Japanese invaders would exploit the unrest—as indeed they were planning to do with the Indian National Army—Wavell, the British commander in chief in India, had to commit 57 infantry battalions to restore order in the countryside. So hard pressed were the British as they tried both to quell the rebellion and to maintain defenses against the Japanese that Slim, on the scene of the trouble, had to form his reserve by drawing upon venereal-disease patients from military hospitals in Calcutta and Barrackpore.

For all these reasons, the British were in no position to mount a major offensive, yet they felt they had to take some initiative to build morale at home and in the army. In late 1942, while broad strategy was still being thrashed out, they mounted a limited operation in Burma. This was an ill-fated venture into Arakan, the coastal region of Burma near India's Bengal Province. The operation's immediate objective was to capture Akyab Island 90 miles down the coast, which would provide a fighter base to cover future operations against Rangoon. Success here would also provide a much-needed propaganda victory, and the British took pains to ensure that a victory would be achieved. Estimating correctly that the Japanese held the region with little more than a regiment, the British planned to attack with an overwhelming superiority of infantry, armor and artillery.

In the fall of 1942, the 14th Division under General W. L. Lloyd thrust south from India down both sides of Burma's Mayu Mountains, a rugged, jungle-covered range lying near the coast. After a slow start, the offensive went smoothly, until the end of the year, when it bogged down about 15 miles short of Akyab. The Japanese brought up reinforcements and established a network of camouflaged bunkers. These strong points proved impregnable to artillery and bombardment, and their interlocking fields of fire stopped a series of ground assaults. As the weeks dragged on without a breakthrough, the British strengthened their troops again and again, until Lloyd's division comprised nine brigades —and one after another the brigades went forward into the lethal meat grinder.

Slim, who had been training his XV Corps, was sent to observe the situation, and it struck him immediately that Lloyd had repeated mistakes the British had made at the beginning of the year in the first campaign in Burma. Because of the difficult terrain, Lloyd had failed to send his troops down through the jungle on the Mayu Range. Instead, the British force had taken the roads on either side of the mountains; consequently it was split and exposed to attack. Moreover, the troops were being wasted in frontal assaults against strongly held positions along the way.

Sensing an opportunity, the Japanese reinforced their troops in late March, and succeeded in doing precisely what the British had been unable to accomplish—they marched into the jungle and over the Mayu Range and launched a series of flanking attacks. One of the British brigades disintegrated when Japanese troops overran its headquarters and killed its brigadier.

For the second time in a year, the High Command called on Slim to take over in a time of trouble. Again, as in the first campaign in Burma, by the time Slim arrived the situation was already all but irretrievable. "In war," he wrote later, "you have to pay for your mistakes, and in Arakan the same mistakes had been made again and again until the troops lost heart." Once more Slim presided over a British retreat. The Arakan force pulled back to India with the army's morale worse than ever—2,500 men were dead, wounded or missing. Churchill himself regarded the operation as disappointing and discreditable.

The stage was now set for the appearance of one of those remarkable and daring figures who have materialized again and again at critical moments in Britain's military history: Gordon at Khartoum, Clive of India and Lawrence of Arabia.

Even in a theater already known for its oddballs and eccentrics, Brigadier Orde C. Wingate, who was suddenly propelled to the forefront at this point, was extraordinary.

Wingate was born in the 20th Century but he really belonged to that Victorian era in which British gentlemen-adventurers roved the globe, exploring, botanizing, climbing mountains, bird-watching and waging war. He was often slovenly and unkempt, dressed in sagging socks, ill-fitting uniforms with undone buttons, and an old pith helmet shaped like an inverted coal scuttle. He ate quantities of raw onions, believing them beneficial for health, and carried strapped to his wrist a miniature alarm clock, the clanging of which signaled the end of his interviews and audiences. He was frequently rude and contentious, and had on occasion struck subordinates when they aroused his wrath. To show his disdain for authority he donned dirty, grease-stained uniforms when he met with superiors, the more orthodox of whom he called "military apes." At times he wore no clothes at all, entertaining his guests or colleagues in the nude; during conversations he rubbed his naked torso with a rubber brush, a method of grooming that he seemed to prefer to bathing. In the field, he strained his tea through his socks and often served it this way to others.

While some of Wingate's associates undoubtedly thought him mad, his madness was not without method, and to some degree his strange behavior may have been calculat-

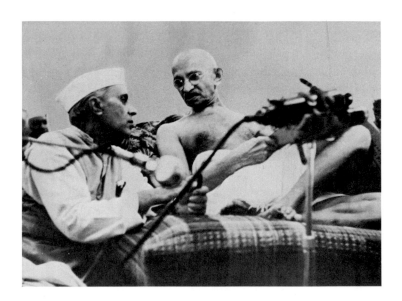

Indian National Congress Party leaders Jawaharlal Nehru (left) and Mohandas K. Gandhi confer in Bombay on August 7, 1942—36 hours before both men were jailed. Nearly 200 party leaders were imprisoned by the British in an attempt to crush Gandhi's civil disobedience campaign against continued British rule. Riots ensued, which meant that the British had to divert some of their badly needed troops from the war effort.

ed. "With English of a certain class," he once said, "the worst crime you can commit is to be different, unorthodox, unexpected. I am all those things. The only way to get these qualities tolerated, if not accepted, is to transform one's 'difference' into eccentricity." For all of his quirks, Wingate had a fierce, driving ambition and a profound, almost mystical sense of his own destiny. Although the comparison enraged him, he was frequently likened to Lawrence of Arabia, who was in fact a distant relative. Both had piercing blue eyes, hawklike noses, and a devotion to the causes of foreign peoples that disturbed and even frightened their own superiors. They also—though Wingate was quick to disparage his kinsman's military theories—shared a commitment to irregular warfare carried out by indigenous troops.

Born into a distinguished Puritan military family, Wingate had a highly erratic career. At times his unorthodox successes brought him notice out of proportion to his rank or station; at other times his behavior and tendency to insubordination brought him to the verge of court-martial. As a young officer he studied Arabic and became proficient enough in the language to wangle a post with the Sudan Defense Force. There, while leading patrols against ivory smugglers and slave traders, he began to store up knowledge about guerrilla warfare, and at the end of his assignment he set off on a personal expedition into the Libyan Sea of Sand, at the eastern end of the Sahara, where he tried unsuccessfully to find a legendary oasis called Zerzura.

In the fall of 1936 he went to Palestine, which was then administered under a British mandate. There he became a passionate advocate of Zionism at a time when Britain—on the whole—was pro-Arab. Wingate importuned his superiors so relentlessly that they allowed him to organize Jews into irregular units called Special Night Squads, which had the assignment of protecting Jewish villages and an important oil pipeline against Arab raiders. Wingate's patrols were so aggressive in their ambushes and night raids that they made British officials uneasy; at one point his enemies alleged that Wingate had offered to lead the Jews in an uprising against his own government. In early 1939, the Special Night Squads were disbanded and Wingate was abruptly recalled. Back in England he found his loyalty questioned, and though his career survived it was under a cloud.

When World War II broke out he was in an obscure post in an antiaircraft brigade in England. But General Wavell, who had once been Wingate's commander in Palestine, now came to the rescue. A cautious man himself, Wavell was nevertheless open to unconventional ideas, and after becoming commander in chief in Africa he sent for the strange young major. Soon Wingate was commanding an Ethiopian partisan army, trying to drive vastly superior Italian forces from Ethiopia and restore Emperor Haile Selassie to the throne. It was Wingate's first experience with a sizable command; he made a number of tactical mistakes but he achieved some stunning triumphs, culminating in an operation in which his force of less than 1,700 bluffed more than 15,000 Italian and colonial troops into surrendering.

In spite of his victories in the field and the successful restoration of the Emperor, Wingate so annoyed his superiors by his refusal to communicate with them or even to obey orders that he was recalled to Cairo. There, depressed because he felt his work was unappreciated, he slashed his throat with a knife. Though the suicide attempt failed, his apparent instability might have ended his military career then and there. But once again Wavell, now commanding in Asia, intervened. In desperate straits as the defense of Burma collapsed, he asked for the audacious Wingate to join him in Delhi. Given the temporary rank of colonel, Wingate was put in charge of guerrilla operations in Burma.

Wingate soon proposed what he called "long-range penetration" (LRP). His plan called for the insertion of conventional forces far behind enemy lines. There, supplied by air and directed by radio, the LRP force would cut the enemy's lines of communication and cause as much disruption as possible. Pressing his proposal on anyone who would listen, Wingate made something of a nuisance of himself around headquarters in Delhi. As Slim recalled, he "fanatically pursued his own purposes without regard to any other consideration or purpose." Most officers with conventional ideas about warfare found him tedious and annoying, and nicknamed him "Tarzan" or "Robin Hood." But others found him mesmerizing. Said one officer: "Soon we had fallen under the spell of his almost hypnotic talk; and by and by we—or some of us—had lost the power of distinguishing between the feasible and the fantastic."

One of those who was persuaded by Wingate's proposal was Wavell. The Allies were still planning to launch the offensive to retake Burma in February of 1943, and it appeared to Wavell that Wingate's long-range penetration force could hobble the Japanese reaction. And so he authorized Wingate to prepare the first LRP group, the 77th Indian Infantry Brigade. Ultimately the unit became known as the Chindits—a name derived from the mythical lions carved in stone that guard Burmese pagodas.

Wingate threw his 3,000 British, Gurkha and Burmese soldiers into intensive training during the monsoon. The men had to learn not only how to fight in the jungle, but also how to cope with the 1,000 mules that would form their heavy transport on the expedition. (Among the troops were draftees from such urban centers as Liverpool and Manchester, and they liked to joke that the decoration called the DCM—Distinguished Combat Medal—stood for "Died Chasing Mules.") At the start of the rigorous training program a staggering proportion of the men fell out sick or exhausted—in some units as many as 70 per cent were either in the hospital or trying to get in. But Wingate ordered his doctors to root out what he called "the prevailing hypochondria," and pointed out in lectures to his troops that behind the enemy lines there would be no hospitals.

Wingate was almost ready to lead his brigade into Burma when the Allies canceled *Anakim*. Without a major operation for the Chindits to support, Wavell felt that Wingate's expedition would be meaningless. As he saw it, the brigade was not strong enough to engage in a major battle, and any damage Wingate's men might inflict on the lines of communication would be temporary. On February 5, Wavell visited Wingate, intending to cancel the operation. But in a two-hour discussion Wingate put up a barrage of arguments; Wavell finally yielded, and in a speech to Wingate's troops said they were embarking on "a great adventure." This proved to be an understatement. In mid-February the Chindits crossed the Chindwin and plunged into Burma's jungles. While two columns—including an officer masquerading as Wingate—created a diversion to the south, Wingate's main force slipped east toward the railway linking Mandalay with the key northern city of Myitkyina.

In the jungle Wingate was a stern taskmaster. He had the notion that marching prevented malaria, and he kept his men on the move constantly. He forbade shaving, to save five minutes in the morning, and he set little personal ambushes to check up on the alertness of his officers and men. He glared so balefully at those who displeased him that the troops took to calling him Brigadier Bela Lugosi. He issued orders couched in Biblical quotations and radioed his column commanders a slogan drawn from Ecclesiastes: "Whatsoever thy hand findeth to do, do it with thy might."

During the first weeks in the jungle the Chindits' operations matched Wingate's hopes. They cut roads, destroyed bridges, attacked outposts, set ambushes and booby traps, and sabotaged the Mandalay-Myitkyina railway in many places. Aerial supply operations worked well, and there were few casualties. The enemy hunted the elusive Chindits in vain, finally committing two divisions to the search.

After much deliberation, Wingate decided to cross the mile-wide Irrawaddy and raid even deeper into enemy territory. It was a grave misjudgment. Wingate now found himself trapped in a hot, dry forest, with the broad river at his back. A Japanese reconnaissance plane spotted some of his troops, and it seemed only a matter of time before the Japanese would catch up with the brigade. Airdrops were hard to arrange, and the men were beginning to wilt from hunger, disease and the constant strain.

For the next several weeks the Chindits kept on the move, living out a nightmare. Water was so scarce they drank the

On a military highway in India, an army truck rolls past a caravan of camels drawing wagons loaded with drums of oil and other supplies. Since motor vehicles and adequate roads were scarce, the Allies and Japanese alike used animals to carry matériel over mountainous jungle country.

Workers at a munitions plant in India prepare a consignment of artillery shells for delivery to Allied units in CBI. When the fighting reached its peak in 1944, the factory, after being reequipped with Lend-Lease machinery, was turning out more than 24 times as many shells as it had in prewar days.

fluid contained in the stems of green bamboo. Unable to bathe, they were crawling with lice, and were tormented by ticks, leeches and vicious red ants. The men became obsessed with thoughts of food and described to each other in loving detail the great meals they would have when they got home. They ate their mules, made soup of their horses, and when all else failed took lessons from their Burmese riflemen in the preparation and consumption of locusts, rats, monkeys and the shoots of jungle plants. Dysentery, malaria and Japanese patrols took an increasing toll. There was no way of evacuating the wounded. Some who could not go on were left in villages in the hope that the Burmese would not turn them over to the Japanese; others were simply left in the jungle to meet their fate alone.

On March 24, Wingate was ordered to return to India before the enemy and disease could annihilate the brigade. Getting out proved much harder than getting in. "Just put yourself in the position of the Jap commander," Wingate told his men. "Your one aim will be to prevent anyone from getting out alive. . . . We can take it for granted that from now on the Jap commander is going to do everything in his power to wipe us out. And the first thing he'll do is to make a strong effort to prevent us recrossing the Irrawaddy."

The brigade split up into small groups with Wingate leading a force of 220. At the river, Wingate's men came under fire from the Japanese. Wingate stalked the river-bank, looking "like some minor prophet with his huge beard and blanket wrapped around his shoulders," according to one of his subordinates. He decided that, rather than attempt a crossing, he would break his force into five small groups and infiltrate back through the enemy lines.

Wingate himself led a group of 43 men. Instead of crossing the river under fire, Wingate and his tiny command remained in a secluded patch of jungle. There the men spent a week resting and feeding on their remaining pack mules and horses, which they slaughtered by cutting their throats to avoid alerting the Japanese with gunfire. In the jungle bivouac Wingate, always talkative, became a compulsive monologuist, quoting the Bible, endlessly arguing and lecturing to his men on ancient and modern literature and religion, 18th Century art, and the relative merits of Popeye the Sailor and Popeye's friend J. Wellington Wimpy.

After a week of rest during which the chief enemies were leeches and the ever-present mosquitoes, Wingate led his men back to the Irrawaddy, which they now crossed without difficulty. For another couple of weeks they marched on through the jungle. They ran out of rations, and the Burmese soldiers killed pythons for them and made soup of roots. One of the officers grew so weak from dysentery that he could not continue; Wingate camped beside the man for

48 hours hoping that he would regain his strength, but in the end he was left to die in the jungle. When another soldier, a lance corporal crippled by sores on his legs, saw that he was holding up the column, he simply walked off into the jungle and disappeared.

At last the party neared the Chindwin. Across the river lay safety, but the Japanese had taken all the available boats and their patrols were everywhere along the east bank. Wingate and a few others who felt strong enough decided to swim the big, fast-flowing river, then contact the British, and send boats for those left behind. To avoid disclosing themselves to enemy patrols, Wingate and his swimmers spent seven hours hacking through dense elephant grass to reach the river. When they finally set off for the far bank, it turned out to be a near thing for all of them. Wingate probably survived only because he rested in midstream by floating on his back with his head cradled in his buoyant old pith helmet. But they made it, and the following night most of the others came across in boats under Japanese fire.

Wingate brought out 34 of the 43 men he had started with. Other Chindit groups took heavier losses. One col-

umn of 150 men headed east and marched all the way to China. Of the 3,000 who had gone into the jungle, fewer than 2,200 returned, and the majority of the survivors were so debilitated by their experience that they could never serve in combat again. Theirs had been an incredible ordeal: they had operated for three months behind enemy lines, had marched 1,500 miles through difficult country and had been forced to leave many of their comrades behind, dead or dying in the jungle. But they had achieved what other British forces had failed to: before crossing the Irrawaddy, they had carried the war to the Japanese, operating far behind their lines, attacking outposts, setting up ambushes and wreaking havoc on communications.

The reaction at British headquarters to Wingate's operation was mixed. To many senior officers it was an unmitigated disaster. Wrote Slim later: "As a military operation the raid had been an expensive failure. It gave little tangible return for the losses it had suffered and the resources it had absorbed. The damage it did to Japanese communications was repaired in a few days, the casualties it inflicted were negligible, and it had no immediate effect on Japanese

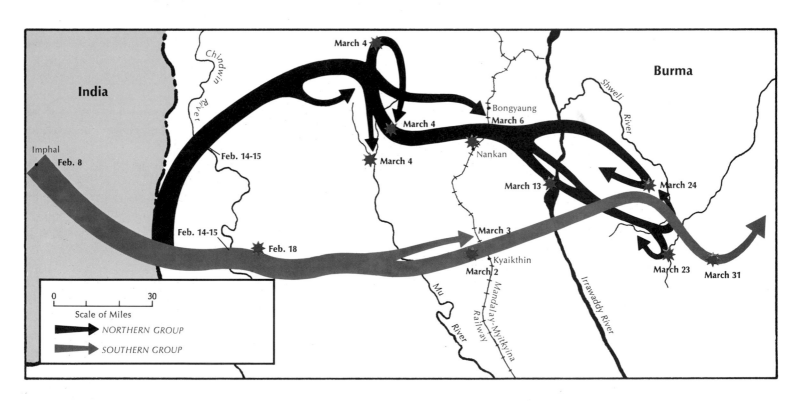

Colonel Orde Wingate's 3,000-man 77th Indian Infantry Brigade, known as the Chindits, set out from Imphal on February 8, 1943, on a raid deep into Burma. The brigade split into two groups and crossed the Chindwin River. Following a series of wide-ranging feints and clashes (stars) with the enemy, the northern group (black arrows) blew up the bridges of the Mandalay-Myitkyina railway near Bongyaung and Nankan, while the southern group (gray arrows) cut the rail line near Kyaikthin. In spite of heavy losses, both groups pushed across the Irrawaddy River separately —only to find air supply difficult and the Japanese closing in. On March 24 the operation was halted. Most of the northern group retreated to India, while the survivors of the southern group slipped into China.

dispositions or plans. . . . If anything was learned of air supply or jungle fighting it was a costly schooling."

The response in other quarters was quite different. Back home in Britain, where the events that had occurred in the Burmese jungle were only dimly perceived, the fact that the British had gone over to the offensive and had penetrated far behind Japanese lines was regarded as a great achievement. In sore need of a victory, the British now had something that could be interpreted as one, and the propaganda mills began churning. Newspapers hailed Wingate as "the Clive of Burma," and the Chindits became overnight heroes.

Among those most impressed was Winston Churchill. After months of what seemed to him indifferent performance by British commanders in Asia, here was a man of daring and imagination who seemed able to win battles. "All the Commanders on the spot," wrote Churchill at the time, "seem to be competing with one another to magnify their demands and the obstacles they have to overcome. . . . I consider Wingate should command the army against Burma. He is a man of genius and audacity . . . and no mere question of seniority must obstruct the advance of real personalities to their proper stations in war."

Churchill's proposal to place the unorthodox and rather peculiar junior brigadier in charge of the Burma campaign stunned senior officers. They succeeded in dissuading the Prime Minister from making such a move. But now a relationship began that paralleled the one existing between Chennault and Roosevelt, in which a daring general formed a personal alliance with his Commander in Chief, much to the discomfiture of his direct superiors. Churchill had Wingate come to England for discussions, and he found Wingate's ideas about long-range penetration, now grown much more grand, quite to his liking.

Wingate held that long-range penetration groups could establish strongholds and airstrips deep in the jungles and defend them against concerted attacks, thus forming a permanent rather than a temporary presence in the enemy's rear. He also argued that LRPs should not be considered mere supplements to conventional troops; they should be the main force. Given a few well-trained brigades, he felt he could turn the tide of war. Churchill found great appeal in the relatively minor effort envisaged by Wingate. Before the Trident Conference, Churchill had expressed his misgiv-ings about the Burma campaign by saying that "going into swampy jungles to fight the Japanese is like going into the water to fight a shark. It is better to entice him into a trap or catch him on a hook and then demolish him with axes after hauling him out on to dry land." While the Americans were agitating for the recapture of Burma so that a land supply route to China could be reopened, Churchill wanted the main thrust in Asia to be toward Sumatra instead and then on toward Singapore. Wingate's proposal seemed to offer a way of satisfying U.S. demands for action, and perhaps a cheap victory over the Japanese as well.

Churchill immediately asked Wingate to accompany him to the Allied Quadrant Conference in Quebec in August 1943. There Wingate presented a plan to insert eight long-range penetration brigades behind enemy lines during the forthcoming dry season. While the plan brought howls of protest from most of the command in India because of the resources it would require, Wingate found substantial support for his proposal at the conference. Churchill liked the idea, as did some of his general staff; the Americans were also impressed. At the conference, Marshall became a great admirer of Wingate, and General Hap Arnold, Chief of Staff of the U.S. Air Forces, wrote of the strange Englishman: "You took one look at that face, like the face of a pale Indian chieftain, topping the uniform still smelling of jungle and sweat and war, and you thought: 'Hell, this man is serious.'" Indeed the American chiefs were so taken with Wingate that they promised an American brigade for his force, as well as planes and gliders to support his operation.

At the Quadrant Conference, in addition to approving the new Wingate campaign, the Allies agreed that there would be an attempt to seize northern Burma in the 1943-1944 dry season. A joint operation was envisaged involving Slim's regular forces, Wingate's Chindits and Stilwell's Chinese troops. The British also decided to alter their own command structure, in accordance with Churchill's feeling that some life had to be pumped into the sluggish India command. Wavell had already been made Viceroy of India and replaced by General Sir Claude Auchinleck, the former commander in chief of British forces in the Middle East. Now the command function was to be split; Auchinleck would take on the responsibility of training and equipping the Indian

Army and developing India as a base for operations. The actual campaign against the Japanese would be conducted by a new organization, the Southeast Asia Command. As Supreme Allied Commander for SEAC, the British chose Acting Vice-Admiral the Lord Louis Mountbatten. A cousin of King George VI, Mountbatten was quite junior in rank and age: he was only 43. But he had distinguished himself in the British raid on Dieppe; he was handsome, charming, enthusiastic and aggressive. Even Stilwell, who rarely met an Englishman he liked, pronounced Lord Louis "a good egg."

SEAC's Deputy Supreme Commander would be Stilwell, who now added that responsibility to his many others. And it was Stilwell who was to be one of Mountbatten's first problems. On October 16, 1943, when Mountbatten arrived in Chungking to visit Chiang Kai-shek, he learned that the Generalissimo had sent a request to Roosevelt asking for Stilwell's recall—an act that would deprive Mountbatten, on the eve of a major offensive, of the services of the one man who appeared able to lead Chinese troops.

Over recent months Stilwell's relationship with the Generalissimo had steadily deteriorated. The American general had experienced mounting frustrations in trying to prepare the Y Force for action in Burma. Partly this was because of Chennault's priority on Hump supplies, and partly it stemmed from Chiang's slowness in designating the units the Y Force required. As usual, Stilwell spilled out his bile in his diary. In a typical entry he called the Generalissimo "obstinate, pig-headed, ignorant, intolerant, arbitrary, unreasonable, illogical, ungrateful, grasping." At least some hint of his attitude—he was making little effort to hide it—got back to both the Generalissimo and to Stilwell's Ameri-

can superiors. At one point Marshall rebuked him with a message telling him to "stop the wisecracks." (Marshall also relayed a suggestion from a British general that while Stilwell did not have to join in the singing when "God Save the King" was played at a British mess, he might at least stand.)

Chiang had a number of reasons for wanting Stilwell out of his way—for one thing, he hoped to replace him with a Chinese general who could represent China on the Combined Chiefs of Staff—but his stated reason for requesting Stilwell's recall was that the American had "lost the confidence of the troops." From Madame Chiang, with whom he had established more cordial relations, Stilwell learned that the Generalissimo had a long list of grievances against him: he was haughty; he had suggested that Chiang use Communist troops; he signed his correspondence "Lieut. Gen., USA" instead of "Chief of Staff to the Generalissimo."

Before presenting his credentials to the Generalissimo, Mountbatten met with Stilwell. "You should not be seen shaking hands with me," the American told him. "It will be bad for you." Appalled at the thought of losing a man he needed, Mountbatten said, "If you want your job back, I'll get it for you." And Mountbatten made good on his promise; he sent word to the Generalissimo that he could not possibly use Chinese troops in the forthcoming offensive if Stilwell were recalled. Faced with such an ultimatum, Chiang backed down. Stilwell on his part made a grudging apology for his alleged misconduct, and the Generalissimo withdrew his demand for Stilwell's recall.

Mountbatten had no such problems with his other principal field commander, Slim, who had been given the command of the British Fourteenth Army on the Burma-India border. First as corps commander, then as army commander, the bulldog-jawed Slim had been working to overcome the problems of health, supply and morale in his woebegone command. He instituted a rigid system to ensure that all his troops took their antimalarial pills, and established malaria-treatment units just behind the front, so that patients could be quickly returned to their units.

To supply the hard-to-reach Arakan front, Slim's engineers had to build roads through country where there was no gravel or other surfacing material. They found a solution by importing Indian artisans, setting up brick kilns every 20

The recently appointed Supreme Allied Commander in Southeast Asia, Admiral the Lord Louis Mountbatten, confers with Chinese Finance Minister H. H. Kung (front left) in Chungking in 1943. During his first visit to the Nationalist Chinese wartime capital as Supreme Allied Commander, Mountbatten helped patch up the growing rift between Generalissimo Chiang Kai-shek and his American Chief of Staff, General Stilwell.

At an airfield 100 miles to the northeast of Chungking, a Chinese ground crew refuels a B-29 from five-gallon gasoline cans after the bomber made an emergency landing. Long-range B-29s arrived in India in the spring of 1944 and bombed Japanese-occupied Bangkok on June 5. Just 10 days later B-29s based near Chengtu in China hit Japan for the first time.

miles or so and surfacing the road with millions of bricks. To improve morale Slim traveled constantly from unit to unit, giving three or four inspirational speeches a day from the hood of his jeep. Since his command included not only Britons, but also Africans, Gurkhas and Indians who spoke a variety of tongues, the language problem was formidable. Slim, like most Indian Army officers, spoke Gurkhali and Urdu. He also knew a smattering of other Indian languages. He was once mortified when an aide informed him he had just addressed a unit of Urdu-speaking Indians in Gurkhali.

Slim passed on to his subordinate commanders some of the lessons he had learned in the first Burma campaign and in the Arakan campaign. Avoid head-on attacks, he said. "Attacks should follow hooks and come in from flank or rear, while pressure holds the enemy in front." Moreover, on finding enemy units in their rear, troops should "regard not themselves, but the Japanese, as 'surrounded.'" Most important, the men must overcome their fear of the jungle.

Slim stressed to them that the tropical rain forest was neither impenetrable nor hostile. The large dangerous animals of the jungle were few and far between, and only rarely were they a threat to man, he said. Certainly there were poisonous snakes, but he noted that they were secretive and rarely encountered. Even the most serious hazards, such diseases as dysentery and malaria, could to some degree be contained by rigid discipline, he told his troops. Once the soldier has learned to live in the jungle, Slim concluded, "He can use it for concealment, covered movement, and surprise."

As his troops became better trained, Slim began to test them in battle. Since the oft-bloodied British soldiers regarded the Japanese as military supermen, Slim set out to destroy the myth of Japanese invincibility with a series of minor operations, all planned to give the British the best advantage. He used battalions to attack platoons, entire brigades with aircraft and artillery support to attack companies. When a critic said that this was like using a steam hammer to crack a walnut, Slim replied: "If you happen to have a steam hammer handy and you don't mind if there's nothing left of the walnut, it's not a bad way to crack it."

By November of 1943, with the dry season in Burma beginning, the Allies were better prepared to start offen-

sive operations. Slim's army was ready for action, and one of Stilwell's X Force divisions from Ramgarh, moving out ahead of the engineers who had begun building the Ledo Road, had already engaged the Japanese. Wingate's new Chindits were 20,000 strong and completing their training. In India, Gandhi's rebellion had been quelled, and lines of communication and supply to the frontier had been improved. With the creation of SEAC, Mountbatten and his staff rushed to complete plans for a dry-season campaign—plans that they would present in a few weeks at the Allies' Sextant Conference, to be held in Cairo and Teheran.

Concluding that his predecessors had been "somewhat pessimistic and unenterprising," Mountbatten wished to take a more aggressive posture. But he did not want to risk another British defeat—he was determined to set a course toward certain victory. Thus he and his staff developed plans for a number of limited operations that added up to something less than an all-out offensive. These operations were to include the north Burma attacks by the Chinese troops of the Ramgarh and Y forces, the Wingate penetration, an advance by Slim's XV Corps in Arakan and his IV Corps across the Chindwin, an airborne attack on the railway line in north Burma and an amphibious assault on the Andaman Islands in the Bay of Bengal.

When the Allies met in Cairo, toward the end of November, Mountbatten's plans had not only to satisfy the British and American chiefs, but also Chiang. For the first time, the Generalissimo was present at a high-level Allied conference, and he made demands of his own. If he was to commit his Y Force to battle in north Burma, he wanted assurances that the British would not only mount a major amphibious operation somewhere in the Bay of Bengal in order to block the Japanese sea-lanes, but would also support the Y Force on the ground by making an airborne attack toward Mandalay. Although Mountbatten's planned attack on the Andamans filled the first of these conditions, the British felt that the thrust toward Mandalay was not feasible; informed of this, Chiang put on an extraordinary display of vacillation.

On November 25, Churchill and Mountbatten met with the Generalissimo and persuaded him to participate in the offensive even without the Mandalay attack. But that same evening, in a meeting with Roosevelt, Chiang made it clear that he had changed his mind. The next day at tea Churchill, Roosevelt and even Madame Chiang ganged up on the Generalissimo and once more obtained his agreement. The next morning, just before leaving Cairo, Chiang reversed himself again, telling Stilwell that he would not take part unless the British went through with the Mandalay operation. The British Chief of Staff, General Sir Alan Brooke, described the meetings as "a ghastly waste of time." Wrote Mountbatten: the chiefs "have been driven absolutely mad, and I shall certainly get more sympathy . . . in the future."

On his way back from Cairo to China, the Generalissimo stopped to visit the training center at Ramgarh. There, perhaps inspired by the trim appearance of the Chinese troops, he reversed himself once more and decided he would commit his Y Force to Burma, even without the British attack on Mandalay. But meanwhile the American and British leaders had moved on from Cairo to Teheran to confer with Stalin. When Stalin promised to join the war against Japan as soon as Germany had been defeated, the British reversed themselves. On the ground that China therefore was no longer of such critical importance, they argued that the landing craft scheduled for the Andaman assault would be better used in the planned invasions of Normandy and Southern France. In the face of British determination, Roosevelt finally agreed. Chiang, informed that the British now refused to meet the second of his major demands, again withdrew his promise to commit the Y Force to battle.

By the end of the Sextant Conference, both British and American planners had begun to view China's role in the War as a very limited one. The prospect of training a large and capable Chinese army seemed unlikely, and now that the Allied advance across the Pacific was showing promise, the need for a China base seemed less acute. Chennault's air offensive, in spite of priority accorded him on supplies flown over the Hump, had not lived up to expectations, and Roosevelt and the American chiefs were now putting more faith in a plan to have B-29s from India fly out of Chengtu in western China to strike the Japanese home islands.

By now a concerted Allied effort on the Asian mainland had become a remote prospect. Of the seven operations Mountbatten had proposed, three—the amphibious assault in the Andamans, the airborne attack on the railway in northern Burma and the advance by the Y Force across the

Salween—had been canceled. All that remained of the Allied plans were the move by the X Force from Ramgarh into Burma, Wingate's second Chindit foray behind the Japanese lines, and advances by Slim's XV Corps in Arakan and by the IV Corps across the Chindwin.

While the Allies' offensive plans for a second Burma campaign were foundering, the Japanese were contemplating large-scale operations of their own. Ironically, the Japanese had been spurred to consider these new offensives by the audacity of two highly unconventional generals, Wingate and Chennault.

The Japanese, like the British, had assumed that it was impossible to launch major operations across the mountains and jungles of the India-Burma border, and thus they felt that Burma was safe against a British offensive. But when the Chindits penetrated from India and began raising an uproar behind their lines, the Japanese reconsidered. There seemed no explanation for Wingate's operation unless it was a reconnaissance in force preparatory to a major Allied offensive. The Japanese concluded that they had better adopt a more aggressive strategy themselves in order to spoil any forthcoming attack.

This view was vigorously championed by Lieut. General Renya Mutaguchi, soon to become commander of the Japanese Fifteenth Army in Burma. A fierce, brave, inflexible soldier who loved battles, drink and women, he had commanded the regiment that sparked the Sino-Japanese War by precipitating an incident at the Marco Polo Bridge near Peking in 1937. He was a man of strong personality, feared and respected throughout the army. Mutaguchi felt that it was possible to launch an offensive across the rugged India-Burma border. He believed such an operation would both disrupt the British and stimulate the seething Indian independence movement. Mutaguchi and other Japanese commanders in Burma played a series of war games, which convinced them that the best move would be a preemptive strike across the Chindwin toward the British base at Imphal, just over the border in northwest India. In July 1943, Imperial General Headquarters told its Burma commanders to plan such an offensive for the coming dry season.

At this point another element was introduced into the situation to prod the Japanese to offensive action. During the summer of 1943, the Fourteenth Air Force had failed to fulfill Chennault's promises. Chennault had predicted that he would achieve air superiority by August, but in spite of the airlift priority Roosevelt had given him, his air force received neither the supplies nor the reinforcements he had asked for. But in September new aircraft and supporting equipment started reaching him in quantities, and he was able to establish new bases in eastern China. With his planes now in range of Taiwan and parts of Japan, Chennault asked permission from Washington to strike at Japan.

General Arnold refused, because he did not want the Japanese to bolster their home-island antiaircraft defenses before he began the planned raids by the India-based B-29s. But Arnold did approve a raid on Taiwan. On Thanksgiving Day the Fourteenth Air Force carried out a devastating attack on the island, destroying 42 Japanese aircraft on the ground in one 12-minute pass. Within the next two weeks, several Japanese cargo ships were successfully attacked in the Taiwan Strait. The Japanese, already disturbed by the growing strength of the Fourteenth Air Force in eastern China, now took alarm.

Chennault had an unquenchable faith in the ability of his air force to stop Japanese ground troops. He still thought that his Flying Tigers had halted the Japanese at the Salween in 1942. And in the fall of 1943 his confidence was reinforced when Japanese ground forces made a major foraging raid against the rice center of Changteh; Chennault threw his planes into the battle, and when the Japanese withdrew after capturing the supplies they had been seeking, Chennault once again credited his air force with a victory over infantry. He therefore thought that his east China bases were secure against ground attack. The Japanese, believing otherwise, began making plans to capture them.

Thus, as 1943 drew to a close the Japanese were preparing for offensives on two fronts. Meanwhile, the Allies were poised to attack in three directions. Slim was planning operations into Arakan and across the Chindwin, Stilwell was heading into the jungle to assume personal command of the Chinese troops trying to open the route for the Ledo Road, and Wingate was ready to plunge deep into Japanese territory to establish strongholds in support of both Stilwell and Slim. In his diary, Stilwell wrote in capital letters: CAN WE PUT IT OVER?

The war's long interlude was coming to an end.

THE JUNGLE FIGHTERS

Before his bold 1944 raid into Burma, Major-General Orde Wingate, copies of Aristotle and Plato under his arm, confers with U.S. Colonel Philip Cochran.

AN ECCENTRIC GENIUS LEADS THE WAY BACK IN

In March of 1942 one of the most unorthodox men ever to wear a British uniform, Orde Charles Wingate, arrived in Burma to take charge of guerrilla operations against the Japanese. Wingate, a colonel at the time, reveled in nonconformity and was given to actions that sent shock waves of disbelief through the upper echelons of the British Army. Both a scholar and a linguist, he would quote from the Bible, hold forth on the social habits of hyenas or discourse on the works of Plato.

This strange man had a wild plan, one that stood in sharp contrast to prevailing military doctrine. Like a great cavalryman of an earlier war, he wanted to insert a small raiding force behind Japanese lines to disrupt communications, destroy supply dumps and generally "wreak havoc out of all proportion" to the force's numbers. His long-range penetration attacks—as he referred to them—were to be supplied by air and directed by radio.

To toughen his raiders for "this most exacting and exhausting" operation, Wingate put them through a merciless regimen. He made them carry out orders on the run, swim rivers, live on short rations, endure painful insect bites and slog through ankle-deep mud in the monsoon season. He accepted only serious illness as an excuse, and those men who passed out on long marches were quickly revived and forced to continue. For study purposes, he had enormous sand tables created, some measuring 400 square yards, with hills, rivers and gun emplacements built to scale.

Finally, on February 13, 1943, Wingate and his Chindits—as his raiders were called, after the fierce sculptured lions guarding Burmese temples—were ready. In addition to a rifle, a bayonet, ammunition and three hand grenades, each man carried a five-day supply of rations, a jackknife, a rope for climbing, a water bottle, four pairs of socks and a spare shirt. The total load weighed 70 pounds. Accompanied by more than 1,000 pack animals and eight messenger dogs, the 3,000-man force began crossing Burma's Chindwin River into Japanese-held territory, embarking upon one of the most daring adventures of the war.

After crossing a jungle waterway with the Chindits, RAF communications specialists check out their radio while waiting for their clothes to dry.

Huddled over a map with an aide, a beardless Wingate discusses plans for the first of his two long-range penetrations behind the Japanese lines in Burma.

Parachuted supplies drift toward trees, where Wingate's men later hid them from Japanese planes.

A DARING FORAY BUILDS TO A NIGHTMARE

In the first few weeks after they crossed the Chindwin River, the Chindits raided and harassed the Japanese. Attacking the rail line, they cut one 30-mile stretch of track in 75 places. But the jungle-wise Japanese held the upper hand. "If they stay in the jungle," said the cocky commander of the Japanese Fifteenth Army, Lieut. General Renya Mutaguchi, "they will starve."

Far from avoiding the jungle, Wingate, emboldened by his success, drove deeper into enemy territory. Airdrops became more difficult; potable water was scarce. Boots disintegrated from jungle rot. The men went for days without food, and casualties mounted. A few lucky ones (right) were evacuated by plane while the rest, when the time for withdrawal came, had to hack their way back to India. A third of the Chindits never made it.

"Our beards grew long and we were tattered and filthy," wrote one survivor of the ordeal. "As we marched through night after night, using the jungle darkness as extra cover against the Japanese, we became desperately weary. . . . We got back in dribs and drabs."

A Chindit officer, in quilted vest, greets a plane crew that has arrived to evacuate casualties.

Sick and wounded Chindits, returning from their trial in the jungle, are attended by a crewman on board a C-47 flying them back to India for medical care.

OUT OF DEFEAT
A SECOND CHANCE

Less than four months after his depleted force stumbled out of the Burmese jungle, Wingate was plotting another expedition against the Japanese. "The first was the experiment," he said confidently. "Now comes the full dress show."

Helping Wingate to orchestrate this new operation was an innovative young American fighter pilot named Philip J. Cochran, whose Air Commandos were to bring a new dimension to jungle fighting. Under Cochran's direction, gliders would be used for the first time in the China-Burma-India Theater; they would transport more than 400 men and ground-clearing equipment behind enemy lines.

The takeoff was set for Sunday, March 5, 1944. Meanwhile, B-25s and P-51s softened up enemy positions with more than 335 sorties. Tow planes practiced getting off the ground with heavily laden gliders attached to them by ropes, while the Chindits themselves practiced getting in and out of mock-glider interiors thrown together out of bamboo.

In a jungle clearing before takeoff, Colonel Cochran briefs his Air Commandos—he called them "sports" and "you guys"—on the flight into Burma. He pulled no punches; some of them, he said, would "find their souls" on the dangerous mission. Cochran served as the prototype for a dashing airman in the American comic strip Terry and the Pirates.

Fifteen minutes before takeoff, shocked Allied officers—including Wingate in pith helmet —examine an aerial photograph (inset) taken two hours earlier. It shows one of their landing zones littered with giant tree trunks. To avoid alerting the enemy, Wingate had banned reconnaissance flights for days, but one of Cochran's pilots had flown over the clearing anyway and taken the picture. The gliders were diverted to another site; later it was discovered that the trunks had been laid out by Burmese woodcutters, not the Japanese.

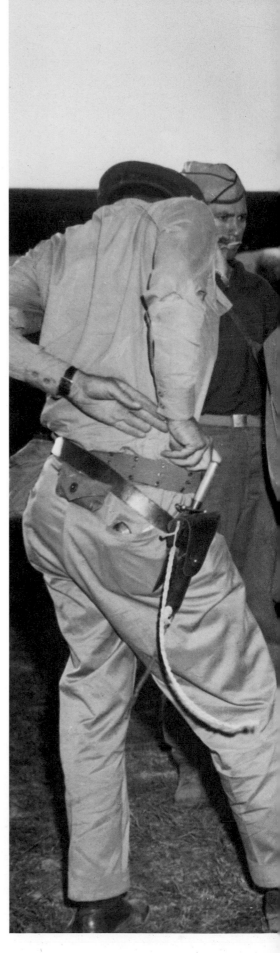

The tail of a C-47 frames a glider skimming over Burma's hills. Some of the transports, towing two gliders, were forced down by overheated engines.

A dejected but lucky pilot sits beside his wrecked glider at Broadway. Each craft could carry 16 men and, freed of its tow line, would glide at 75 mph.

A NEW YORK NAMESAKE BECOMES A DEATH TRAP

At 12 minutes past 6 o'clock on the evening of March 5, a C-47 towing two Waco gliders roared down the runway of the Lalaghat airfield in eastern India. The second Chindit foray into Burma was under way. Within two hours, waves of gliders slammed down on an obstacle-ridden jungle clearing dubbed "Broadway."

Most of them landed safely, but some somersaulted over ditches, smashed into trees or hurtled into other wrecked aircraft. Seventeen had snapped loose from their tow lines while in the air, and nine of them had come down in Japanese territory. Confused Chindits in one downed glider fought a pitched battle with a rescue team of British troops.

Air Commandos patch up the damaged wing of a C-47, which dwarfs a bulldozer airlifted into Burma. To clear Chindit landing strips, the bulldozers sometimes worked in pairs, pulling a log between them to level dirt dikes, called bunds, in rice fields. They were used also to haul away gasoline tanks filled with drinking water dropped to the troops by P-51s.

Sappers lay charges to blow up a bridge on a rail line used by the Japanese; after the blast, they carted off track and railroad ties to reinforce their bunkers.

Chindits in bush hats—which the Japanese thought were Australian—survey damage in a village.

BARBED-WIRE BASTIONS INSIDE ENEMY TERRITORY

Within a week after the landing at Broadway, Wingate had nearly 12,000 troops in Burma, three quarters of whom had arrived by air. Other strips were quickly established, each protected by its own stronghold. The Chindits dug bunkers, laid telephone lines, aligned their heavy weapons and strung miles of barbed wire not only around entire positions, but around individual platoons, companies and battalions as well. The stronghold at Broadway eventually included a hospital, cultivated fields, a chicken farm and shops.

From these fortresses in the jungle, Wingate's raiders slashed out time and again at enemy lines of communication, tearing up railroad tracks and destroying supplies. And when the Japanese moved to eject the invaders from their bases, the Chindits fought back fiercely in hand-to-hand combat. Chindit Major John Masters, in his book *The Road Past Mandalay*, described the terrible aftermath of the fighting in vivid wasteland terms: ". . . blasted trees, feet and twisted hands sticking up out of the earth, bloody shirts, ammunition clips, holes half-full of water . . . and over all the heavy, sweet stench of death, from our own bodies and entrails lying unknown in the shattered ground, from Japanese corpses on the wire, or fastened, dead and rotting, in the trees. . . ."

After visiting a Chindit stronghold Wingate, armed with a Lee Enfield bolt-action rifle, climbs aboard his plane for the next leg of a battlefield tour. Seeing him off on the trip is Lieut. Colonel Michael Calvert, one of his most brilliant commanders. Wingate was killed shortly afterward.

Versatile P-51 Mustangs, sporting the five-striped insignia of Cochran's Air Commandos, roar over the airstrip at Broadway. Like the B-25 bomber on the ground below them, such fighters provided support for the Chindits by bombing bridges and interdicting enemy supply columns.

THE GENERAL'S LAST FLIGHT

The Chindits fought on valiantly in Burma until they were finally withdrawn in August. With the help of close air support, they had defeated 11 Japanese battalions and tied up troops the enemy desperately needed elsewhere.

But their inspiring, eccentric leader was not on hand to share their success. On the evening of March 24, 1944, Wingate was returning to Lalaghat field from a visit to his troops when the B-25 he was in suddenly plunged into the rugged hills west of Imphal. So violent was the crash and the ensuing fire that little more than Wingate's battered pith helmet and some charred letters from home remained with which to make positive identification. His death was regarded by many as a blow to the Allied cause in Burma. "A bright flame was extinguished," said Prime Minister Winston Churchill in tribute.

4

Even as he struggled out of Burma at the head of his ragtag column in 1942, Joseph Stilwell was making plans to fight his way back in. Now in October 1943—16 months after his humiliating retreat—his troops were finally ready to re-enter the country.

Stilwell had hoped to invade Burma as early as the fall of 1942, but the Allies had been unable to agree on a coordinated strategy. Chiang refused at first to commit his troops to a Burma campaign without assurance that the British would join in. The British, burdened by commitments in Asia and Europe and still smarting from their defeat in Burma months before, were reluctant to court disaster again.

At the Trident Conference in Washington in May 1943 and the Quadrant Conference in Quebec in August a limited strategy was agreed upon. For the time being the reconquest of all of Burma—which Stilwell had been urging—would not be attempted. Instead, north Burma would be occupied and a land route from India to China opened, breaking the Japanese blockade of the country.

To carry out that plan, a four-pronged offensive was subsequently devised. Stilwell's India-based Chinese troops would cross into Burma and attack down the valleys of the Hukawng and Mogaung rivers, lying end on end in a north-south direction. Their objectives would be to drive the Japanese out of north Burma, clear the way to open the land route to China, and capture the vital airstrip and communications hub at Myitkyina. Wingate's Chindits—whose daring airborne foray into the Burmese jungles in February of 1943 excited the admiration of Churchill, Roosevelt and the American Joint Chiefs of Staff—would be landed in the rear of whatever Japanese forces might oppose Stilwell's troops. Their mission would be to cut the enemy's communications. Meanwhile, Slim's IV Corps would cross into Burma to prevent Japanese troops from attacking Stilwell from the rear, and his XV Corps would advance down through the Arakan peninsula to Akyab 300 miles to the south.

The key to the offensive in north Burma was the effort to establish an overland line of communication to China. Since the fall of 1942, U.S. Army engineers had been constructing a two-way, all-weather road southward from Ledo in Assam that was to cross over into Burma and follow the Hukawng Valley, then enter the valley of the Mogaung River and eventually run past the towns of Mogaung and Myitkyina.

THE DRIVE TO "MITCH"

South of Myitkyina, the Ledo Road, as it was called, would hook up with existing British-built roads, which in turn joined the old Burma Road. This war-torn route would be repaired and resurfaced as far as Kunming. Completion of the entire project would make it possible to truck supplies from India to Kunming, Chungking and points beyond.

Engineers figured that 65,000 tons of supplies a month could be hauled over the Ledo-Burma Road. Moreover, a six-inch pipeline to be constructed along its length would provide gasoline for the Hump operation and for Chennault's Fourteenth Air Force, flying out of newly built bases in east China. The new flow of supplies would enable Stilwell to bolster the Y Force, the Chinese troops now being trained across the Salween River on Chinese soil.

The taking of Myitkyina's airstrip would further improve the supply situation in China by enabling the U.S. Air Transport Command to reduce traffic along the dangerous and congested Hump route, and to fly heavier payloads over Myitkyina to Kunming, an easier, less mountainous route.

Stilwell's intention was to seize Myitkyina before the 1944 monsoon season. He knew that many in CBI considered such a goal unrealistic. Admiral Mountbatten and his staff were convinced that Myitkyina, the key to success in any north Burma campaign, could not be won without major British participation, at a cost in men and matériel that the British could ill afford. Once Myitkyina was taken, the British felt, it would be all but impossible to hold. In the face of this skepticism, Stilwell did not tell Slim the details of his plan to take Myitkyina until March, when his troops were far down the Hukawng Valley, and even then asked Slim not to speak of the operation to anyone, including his superiors. Stilwell explained his secretiveness by saying that he was afraid that the plan would be leaked, but Slim concluded that "the real reason was that if the operation did not come off, or misfired, he did not want anyone to be able to say he had a failure."

The command structure for Stilwell's north Burma campaign had a comic-opera aspect. As Acting Deputy Supreme Allied Commander for the Southeast Asia Command, Stilwell was answerable only to Mountbatten. But as commanding general of the Chinese Army in India, the X Force, he was technically only a corps commander who would logically come under the control of General Sir George Giffard, Commander-in-Chief of the British Eleventh Army Group in Delhi. Giffard had command—in name, at least—of all Allied forces on the subcontinent. However, Stilwell did not respect Giffard and refused to serve under him. When he was pressed by Mountbatten at a conference, Stilwell astonished everyone by suggesting that he serve under General Slim. Slim, commander of the Fourteenth Army, was in fact Stilwell's subordinate. Nevertheless the American general's request was granted.

According to one story, Stilwell saluted Slim after the conference and said, "Sir, as Fourteenth Army commander, do you have any orders for me?"

"No, sir," replied Slim. "As Deputy Supreme Allied Commander, do you have any orders for me, sir?"

"Not on your life," said Stilwell.

During the course of the north Burma campaign, Slim gave Stilwell few orders, and those few Stilwell accepted graciously. Strikingly different in temperament, the two men shared the same military convictions, and there was no friction between them.

Stilwell recognized that the task confronting him would be one of the hardest of his career. "We have to go in through a rat hole and dig the hole as we go," he said.

The country that lay ahead was indeed forbidding. From the India-Burma border the attack route ran through a wilderness of steep jungle-clad mountains, cut from north to south by torrential rivers fed by the snowy eastern spurs of the Himalayas. Hacking a half-mile path through the undergrowth could take a day, and during the monsoon even longer. The heavy rains forced wild animals onto high ground; among them were snakes ranging from pythons more than 20 feet in length to six-inch kraits with a nerve-paralyzing venom that could kill a man in a matter of minutes. Insects and bloodsucking leeches abounded.

To carry out Stilwell's part of the north Burma campaign, planners at his Delhi headquarters mapped out a three-stage campaign. In stage one, Chinese troops of the X Force would move across the Indian border through the Naga Hills into Burma and provide protection for the American engineers building the Ledo Road. In stage two, they would push on to the Hukawng Valley, seize the town of Shingbwiyang at the head of the valley and occupy ground that would be the jumping-off point for stage three. The final phase would involve a drive down through the Hukawng and Mogaung valleys to capture Mogaung and Myitkyina and clear the way to the south.

The Chinese 38th Division led by General Sun Li-jen crossed into Burma from India at the end of October 1943 —actually before the Combined Chiefs of Staff had approved the overall plan for the campaign. Following some of the trails refugees had used to escape to India in 1942, the Chinese came upon grim evidence of the terrible toll that the pell-mell retreat from Burma a year earlier had taken. Thousands of skeletons lay scattered beside waterholes and campsites, as well as along the steep mountain slopes where refugees had died of starvation, disease or exhaustion. Where roads existed, the rusting hulks of abandoned cars and trucks loomed by the wayside.

Although intelligence reports had given no indication that Japanese forces were present in this part of north Burma, the operation ran into trouble from the start. While preparations for the campaign had been going forward, the Japanese had been moving troops into the hills north of the Hukawng Valley to oppose any Allied intrusion and to prepare for their own invasion of India.

The 38th Chinese Division had not gone far into Burma when troops of the 112th Regiment's 2nd Battalion came upon a Japanese outpost near the village of Sharaw Ga. They beat back the defenders, but soon found themselves under heavy machine-gun and mortar fire. They spent three days trying to take Sharaw Ga and in the process incurred such heavy casualties that they were forced to dig in. The 1st Battalion encountered the same kind of determined opposition outside the nearby village of Yupbang Ga, as did the 3rd Battalion farther south at Ngajatzup.

It was clear now that the Chinese troops were up against a stubborn and experienced enemy. What they were facing, in fact, were troops of the crack Japanese 18th Division, veterans of the conquests of Singapore and Rangoon, led by a tenacious and resourceful commander, Lieut. General Shinichi Tanaka.

In its initial stage, the movement into Burma was led by Stilwell's deputy, Brigadier General Haydon L. Boatner. Stilwell had to leave CBI on November 20 for the Sextant Conference in Cairo, where he argued CBI strategy before Roosevelt, Churchill and Chiang, and was ordered to complete the occupation of north Burma by the spring of 1944.

By the time Stilwell returned to CBI on December 21, the fighting in the Hukawng Valley had reached a stalemate. It was at this point that Chiang put the American in full command—"without strings," as Stilwell noted in his diary—of the remaining X Force in India and of the troops now in Burma. Stilwell went immediately to the front to direct operations and spent two days conferring with General Sun of the 38th Division. Stilwell was itching to demonstrate to Chiang that properly trained and well-led Chinese soldiers could beat the Japanese. A few triumphs, he reasoned, might persuade Chiang to send the Y Force across the Salween into Burma. Stilwell had hopes that elements of the X Force would be able to link up with elements of the Y Force in the vicinity of Myitkyina. Before this could happen, however, the stalemate in the Hukawng would have to be broken. Accordingly, he planned a strong attack at Yupbang Ga that was designed to hook around a portion of the Japanese 18th Division and cut it off from the rest of the Japanese force.

Stilwell made a speech to the troops at Yupbang Ga, telling them that the attack was "important and must go." The Chinese responded well to his urging. Their assault was preceded by an accurate artillery barrage, and the attack itself was pressed home with vigor against stubborn resistance. A pocket of enemy troops was wiped out, and the Chinese gained the heady impression that they could indeed beat the Japanese.

Though headquarters in Chungking and Delhi were howling for his presence, Stilwell remained in the field. Between December 1943 and July 1944, he would spend most of his time at the front. For doing so he became the target of considerable criticism from the British and even from a good many Americans. He was referred to snidely as "the best three-star company commander in the U.S. Army," and as the leader of "the platoon war in Burma."

While at the front Stilwell lived under conditions that even Slim, who did not overindulge himself in luxuries, described after a visit as "unnecessarily primitive." He slept on a cot in fly-covered blankets, used a packing crate for a desk when a folding field desk was not available, bathed

Launching Stilwell's drive into northern Burma, American-trained Chinese troops, covered by a P-40 fighter, march down a new portion of the Ledo Road in October 1943. For the operation, which was aimed at taking Myitkyina's vital airstrip, more than 23,000 Chinese soldiers, known as the X Force, were trained under Stilwell at Ramgarh in northeast India.

out of his helmet and ate from a regular field mess kit. Each day he hiked for miles to visit his forward units. "Up the river, over the hogback," he wrote in his diary. "Slip, struggle, curse and tumble." And in a letter to his wife he reported: "Progress is slow; the jungle is everywhere and very nearly impenetrable. Yesterday, on a cut trail I took 3½ hours to do three miles, tripping and cursing at every step. I expect to see Tarzan any day now." One officer who served with Stilwell later observed that the general came to know every footbridge and detail of terrain in the Hukawng Valley: "You had to really be on your toes when you talked to the old man about where you were operating in the field."

Stilwell continued to keep up the pressure on the Chinese troops under his command and succeeded—at least for the moment—in getting victories out of them. "Good work by Chinese," he wrote exultantly after one action. "Aggressive attack, good fire control, quick action. They are full of beans and tickled to death at beating the Japs!" After another successful action, a victorious Chinese company horrified an American liaison officer by parading about carrying

bamboo poles on which Japanese heads had been impaled.

But though the Chinese won some victories, their successes were infrequent and fell far short of Stilwell's hopes for his troops—which were not simply to drive the Japanese 18th Division back, but to trap and destroy it.

As the struggle moved slowly down into the tangled jungle basin of the Hukawng Valley, with the Chinese 22nd Division now revitalized and available to strengthen his hand, Stilwell tried encircling the 18th. On two separate occasions the Chinese started moving around the 18th Division from opposite directions. But instead of closing the gap between them, they allowed the Japanese to withdraw through the opening. Were they inept, or did they have some motive of their own? It has been suggested that they were following an ancient Chinese military maxim: "When you surround an army, leave an outlet free. Do not press a desperate foe too hard."

Stilwell did not give up easily, and before the end of February he decided to try encircling the Japanese once more. Now he had some moral support from Washington:

President Roosevelt had indicated that he was in complete sympathy with a drive on Myitkyina. Stilwell dryly told a staff member that he would trade the sympathy for one U.S. division. But Roosevelt was backing his sympathy in a way that was almost as good as sending a division: he informed Prime Minister Churchill that he was expecting Stilwell to take Myitkyina by the end of the dry season and that he thought Stilwell could hold it if he continued to have British backup in Burma. Churchill reassured Roosevelt that Mountbatten would not withdraw British troops from Burma for the sake of his own plans.

In addition Stilwell actually did get an American combat unit—the first to reach the Asian mainland. This organization bore a cumbersome title: 5307th Composite Unit (Provisional). In official dispatches, it was called by its operational code name, *Galahad*. But it would come to be known as Merrill's Marauders, after Brigadier General Frank Merrill, whom Stilwell had selected as its leader. Merrill had walked out of Burma with Stilwell in 1942 and within two

years had risen from major to brigadier general. An open, amiable man, he exuded optimism and self-confidence. He had been an assistant military attaché in Tokyo before the war and knew the Japanese and their language. His liabilities were a weak heart—which had already given him trouble once during the arduous retreat—and a lack of experience with infantry, his background having been primarily in cavalry and staff work.

Merrill's Marauders totaled only 3,000 men, but they were to achieve a reputation far out of proportion to their numbers. Lieut. Colonel Charles N. Hunter, Merrill's classmate at West Point and the unit's executive officer through most of the Burma action, called the Marauders "the most beat upon, most misunderstood, most mishandled, most written about, most heroic and yet most unrewarded regimental sized unit in World War II."

To be sure, commanders commonly talk about their outfits in superlatives, but this unit deserved them. In its short lifetime it was to engage in uncommon exploits, suffer uncommon ordeals, get into an inordinate amount of trouble and stir up an exceptional fuss.

The 5307th was created originally for the sole purpose of operating behind enemy lines in Burma; the U.S. War Department fully expected that by the time the unit was withdrawn from this assignment it would have suffered 85 per cent casualties through combat and sickness, and that the survivors might require three months of hospitalization and rest before being fit to return to duty. The outfit included many veterans of jungle combat in the Pacific who had volunteered for what the War Department called a "particularly hazardous, self-sacrificing operation." It also had its fair share of drunks, misfits and violence-prone characters intimately familiar with the inside of the guardhouse—many of whom had been "encouraged" to volunteer. Their behavior was, at best, unpredictable; on at least one occasion some of them amused themselves by shooting at Indian civilians, just to see them jump.

The Marauders had been organized as an American contingent to fight with Britain's Orde Wingate in the second Chindit operation in central Burma. They had even trained with the Chindits in India for three months. But Stilwell wanted the unit for his own purposes in northern Burma, and he lobbied fiercely to get it. (When he succeeded,

During the drive on Myitkyina airstrip, Joseph Stilwell (center) maps out strategy in March 1944 with his two top Chinese commanders, Lieut. General Sun Li-jen (left) of the 38th Division and Lieut. General Liao Yao-hsiang of the 22nd Division. After a faltering start, both American-trained divisions made a major contribution to the success of the campaign.

Wingate was furious. "You can tell General Stilwell," he raged, "he can take his Americans and stick 'em.")

The Marauders were divided into three battalions, with each battalion split into two combat teams. Like the Chindits, they were originally intended to function as a mobile, wide-ranging force that used animal transport and relied on airdrops for resupply. But Stilwell had other plans. Instead of making hit-and-run, Chindit-style raids against the Japanese lines of communication—which Stilwell characterized as "shadowboxing"—the Marauders were to be used where they would be needed most. Stilwell intended to send them around and behind the 18th Division in what he called a "left hook," while the Chinese pressed the Japanese frontally and on the flanks. He hoped that by planting the Marauders firmly in the rear of the 18th he would force Tanaka—who had been conducting a series of successful delaying actions as he fell back slowly before the Chinese—to stand and fight it out.

From India the Marauders moved by train to Ledo, then marched 140 miles over the Naga Hills to Stilwell's headquarters at Shingbwiyang. On February 24 they left Shingbwiyang on their first mission, which was to set up a roadblock behind the 18th Division at Walawbum, a village near the southern end of the Hukawng Valley.

But the wily Tanaka sensed what was up. He knew that Stilwell would try to surround him again and that the American general would make every effort to close the gap that the Chinese had previously left open. Instead of wasting his energies battling the Chinese, Tanaka decided to throw the bulk of the 18th against the force closing the gap in order to destroy it.

On March 1, Tanaka learned that this force, which consisted of Americans, had moved into position behind him at Walawbum. Here was the opportunity he had been waiting for. He promptly attacked, and thus brought about the first pitched battle between Americans and Japanese on the Asian mainland.

The Japanese launched one bayonet charge after another, but the Marauders clung to their positions. In this initial combat action they proved to be both tough and tenacious. When the Japanese came at them with cries of "Banzai!" the Americans responded with a war cry of their own—a two-syllable obscenity delivered in a kind of wolf howl.

During a particularly vicious attack, two bullets punctured the water-cooling jacket of an American machine gun; the crew poured in water from their canteens and kept on firing. One battalion went for 36 hours without food or water, but managed to beat off every assault.

At last Tanaka called off the attack. But before the main Chinese force could catch up with him, he withdrew his division over a secret trail that his engineers had cleared just a few days before. His losses had been high; in five days of battle 800 of his men had been killed. On the American side there were only eight dead and 37 wounded.

Stilwell had won his first major victory in Burma, and his forces now dominated the Hukawng Valley. But Tanaka and his 18th Division had slipped away; they would have to be dealt with again.

On March 5, with Stilwell in control of the Hukawng Valley, Wingate to the south began fulfilling his part of the strategy, inserting five Chindit brigades—as he put it—"in the enemy's guts." By concentrating three of the brigades around Indaw, below Stilwell and Tanaka, he hoped to cut off the 18th from the rest of the Japanese occupying the country and compel Tanaka to pull out of northern Burma. Although the Chindit operation got off to a bad start when a dozen of the gliders crashed in the jungle landing zone, killing 23 men and injuring 30 others, Wingate's forces soon established themselves near Indaw. There they managed to cut the rail line, guaranteeing that the 18th would soon run short of supplies.

By the middle of March, Stilwell's Chinese troops had fought their way down the Hukawng Valley and were approaching the Jambu Bum ridge, which barred entry into the Mogaung valley. Vinegar Joe now decided to try once again to trap Tanaka by sending the Marauders on two sweeps that would take them around through the mountains to the east and bring them in behind the 18th Division. The Marauders' 1st Battalion was to make a swing through the mountains and set up a block near Shaduzup, on the road running south of the Jambu Bum ridge. The other two battalions—the 2nd and 3rd—were to make a much wider and longer hook to the east, follow the valleys of the Tanai and Hkuma rivers south, come in behind Tanaka and take up a blocking position farther down the Mogaung valley.

The 1st Battalion had the shorter but more difficult route, along a trail that skirted the Jambu Bum Mountains. Since the trail ran close to the Japanese, the Marauders kept running into enemy patrols; within one stretch of a mile and a half the battalion had to fight eight minor engagements. At last, in an attempt to avoid the Japanese, the battalion commander elected to leave the trail and strike off into the mountains.

From that point on, the march became a nightmare. It took the battalion two weeks to cover 30 miles. Muleteers had to cut trails through thickets of dense, tough bamboo, foot by foot, while the rest of the column waited, standing in place, rather than sitting down, because the slopes were so steep. Many of the men were suffering from dysentery, and all endured relentless attacks by jungle pests.

There were dumdum flies, whose bites produced fierce itching; tiny buffalo flies, which passed right through mosquito netting and bit all night long; and leeches—the inch-long common leech, the three-inch buffalo leech and the monster elephant leech that grew to nearly half a foot in length. The leeches lived at different levels in the vegetation, from the ground up to the low-lying branches of trees. They dropped off onto passersby, fastening themselves to exposed skin or working their way to the skin through layers of clothing.

All of the Marauders soon were oozing blood from leech bites. They burned the leeches off their bodies with lighted cigarettes or removed them with a hill-tribe concoction of quicklime, tobacco juice and kerosene. Neglected bites festered into ulcers that could eat through a man's leg. The mules suffered even more; their fetlocks were running with blood and crawling with the maggots that hatched in the open wounds.

The men were constantly hungry. Their basic fare consisted of K rations—canned meats, date bars, chocolate, cheese, coarse biscuits, powdered coffee and the inevitable sticks of chewing gum. But there were never enough K rations; the airdrops to an outfit on the march were of necessity few and far between. Moreover, the rations, formulated to see soldiers through short-term emergencies, contained neither the bulk nor the calories nor the vitamins the Marauders needed in their prolonged exertions.

As their hunger grew, the men became obsessed with thoughts of food and evolved elaborate barter systems for trading choice items. Charlton Ogburn Jr., a signal officer who served with Merrill, later recalled the system in his book *The Marauders:* "There is the sound of voices habitually subdued, addressed unendingly to the one subject of unfailing interest: 'Pack of Cavaliers for two lumps of sugar, anyone?' 'Pork-and-egg-yolk for a cheese component?' 'Coffee for a fruit bar?' " The hunger and the thirst, said Ogburn, led to a feeling of "utter despondency, if we have been marching down a dry ridge all afternoon, of having to endure an evening, a night, and at least part of a morning without water or coffee and consequently without food either, for a dry throat will pass no part of a K-ration."

Exhausted by the journey and its privations, the 1st Battalion finally made its way down into the Mogaung valley after more than two weeks, only to find the Japanese encamped in the area where they had expected to set up their block. The Marauders lay still through the night, waiting until the Japanese started building early-morning cooking fires before launching their attack. The Japanese were taken completely by surprise, and a bayonet charge put them to flight. The 1st Battalion then set up a roadblock on the valley road south of Shaduzup. Their work done, they were relieved by a regiment of the Chinese 38th Division.

While the Chinese were lying in wait, the elusive Japanese division coolly slipped around to the west and extricated itself from the trap. Meanwhile, the 2nd and 3rd battalions were making their wider sweep around to the east and down through the Tanai and Hkuma valleys. The 2nd Battalion crossed the Mogaung River and the 3rd Battalion remained on the other side of the river to protect the rear. When the 2nd Battalion attempted to set up its roadblock in the vicinity of a village called Inkangahtawng, it ran headlong into a Japanese force of about 2,500 men. A series of strong attacks forced the battalion to withdraw across the river. At that point the effort to trap Tanaka in the Mogaung valley was abandoned.

While the Marauders were sweeping around to the east and vainly attempting to block the Japanese in the Mogaung valley, Stilwell's Chinese troops to the north were pushing down across the Jambu Bum ridge in an effort to break into the valley. The Japanese defended the ridge so stubbornly

Top Japanese officers in the China-Burma-India Theater as the fighting neared a climax were Lieutenant Generals (from left to right) Shinichi Tanaka, Renya Mutaguchi and Kotuku Sato. Tanaka, whose 18th Division bitterly opposed Stilwell's drive into northern Burma, and Sato, who hurled his 31st Division against the British garrison at Kohima in India, were both commanders in Mutaguchi's formidable Fifteenth Army.

that Stilwell ordered up some armor and tried to take it with a coordinated tank and infantry attack. But the tankers—Chinese troops with American advisers—found it difficult to distinguish their own infantry from the Japanese. As a result the infantrymen became extremely wary of getting close to the tanks, and the effectiveness of the tank and infantry attacks was sharply reduced.

It took two days of hard fighting to reach the crest of the ridge, and the resistance was every bit as fierce on the other side. The dirt road leading down the far slope was mined, and the Japanese had felled trees to bar passage of the tanks. After two days had been spent clearing the road, Stilwell ordered another tank and infantry attack, but again the infantry would not keep up with the tanks. To avoid being mistaken for Japanese, the infantrymen hit upon the device of waving white cloths. But the Japanese caught on to this, and waving white cloths of their own they managed to lure five tanks into an antitank trap and destroy them.

As the Chinese forces laboriously ground their way down toward Shaduzup, an alarming new threat to their safety emerged. Stilwell's staff obtained a captured sketch showing an enemy battalion heading north in the Tanai valley with the intention of crossing into the Hukawng Valley to attack the Chinese in the rear and on the side. Stilwell ordered Merrill to block the trail north of the village of Nhpum Ga and stop the Japanese from reaching their objective. Merrill chose the 2nd and 3rd battalions for the job. Though the men were still weary from their long march and encounter with the enemy at Inkangahtawng, they managed to reach their destinations in two days. The 2nd Battalion occupied Nhpum Ga, while the 3rd Battalion went three miles farther north to Hsamshingyang.

At Nhpum Ga, the men of the 2nd Battalion dug a defensive perimeter about 400 yards long and a couple of hundred feet wide on a hilltop. They had barely occupied this position when the Japanese attacked. For a week the Marauders were pounded by artillery and mortar fire. During the barrages, more than a hundred of the Marauders' pack animals were killed. The ground was so rocky—and the Japanese fire so withering—that the Americans could not bury the mules and had to live with the almost unendurable stench of the bloated carcasses rotting in the tropical heat. To add to their misery, they were running out of water and were restricted to half a cup a day of stagnant, muddy liquid. Whenever the artillery fire stopped, the Japanese charged the ridge. At one point they subjected the battalion to 16 successive do-or-die charges.

The Americans were able to hold their ground partly because of the guile and bravery of a Japanese-American sergeant, Roy H. Matsumoto. Each night he would crawl past the perimeter and sneak within earshot of the Japanese. With the information he gathered about their plans the Marauders were ready for the next Japanese moves.

One night Matsumoto learned that the Japanese were going to attack a particular point on the perimeter the following morning. After booby-trapping their foxholes, the men in this section withdrew to high ground. The Japanese launched their attack and rushed straight into fire from above. When Matsumoto yelled "Charge, Charge!" in Japanese, a follow-up wave of Japanese soldiers leaped into

the booby-trapped foxholes. Fifty-four Japanese were killed in the assault.

As the siege was going on, General Merrill, leading the 3rd Battalion to the relief of the 2nd, was struck down by a heart attack only three miles outside of Nhpum Ga. Stilwell ordered Merrill evacuated by plane on March 31, in spite of the ill man's protests. Command of the Marauders now passed on to the executive officer, Lieut. Colonel Hunter, a tough, old-line infantryman whose extensive service in the Philippines and Panama had turned him into an expert in jungle warfare.

On April 3, Hunter assembled the officers of the 3rd Battalion and told them: "Gentlemen, in the morning we start an attack that will drive through to the 2nd Battalion. It may take two or three days, but we *will* get through." He resorted to several tricks to confuse the Japanese. To draw some of them off in another direction, he staged a fake fire fight in the jungle, with some of his men using regular weapons and the rest using carbines, which sounded like the enemy's rifles. And he had a message dropped by plane into the Japanese lines, ostensibly by accident. The message said that an Allied airborne battalion would be parachuting in some distance away.

On April 4, the 3rd Battalion attacked with everything it had. Hunter knew that it was common practice for the Japanese to withdraw under artillery fire or bombing attack, then race back to their positions in time to stop any follow-up infantry assault. Now the Marauders exploited this habit by creeping forward as far as possible under their own mortar barrage and then, when it lifted, sprinting toward the momentarily unoccupied Japanese trenches. The Americans won the foot race, advancing 200 precious yards.

While the 2nd and 3rd battalions were battling the Japanese, the 1st Battalion started a round-the-clock forced march to Nhpum Ga from the Shaduzup area. In the dense jungles at night, each man carried a luminous compass or a phosphorescent chip of wood on his back to keep the man behind from stumbling off in the dark.

When the 1st Battalion arrived in the Nhpum Ga area at last, seven days after starting out, and combined forces with the 2nd and 3rd battalions, the outnumbered Japanese began slipping away into the jungle. On Easter Sunday the 13-day siege was over. It had cost the Marauders 59 men dead

and 314 wounded. Some 400 Japanese bodies lay on the slopes of the ridge where the 2nd Battalion had first set up its perimeter.

By this point the drive down the Hukawng and Mogaung valleys and the roadblocking efforts of the Marauders had proved so costly that officials in the highest Allied circles were beginning to question whether the capture of Myitkyina would be worth the price. Admiral Mountbatten, who had viewed the whole enterprise with misgivings from the start, was asked his opinion by the Joint Chiefs of Staff. He replied that in his judgment continuation of the campaign was "unsound and should not be attempted." He proposed instead that an operation be undertaken against the Prome-Rangoon area of southern Burma.

But Marshall and the Joint Chiefs of Staff favored pushing on to Myitkyina. At the end of April, Marshall sent Stilwell a radio message to that effect, and on May 3 the Joint Chiefs affirmed this decision formally in a directive to Stilwell instructing him to go ahead and take Myitkyina.

By now their directive was almost superfluous. Stilwell's strategy for taking Myitkyina was well advanced. The burden of the operation would fall on the Marauders, even though they had been in Burma for two months and were exhausted. They knew that the Chindits were supposed to be relieved after three months' duty in the jungle, and they had expected the same treatment. But Stilwell had made them no such promise and had other plans.

Using the main body of his Chinese troops, reinforced with elements of three new Chinese divisions provided by Chiang, Stilwell intended to continue pressing Tanaka's 18th Division down the Mogaung valley. To prod the Chinese generals and their troops, Stilwell went to the front. "It pays to go up and push," he wrote in his diary. "At least, it's a coincidence that every time I do, they spurt a bit."

At the front, he bullied, cajoled and flattered the Chinese commanders, Generals Sun and Liao. Then he deliberately walked to forward positions, exposing himself to danger. The Chinese officers in charge responded immediately; fearing the wrath that would befall them if the American were killed, they ordered their men to press forward.

Stilwell felt it necessary to keep up the pressure on Sun and Liao because he had been told by a senior Chinese officer that the Generalissimo had secretly instructed the Chinese generals not to push too hard. In any case, Stilwell wanted to tie down as many Japanese troops as possible on this front and prevent them from interfering with the thrust to Myitkyina. The pressure might even draw away some of Myitkyina's defenders. Then, while Tanaka was engaged, a Marauder task force would move off to the east in a long sweep aimed directly at Myitkyina.

The operation was code-named *End Run,* and the Marauders were divided up into three combat teams for this assignment. To increase their numbers, Stilwell assigned to the Marauders two Chinese regiments, as well as 300 Kachin guerrillas—warlike Burmese mountain tribesmen—borrowed from Office of Strategic Services Detachment 101, an American unit that had been operating clandestinely in Burma since late 1942.

Under the leadership of Lieut. Colonel William R. Peers, OSS Detachment 101 had already performed many valuable services in Burma. The original band of 21 men was the first American unit organized to operate on a broad scale behind enemy lines. Their daredevil missions involved parachuting deep into Japanese-held territory to radio back military intelligence and rescue downed Allied airmen. In time they organized the Kachins into a guerrilla force that conducted hit-and-run raids on enemy installations, ambushed marching columns and created havoc in the Japanese rear areas.

The Kachins would be extremely useful in the *End Run* mission, but Stilwell was more concerned about Merrill's men; he knew he was asking the tired Marauders to perform more than their fair share of the fighting. He explained to Merrill, who was recuperating from a heart attack, that he had no other choice.

The Marauders themselves treated rumors of their new assignment as a grim joke. Battle casualties and disease had reduced their original numbers by about half. Myitkyina was some 90 miles away across the rugged Kumon Range; for men in their weakened condition, simply getting there would require a supreme effort. Merrill could do little to motivate them, but he let it be known that once they had captured the Myitkyina airstrip no more would be asked of them; they would be sent to a specially prepared camp in India for rest and recuperation.

The Marauders' morale was at rock bottom. They were

still formally designated only as the 5307th Composite Unit (Provisional). They had no colors, no insignia. Not a single Marauder had received a promotion or decoration in spite of the valor displayed by the unit. Some of the junior officers had been in grade so long that Hunter wryly proposed that they be awarded oak leaf clusters—the Army's device for showing that a decoration has been given more than once—for their lieutenant's and captain's bars. When Hunter complained to Stilwell's staff about the situation, he was told that the Marauders should spend more time fighting and less time worrying about promotions.

Stilwell himself had rarely visited the Marauders, possibly because he felt that his Chinese troops required more of his attention. Stilwell was respected and even deified by men who worked closely with him, but he was regarded less affectionately by some of the troops in the field. While he was generally portrayed as being a soldier's soldier and the

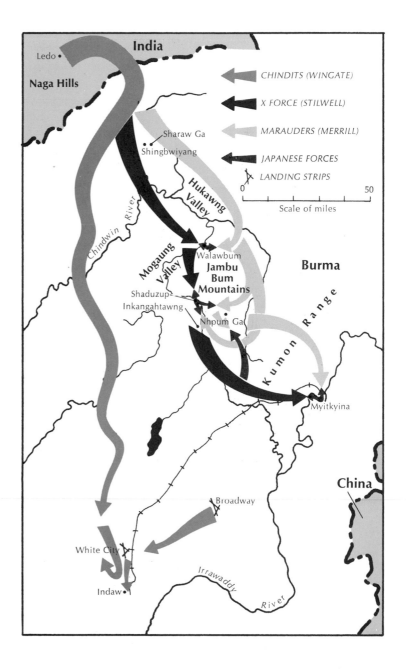

General Stilwell's drive to Myitkyina in 1944 was spearheaded by the Chinese X Force and Merrill's Marauders. Stilwell's men pushed into the Hukawng Valley and made an attempt to trap the Japanese 18th Division at Walawbum. After the enemy retreated into the Mogaung valley, the Marauders circled through the Jambu Bum Mountains to block the Japanese from the rear at Shaduzup and Inkangahtawng. The Marauders then went to Nhpum Ga to confront an enemy relief force advancing from the south. After defeating the Japanese at Nhpum Ga, they crossed the Kumon Range, captured the Myitkyina airstrip and finally took Myitkyina, aided by Chinese troops. To support Stilwell, Wingate's Chindits traveled by foot from Ledo to seize the airfield at Indaw and, simultaneously, by glider to a jungle clearing called Broadway. From there they launched an attack on White City, before cutting the north-south rail line.

GI's Uncle Joe, he was considered cold, uncommunicative and unapproachable by the Marauder officers. To the Marauders in general, wrote Ogburn, "his name was as a red flag to a bull." One day after Stilwell visited the Marauders briefly, an enlisted man said, "I had him in my rifle sights, I coulda squeezed one off and no one woulda known it wasn't a Jap that got the sonofabitch." Similar sentiments toward disliked officers were often voiced by combat soldiers, but the nature of the Marauders and the state of their morale gave this utterance chilling overtones.

Adding to the Marauders' woes was the monsoon. In theory, the heavy rains were not supposed to begin until the middle of May, but as Stilwell noted in his diary, "the dry season in this country is a joke. . . . We have had rain in December, 12 days in January, 18 in February, 10 in March, 10 in April, and now it is really going to rain."

The Marauders set out on April 28 and the rain came on May 1. Stilwell, still under pressure from those who did not believe in the operation, was deeply depressed by

the weather. "Depression days, commander's worries," he wrote in his diary on the 1st of May, three days after the operation had gotten under way. "I start them off for Myitkyina, it rains, the resistance grows here. Why didn't I use them on our front? Is the gap too big? Will they meet a reinforced garrison? Does it mean we'll fail on both sides, instead of only one? Can I get them out? Are the Japs being sucked toward the Mogaung or . . . staying in Mitch? . . . Nothing can be done about it. The die is cast, and it's sink or swim. But the nervous wear and tear is terrible. Pity the poor commanding officer."

The Kachins had warned that an outfit as big as that involved in the *End Run* force would find it impossible to cross the Kumon Range during the rains. As the men slogged toward the 6,100-foot pass over the spine of the range, they were even reduced at times to crawling up the slippery hillsides on their hands and knees. "It was so bad," Ogburn wrote, "it was preposterous." Steps had to be hacked out of the slopes for the ailing, exhausted pack animals. Even so, the mules kept slipping and falling. Some broke their necks; each time one died its load of valuable supplies had to be either abandoned or redistributed among the others. In a single exasperating day, the 3rd Battalion lost 20 mules and was forced to leave behind some 4,000 pounds of sorely needed equipment. Only half the pack animals survived the trek to Myitkyina.

The officers could no longer enforce march discipline. Men straggled into bivouac hours after the head of the column. Some, instead of boiling water to sterilize it or putting purifying halazone pills into their canteens and waiting the prescribed time to allow them to work, simply washed down the tablets with swigs of water taken straight from a stream—thus exposing themselves to amoebic dysentery, a wide range of debilitating microbes and snail-carried schistosomiasis, which could be fatal.

On the way, the Marauders surrounded and destroyed a small Japanese garrison at a remote village called Ritpong. When they moved into the settlement they discovered that the garrison had been living in indescribable squalor. Soon afterward they began falling out with a fever that the doctors first called FUO—fever of unknown origin. The illness later proved to be a mite-borne typhus, a raging killer that the Japanese had carried into Burma. In all, 149 Marauders

Brigadier General Frank D. Merrill, leader of the Marauders, the first U.S. ground combat force to see action in Asia, emerges from a Burmese hut. Merrill's regiment-sized unit, which spearheaded the capture of the airstrip at Myitkyina, was deactivated in August 1944. But during the short span of only 11 months, the Marauders fought more than 20 engagements and marched more than 600 miles over northern Burma.

out of the *End Run* force got the disease, which was characterized by a high fever and skin lesions and lasted about two weeks. Many died, including Colonel Henry I. Kinnison, commander of one of the Marauder combat teams.

The *End Run* force had nearly reached Myitkyina by the 13th of May, 15 days after setting out. Merrill, who had returned to duty at the start of *End Run*, radioed Stilwell: "Can stop this show up till noon tomorrow, when die will be cast, if you think it too much of a gamble. Personal opinion is that we have a fair chance and that we should try." Stilwell replied: "Roll on in and swing on 'em."

On the 16th, Hunter, commanding the assaulting force, bivouacked near the Myitkyina airstrip after putting local villagers under guard to make sure that they would not alert the Japanese. Kachin scouts found the airstrip only lightly defended. At 10 the next morning, Hunter launched the attack, with the Marauders and the two Chinese regiments hitting both the airstrip and a nearby ferry landing on the Irrawaddy. Taken by surprise, the Japanese offered only ineffective resistance and at 3:30 p.m. Hunter could send Stilwell the coded message "Merchant of Venice," meaning that the strip had fallen and transport planes could land.

Stilwell was jubilant. He wrote in his diary in capital letters: "WILL THIS BURN UP THE LIMEYS." In fact, the British were both astonished and annoyed. Few of them had believed that Stilwell could carry out his drive on Myitkyina without asking first for direct British involvement. Churchill sent a message to Mountbatten demanding an explanation of how "the Americans by a brilliant feat of arms have landed us in Myitkyina." This was the first Japanese stronghold on the Asian mainland to be seized by the Allies, and incredibly, Mountbatten had not even been informed it was being attacked. He had been too preoccupied with current British offensives in Burma and India—and with planning an amphibious landing on Sumatra and a push toward Singapore—to pay much attention to Stilwell's advance.

Mountbatten, angry at not having been better informed by Stilwell, told Churchill that he intended to write the American a letter saying so. Wiser counsel seems to have prevailed. When an Order of the Day was finally addressed to Stilwell over Mountbatten's signature, it read: "By the boldness of your leadership, backed by the courage and endurance of your American and Chinese troops, you have taken the enemy completely by surprise and achieved a most outstanding success by seizing the Myitkyina airfield." Mountbatten also praised the crossing of the Kumon Range as a feat that would live in military history.

The capture of the Myitkyina airstrip was indeed a bold and brilliant military enterprise, the high point of Stilwell's career. But things were now about to go desperately wrong. Though Hunter could easily have taken the town of Myitkyina itself, with its small garrison of some 700 Japanese, he had no orders to do so. Merrill, who was at field command headquarters with Stilwell, had said he would be the first man to land once the strip was secure and that he would personally direct operations against the adjacent city. But, inexplicably, Merrill did not appear for 24 hours.

It had been Hunter's understanding that the first arriving aircraft would deliver ammunition and food, and that subsequent flights would bring in other combat equipment and more infantrymen. But cargo planes did not come. Instead —to Hunter's astonishment—aircraft swept toward the field with gliders in tow. An officer stepped out of one of the planes and said proudly to Hunter: "See those gliders? Those are aviation engineers, my engineers."

"What the hell are they for?" asked Hunter.

"To repair the runway."

But the airstrip did not need repairing, said the exasperated Hunter: Where was Merrill? Where was the promised ammunition? Nobody knew.

A short while later, the first of the cargo planes touched down. But instead of ammunition they carried antiaircraft units that the Army Air Forces commander for India and Burma, Major General George E. Stratemeyer, had decided were necessary for defense of the strip. Merrill himself arrived at Myitkyina the next day, was stricken by another heart attack and was once more out of action.

On the afternoon of May 17, Hunter sent two battalions of the Chinese 150th Regiment (part of the 50th Division, which had only recently entered Burma) against the Japanese garrison. There is some uncertainty about what happened next. According to one account, there were Japanese intelligence agents hiding in some trees nearby; they fired into the two Chinese battalions, and in the resulting confusion the battalions began shooting at each other. The following day Hunter sent both battalions back to attack Myitkyina. The Japanese tried the same trick again; once again the two battalions began to fight each other. The performance of the Chinese 150th Regiment became a scandal, and the regiment was soon withdrawn.

In the meantime, the Japanese were reinforcing their Myitkyina garrison, infiltrating troops at night before Stilwell's forces closed in on the city. They now had 3,500 troops defending the town. They quickly dug in behind elaborate earthworks; they had plenty of weapons and ammunition, their morale was high and they were under orders to hang on. The *End Run* force was now confronted by a situation resembling the static trench warfare of the First World War; the two sides occupied fixed positions facing each other. With little artillery, little air support because of monsoon rain clouds, and no armor, the Marauders could not do much to alter the situation.

By now, 80 per cent of the men had dysentery, some so acutely that they cut their pants seats open so as to be able to relieve themselves instantly. Between 75 and 100 sick Marauders were being airlifted out daily; 15 to 30 a day were turning up with symptoms of deadly mite typhus. Under pressure to keep soldiers in the line, medical officers refused to send any man back to hospitals in Assam until he had run a temperature of 102° for three consecutive days and had passed a board of doctors. In the 2nd Battalion—the unit that had been besieged at Nhpum Ga—men were so tired that they fell asleep during the battle, and their colonel fainted three times while directing the fighting. Eventually, the 2nd Battalion was reduced to 12 effectives.

The Marauders felt that they had been betrayed, and that Merrill's promise of relief had been broken. On May 25 on the Myitkyina front, Hunter handed Stilwell a note in which he claimed that his troops had been abused and neglected, and were now all but useless as a fighting force, and he recommended that the Marauders be disbanded. By the end of May, only 200 of the original 3,000 Marauders remained in battle.

The Chindits near Indaw were no better off. They had been in the jungle for four months, and their commanders were asking for relief. Fearing that the withdrawal of the Chindits would endanger his operations, Stilwell refused their pleas—indeed, he kept one Chindit column in the field so long, and made so many demands upon it, that the unit was reduced from 1,300 men to barely 30, the strength of a platoon, before it was finally relieved.

Stilwell felt that he could not make an exception of the Americans at this point. Accordingly, his staff began placing enormous pressure on rear-area hospitals to return to combat any sick or wounded Marauders who were capable of bearing arms. Convalescents were dragooned and shipped back to Myitkyina over the objections of the medical officers. On one occasion angry doctors literally chased a truck convoy full of shanghaied sick and wounded and forced it to turn back. Another group of Marauder convalescents were found to be so sick when they arrived at Myitkyina that they were declared unfit for combat duty and were immediately reevacuated.

Conditions at the hospitals were almost as bad as those at the front. The convalescent camp at Margherita in Assam was located in a pasture and was described as a "pest hole." The bamboo buildings were collapsing from the ravages of termites; wards were overcrowded and had dirt floors. In the wet months, from May to October, it poured most of the time; when the rains stopped it was so hot that, in the words of Ogburn, "it was like the inside of a tea kettle."

But perhaps the most appalling conditions were created by the ailing soldiers themselves. The Marauders had been a rough crew to begin with. Many of those evacuated from Myitkyina were suffering from acute nervous strain, a condition that was exacerbated by the fear of being sent back. Some men went berserk. They got drunk, ransacked officers' quarters, roamed the camp, terrified Red Cross girls and demolished their own canteen. The MPs were afraid to enter the camp to restore order. Ogburn, himself a convalescent at Margherita, wrote later: "Orders were all but impossible to enforce and work details were not worth the effort of trying to assemble. There was nothing with which to threaten the rebellious but the guardhouse, and this would have appealed to most of them as a luxurious alternative to Burma."

To shore up the crumbling Marauders still fighting at Myitkyina, Stilwell sent in additional Chinese troops, two battalions of American combat engineers from the Ledo Road and two battalions of replacements—truck drivers, MPs and artillerymen, all classed as infantry. Many of these men had not fired a weapon since basic training. Most had not even met one another or their officers until three days before departing from the United States.

The four battalions were thrown into the Myitkyina siege not only ill trained but mentally unprepared for the extreme conditions of warfare during a monsoon. Their introduction to combat was disastrous. Some of the engineer units broke and ran under fire, leaving their wounded behind. On one occasion Japanese soldiers dressed in Chinese uniforms beckoned to a company of replacement infantrymen. The Americans walked right up to the Japanese and were cut down with machine guns. Fifty of the replacements became mental cases. Some quit taking their mepacrine tablets in order to get malaria or deliberately wounded themselves—shooting off toes—to escape combat.

However awful things were at Myitkyina, elsewhere in Burma Allied prospects were brightening. In April, Stilwell, on instructions from Marshall, had threatened to divert Lend-Lease supplies from the Chinese Y Force unless it

Members of the Kachin Rangers receive a map briefing from their American patrol leader (right) prior to setting forth on a raid south of Myitkyina in 1944. Equipped and trained by Detachment 101 of the Office of Strategic Services, these tribesmen from the Burmese mountains were vigorous in carrying out guerrilla operations against the Japanese.

131

At Myitkyina airstrip, Dr. Gordon Seagrave's Hospital Unit treats Chinese soldiers. Using cots and litters as makeshift operating tables, Seagrave (right center, in undershirt and hat) and his fellow surgeons performed as many as 190 operations a day, often working until three in the morning and under Japanese shelling. In spite of adverse conditions, they managed to save more than 95 per cent of the casualties they treated.

crossed the Salween and joined in the battle for northern Burma. On the 11th of May, the first of 72,000 Chinese troops crossed the river on bamboo rafts and rubber boats, and set forth to engage the Japanese. Also in May, Stilwell's Chinese divisions in the Mogaung valley suddenly showed new signs of life. For weeks the Americans had tried unsuccessfully to get General Sun to press down the valley and wrest the town of Kamaing, south of Myitkyina, from Tanaka. On May 19, Sun suddenly said to his American liaison officer, "We go to take Kamaing now."

The timing was right. Tanaka's men were near the end of their rope. Their supply dumps had been destroyed by Allied bombers, and they were now subsisting on a daily ration of 100 grams of rice. They were running out of artillery ammunition, and companies had been reduced from an average strength of 50 men in April to 30 in June. On June 29, Tanaka broke off contact with the Chinese and led the tattered remnant of his command out of the Mogaung valley. He had only 3,000 men left of his original 6,000-man force. The once-invincible 18th Division had finally been broken.

Through June and into July the Japanese clung tenaciously to Myitkyina. Living and fighting in mud and water, Americans, Chinese and Japanese came down with trench foot, jungle rot and an ailment called Naga sores—painful ulcers that sometimes ate through to the bone. Aerial resupply was hampered by the monsoon, a dozen wrecked transports littered the airstrip and the troops were continually short of food and ammunition. Combat operations ended each day when the medical units could handle no more casualties. Evacuations of the sick and wounded reached a high of 130 a day. "Rain, rain, rain," Stilwell wrote in a letter to his wife. "Mud, mud, mud, typhus, malaria, dysentery, exhaustion, rotting feet, body sores. If we are badly off, what about the Japs?"

The Japanese had been fighting in Myitkyina since May 17. By the middle of July their garrison, which at its peak had probably numbered around 3,500 men, had lost 790 dead and 1,180 wounded. Moreover, the Allied lines were steadily constricting around it.

By the end of the month, the Japanese were cut off from the outer world, and it was clear that the garrison's strength was ebbing. Hospital patients were being evacuated from Myitkyina by raft down the river and the less severely wounded were being returned to the fighting. When Colonel Fusayasu Maruyama, commander of the 18th Division's 114th Regiment, requested that his unit be pulled out of Myitkyina, Major General Genzu Mizukami, the garrison commander, agreed, even though he had intended every man to fight to the last. On August 1, Mizukami made his apology to the Emperor for his defeat and committed hara-kiri. Maruyama made his escape across the river by raft.

One hundred and eighty-seven Japanese were taken prisoner, most of them sick or wounded. About 600 others managed to escape. There were only two routes they could take: by raft down the Irrawaddy River, or across the river and overland to the east. The Americans were not about to let them get away. Two OSS Detachment 101 guerrilla groups intercepted them. One group lay in ambush on the river 20 miles to the south. The other group harassed those who crossed the river to the east with repeated raids and ambushes. Between them, they killed between five and six hundred Japanese.

The siege of Myitkyina had taken a heavy toll of the Allied forces, too. The Chinese lost 972 men; 3,184 more were wounded. The Americans counted 272 dead and 955 wounded; another 980 were severely ill.

In terms of the size of the enemy force overcome and the Allied casualties suffered in the process, the fight for Myitkyina was roughly comparable to the Marines' taking of Tarawa in the Pacific, one of the bloodiest battles of the island campaign. And at Myitkyina the Chinese and American armies had to do the job without the massive air support and naval gunfire that had been available to the United States Marines.

With Myitkyina in Allied hands, transports immediately began flying the lower, less hazardous route to China, bypassing the Hump, and the tonnage delivered to Kunming quickly doubled. And as soon as the Ledo Road—and the pipeline being laid beside it—could be brought up to Myitkyina, the supply situation would improve even more.

On the day that General Mizukami committed suicide in Myitkyina, Stilwell received news of his own promotion to full general. Three days later he was able to write in his diary: "Myitkyina over at last. Thank God."

BURMA'S CRUEL TORMENTS

Chinese foot soldiers, maneuvering against Japanese positions in north Burma in May of 1944, find tough going and poor fields of fire in a bamboo thicket.

A WAR ZONE OF UNCOMMON MISERY

The men who fought in Burma were up against one of the world's worst climates and some of its most forbidding terrain. They had to scale jagged mountains, hack their way through almost impenetrable jungles, cross swiftly flowing rivers and pass over dusty plains where temperatures ranged as high as 130° F. Some units were forced to beat their way through razor-sharp elephant grass; others, using roads, found their way blocked by mounds of debris pushed up by the Japanese. In the mountains, the roads were sometimes so narrow that tanks crept along with half the outside track hanging over the edge.

The monsoon added its own torments to the fighting. In some places it rained as much as 15 inches a day, and soldiers were mired up to their calves in porridge-thick mud. Diseases and vicious biting and stinging insects were rampant. Men came down with malaria, dengue fever, cholera, scabies, yaws, mite typhus and dysentery. At one point casualties from tropical illness outweighed those from combat by a ratio of 14 to 1, with malaria accounting for 90 per cent of the cases. Swarms of black flies drove men to frenzy. After heavy rains, trees and bushes became so heavily laden with bloodsucking leeches that one officer described the foliage as looking like a "wheat field waving in the wind."

Compounding these torments was the enemy, a fanatical fighter who would rather die than be taken alive. At Pinwe, in north Burma, a Japanese sniper dubbed "Little Willie" by British troops fired away from a hole in a tree for three weeks, picking off eight officers, despite frantic efforts to get him with mortar or rifle fire; he eventually slipped away unscathed. At Ngazun, Japanese attacked British tanks with nothing more than swords.

There was almost no respite from the enemy, the terrain or the climate, and few of the soldiers would ever forget the ordeal of Burma. Charlton Ogburn Jr., a lieutenant who served there with Merrill's Marauders, described it as "the worst experience I have ever been through. It was so incomparably the worst that I could hardly believe in the rest of my life at all."

A dead Japanese—a human antitank mine—sits with a 250-pound bomb in his lap. He was shot before he had a chance to detonate the bomb.

Roadblocks like this one across the Imphal-Kohima road in India were a favorite device for containing or slowing British forces during the Burma campaign.

A HORROR CALLED THE MONSOON

Flying over the northern part of Burma in the monsoon season, the Supreme Allied Commander in Southeast Asia, Admiral the Lord Louis Mountbatten, peered out the window of his airplane and asked what river was below him. "That's not a river," answered an American officer aboard the plane, "it's the Ledo Road."

During the four-month monsoon season it rained as much as 375 inches in some places. The rain came down so hard at times, one veteran said later, "you *literally* couldn't see your hand in front of your face." Valleys were turned into lakes, rivers rose as much as 30 feet in a single night and trails became ribbons of ankle-deep mud. Travel was slowed to little more than a mile an hour. Often during a downpour the bodies of soldiers who had been killed in combat and properly buried bobbed to the surface. Units became isolated, and one officer had to be ferried by raft to his mess hall a few yards away.

Although the monsoon presented some nightmarish problems, it was not the worst of the jungle's tortures. The monsoon rain was cool, and the fighting men liked to take off their shirts and let the water run over the sores and insect bites on their bodies. The really bad part came after the rain stopped, for in the sweltering jungle the temperature climbed steadily every day and the humidity became overpowering. Fungi and bacteria multiplied, breeding rot and disease, and sweating soldiers found breathing difficult and sleeping almost impossible.

Chinese reinforcements, carrying their worldly goods on poles, slog up the monsoon-drenched Ledo Road in October 1944. In Burma, the rains started in May and ended in September.

Mule drivers and Burmese rivermen coax a reluctant animal into the Irrawaddy River. Once in the water, terrified mules often had to be towed by boat.

WATERY CHALLENGE TO ALLIED INGENUITY

Burma's rivers presented a major logistical problem for troops fighting in the jungle. Both bridges and boats were scarce, and Allied engineers had to build hundreds of teak-log barges that looked to one officer "like Noah's arks without the houses." Each barge carried 10 tons of equipment, and three of them lashed together could ferry anything up to a Sherman tank. To tow the barges, tugboats were transported to crossing sites in sections, then welded together on the riverbanks; outboard motors to power the barges were flown in from Calcutta.

When floods destroyed existing bridges, replacements were quickly erected. One unit constructed 40 bridges in 40 miles. Spans were built of everything from simple planks to 150-foot girders, including parts hauled by truck more than 300 miles across the mountains.

Salvage operations dredged up Japanese landing craft, even small steamers. Everything that floated was put to use. But often it remained for soldiers and pack animals to ford Burma's waterways on their own.

General Stilwell leads his men across the Tarung River on a bridge constructed from jungle materials.

Bare-chested British troops, tugging on tow ropes, struggle to drag a jeep across a shallow river during their division's advance on Indaw in north Burma.

In a jungle in north Burma, a Kachin scout leads a group of Merrill's Marauders over a crude log bridge.

LIFE IN A VINE-TANGLED NO MAN'S LAND

Of all of Burma's natural obstacles, jungles were the most forbidding. Bamboo thickets were so dense that soldiers were forced to cut tunnels through them. Underbrush was a tangle of vines and briers, and clearings were dominated by elephant grass as tall as a man. "You never knew from one moment to the next when you'd run into the Japs," wrote Charlton Ogburn. The soldiers lived constantly in agonizing anticipation of a sniper's bullet, and were so jittery that an entire battery of artillery would open up on a suspected sniper.

The terrors of the jungle left an indelible mark on the men who fought in Burma. Many came down with "jungle happiness." When they returned to civilian life, they found themselves ill at ease around crowds and bright lights and sometimes even their families and friends.

British and Indian troops clamber up a jungle hillside in Arakan. Ridges here were so steep that ladders sometimes had to be used to reach enemy positions.

Indian soldiers on patrol in the Chin Hills thread their way through undergrowth so dense that they run the risk of stumbling upon the hidden enemy.

British infantrymen fan out as they cross a broad, treeless expanse along the Irrawaddy River Valley. The soft sand was an obstacle to vehicular crossings, and it

mired trucks up to the axles. When the monsoon rains began to fall, this entire area became inundated and the floodwater rose until it was over a man's head.

5

At the beginning of 1944, as Stilwell's forces hacked their way down the Hukawng Valley, two great forces were squaring off along the India-Burma border, about to engage in the largest land battle yet to be fought in the China-Burma-India Theater.

To the east, deployed along the Chindwin River, was the Japanese Fifteenth Army with two divisions—the 31st and the 33rd. The commander of the Fifteenth Army was the hot-tempered Lieut. General Renya Mutaguchi. A strict believer in the stern, sacrificial warriors' code of *Bushido*—the feudal Japanese code of chivalry that valued honor above life itself—Mutaguchi habitually drove his soldiers to the point of exhaustion, and he was capable of such apoplectic rages that his subordinates were fearful of bringing him any news that might displease him. Mutaguchi had a plan: his troops would cross into India and annihilate the British forces around their base on the Imphal Plain, thereby forestalling a British offensive into north-central Burma, and perhaps fomenting at the same time an uprising by dissident Indian nationalists.

On the west was the IV Corps of General Slim's Fourteenth Army, comprising the 17th Indian Division and the 20th Indian Division, which were dispersed along the Burmese border, and the 23rd Indian Division, which was being held in reserve at Imphal—IV Corps headquarters. Three hundred miles to the south in Arakan was Slim's XV Corps, which had already taken the offensive against the Japanese.

In his planning Slim had been handicapped by a lack of intelligence about Japanese operations. The thick jungle and the enemy's habit of moving by night limited the effectiveness of aerial reconnaissance. Moreover, since the Japanese soldier usually preferred death, even at his own hand, to capture, there was little information to be obtained from prisoners. Indeed, before March of 1944 only one prisoner had been available for interrogation on the entire IV Corps front.

For intelligence about the enemy, the British had to rely almost entirely on captured diaries, directives and maps. Nevertheless, as early as January enough evidence of a Japanese build-up had been gathered to be disturbing. Documents revealed the presence of new enemy units along the India-Burma border, and British pilots reported that large numbers of logs were being stock-piled along the Chin-

THE JAPANESE LOSE FACE

dwin—apparently for the construction of rafts. A British agent discovered that a secret road had been cut through the jungle toward the border, and that numbers of animals, including elephants for transport and herds of cattle, presumably for use as meat on the hoof, were being assembled by the Japanese.

Both the British and the Japanese had once believed that it was almost impossible for either side to launch and sustain a major offensive in the mountainous country along the India-Burma frontier. It was now evident, however, to Slim and to his IV Corps commander, Lieut. General Geoffrey A. P. Scoones, that Mutaguchi was preparing to do just that. Pondering ways to counter such a drive, Slim came up with three alternatives.

The first was to cross the Chindwin and attack the Fifteenth Army before it started its advance. This course of action had all the appeal of an aggressive stroke, and was urged by rear-echelon officers, but Slim did not much care for it. He would have to engage superior numbers of the enemy with a great river at his back, and with a long and vulnerable line of communication stretching all the way to Imphal, 120 miles distant.

Slim's second alternative was to move IV Corps up to the west bank of the Chindwin and attack Mutaguchi while his forces were crossing the river. But this plan too would leave him with a precarious line of communication.

The third option was to pull back the IV Corps' 17th and 20th divisions from their present forward positions and concentrate them on the Imphal Plain, an open area 20 miles by 40 miles in the middle of the mountains. Here Slim would be able to fight on ground of his own choosing, with a good line of communication at his back. The Japanese, on the other hand, would have only a single road over which to move their supplies.

Slim decided in favor of the third alternative. He knew that the Japanese could be aggressive to the point of foolhardiness, allowing their lines of communication to become dangerously overextended, as long as there existed a good opportunity of capturing supplies with which to carry on the fight. Slim also knew that the Japanese often pressed ahead with their plans even when things started going badly, and that Japanese commanders were apt to fling the last of their reserves into battle when prudence would dictate otherwise.

Slim was of the opinion that if Mutaguchi did not capture Imphal and its supplies by the onset of the monsoon in May, the Fifteenth Army would be in serious trouble—but doubtless would press the offensive all the harder and be much easier to destroy.

But when should the two British divisions on the India-Burma border be pulled back? If Slim was misreading Japanese intentions, the British would be yielding a lot of ground. He decided that the order to withdraw would be given by Scoones only when he was absolutely certain that the Japanese offensive was imminent.

Mutaguchi, meanwhile, was making plans of his own. First of all, to distract the British and force them to commit their reserves, he would have his 55th Division stage an attack against the XV Corps in Arakan to the south. Once the British were diverted by developments there, he would drive on Imphal with three divisions—the 31st, the 33rd and the 15th, which had been undergoing jungle training in Thailand—as well as a division of the Indian National Army (INA). He could not depend on the INA, however; it was led by inexperienced officers and many of the men, captured by the Japanese in Burma and indoctrinated by the fiery Indian nationalist leader Subhas Chandra Bose, might well have divided loyalties.

To oppose three British divisions with only three reliable divisions of his own—and with a drawn-out line of communication as well—could not have struck Mutaguchi as very good odds for an attacker. But he had a scheme to improve the odds. He would have part of his 33rd Division block the road behind the 17th Division at Tiddim, thus cutting them off from Imphal, and he would order the remainder of the 33rd to attack the 20th Division in the Kabaw Valley. By cutting off one division and pinning down the other, Mutaguchi hoped to force Scoones to commit the bulk of his reserve, the 23rd Division at Imphal, to the rescue of the 20th and 17th divisions, leaving the city virtually unprotected. Then, while the British were occupied with his 33rd Division, Mutaguchi would send his 31st Division to sever Scoones's communications near the town of Kohima, some 65 miles to the north of Imphal. That left one more Japanese division, the 15th; he would unleash the 15th on Imphal.

The prelude to what was to become known as the battle of Imphal-Kohima took place in February, when Mutaguchi's 55th Division launched its diversionary action against the XV Corps in Arakan. Just as the Japanese general had planned, Slim was thus deprived of any support he might have had from his troops in the south and was faced with the possibility that he might have to send forces to the rescue of the XV Corps. In early March, Mutaguchi was ready to launch what Tokyo radio—somewhat overstating the objective—heralded as the "March on Delhi."

Resorting to the high-flown rhetoric that Japanese generals customarily used to inspire their troops, Mutaguchi issued orders to his men: "The Army has now reached the state of invincibility, and the day when the Rising Sun shall proclaim our definite victory in India is not far off. When we strike we must reach our objectives with the speed of wildfire despite all the obstacles of the river, mountain and labyrinthine jungle.

"We must sweep aside the paltry opposition we encounter and add luster to Army tradition by achieving a victory of annihilation. Both officers and men must fight to the death for their country and accept the burden of duties that are the lot of a soldier of Japan."

The Japanese offensive got under way on March 8, but the British failed to recognize it as such. Although a Gurkha patrol spotted 2,000 Japanese moving westward near Mual-

bem on the 8th, Scoones did not move. Only on March 13, when a Japanese force attacked the road between the 17th Division and Imphal, did Scoones finally give the withdrawal order, and it was not until the following day that the 17th began to pull back. By then it was too late.

The Japanese had blocked the road leading to Imphal in four places, and the 17th was cut off. Scoones was forced to send first one, then a second, brigade from his reserve 23rd Division down the road to help the 17th fight its way out. The Japanese, moving quickly through the jungle, soon cut off the reserve brigades as well. While this was happening, another Japanese force engaged Scoones's 20th Division in a similar attempt to block its withdrawal from the Kabaw Valley. As Slim aptly put it, British and Japanese troops were now layered like "Neapolitan ice" on the road to Imphal.

Things seemed to be going very much according to Mutaguchi's plan. By March 19, less than two weeks after their offensive started, the Japanese had pushed within 36 miles of Imphal. But Slim and Scoones had an ace in the hole. They began supplying men and matériel by plane to the units trapped on the road. The airlift was carried out by the RAF and the U.S. Troop Carrier Command. Although some C-47s were used, the mainstay of the operation was the C-46, which could carry four tons—almost twice the C-47's capacity. The crews had developed a high degree of proficiency in supplying Chinese and U.S. forces in northern Burma and could drop a complete load of bagged rice into an area 100 yards or so in diameter.

Thanks to the airlift and the support of the 23rd Division's two brigades, the 17th and 20th divisions were able to break through the roadblocks. And there was good news from Arakan; the British there had taken the offensive against the Japanese 55th Division. Now, with the backing of Mountbatten—who, acting on his own authority, had diverted aircraft from the Hump operation—Slim began airlifting from Arakan to Imphal the battle-hardened "Ball of Fire" 5th Indian Division. In an incredible logistical feat for the time, the entire outfit—with artillery, mules and jeeps—was moved in 11 days, some of the men going straight into battle from the planes.

By early April, the XXXIII Corps—which had recently joined the Fourteenth Army—arrived to take command of the Dimapur-Kohima sector, and the IV Corps was fully

Subhas Chandra Bose (on the left), head of the Japanese-supported Indian Nationalist Army, confers (through an interpreter) with mustachioed Lieut. General Masakazu Kawabe, commander of the Japanese Burma Area Army, in November 1943. An ardent advocate of Indian independence, Bose placed one of his divisions of Indian insurgents at Kawabe's disposal for the assault on British IV Corps headquarters at Imphal.

concentrated on the Imphal Plain. And with the addition of the 5th Division from Arakan, Mutaguchi now found himself facing not three divisions, but four.

Farther to the north, things were about to go wrong for the British. Slim had expected a Japanese thrust somewhere along the IV Corps' line of communication, a road that stretched 111 miles from Imphal through Kohima to Dimapur. He could not predict precisely where the Japanese might strike, but he knew that there were two likely places.

The first was Dimapur itself, a railhead on the Bengal-Assam railway. If the Japanese were able to take this junction, they would not only capture large amounts of stores and cut off IV Corps from either retreat or reinforcement, but they would also sever the whole Assam line of communication supporting Stilwell's army and the China air ferry over the Hump.

The other probable Japanese target was the pretty mountain village of Kohima astride the Imphal-Dimapur road. Kohima, the gateway to northeast India, sat high on a saddle between two mountain ranges, and was virtually unapproachable except by that one road. If the Japanese were able to take Kohima, they would be almost impossible to dislodge. While the capture of Kohima would not have the same theater-wide ramifications as the seizure of Dimapur, it would isolate IV Corps just as effectively.

Whichever target the Japanese decided on, they would find it weakly defended. Kohima had only a small garrison, and Dimapur had no garrison at all. Late in March, the 161st Brigade of the 5th Indian Division was placed under Scoones's control, but then a serious argument ensued as to whether the brigade should be positioned at Kohima or Dimapur. As the brigade marched and countermarched between the two villages, the Japanese surprised everyone by moving their entire 31st Division from the Chindwin across the rugged mountains along the India-Burma border into the Kohima area and threatening the garrison there with encirclement.

The Japanese attacked on the night of April 4. The Kohima garrison was ill prepared. Only about one thousand men in the village were capable of bearing arms, and these included convalescents, rear-echelon troops, state police forces and some mountain tribesmen of the 1st Assam

Regiment who were exhausted from an earlier battle. The defenders of Kohima did not have barbed wire, and the pipe that led to their only source of water lay in an exposed position on an adjacent ridge that the Japanese were bound to capture.

At dawn on the following morning, elements of the British 161st Brigade attempted to reinforce the garrison from the north. But the defensive perimeter had already shrunk so drastically that only one battalion of the Royal West Kents could squeeze into town; the remainder of the 161st Brigade had to take up a position two and a half miles to the northwest. There it would offer artillery support for the beleaguered garrison.

The Japanese 31st Division included 20,000 men and was commanded by Lieut. General Kotuku Sato, who had only limited combat experience—and who was probably feeling less than total enthusiasm for his present assignment. The division's march to Kohima over the mountains had been

At a February 1944 rally near Delhi, smoke wafts through the roof of a giant tent where 1,000 Hindu priests gathered to pray for an end to the War. During their 10 days of worship—the first mass prayer meeting in India since the 17th Century—the priests chanted more than 10 million prayers.

arduous in the extreme. Almost all of the animal transport had been lost on the trail, and the men were short of food and supplies. Nevertheless, Sato kept up the attack, forcing Kohima's defenders to contract their perimeter not just once but twice in the first 24 hours of battle. He also managed to block the Dimapur road behind the 161st Brigade, and thereby prevented further British reinforcements from reaching Kohima.

With the garrison under siege and the 161st pinned down, Sato was now presented with a splendid military opportunity. Just 46 miles to the north lay the great undefended prize of the Dimapur railhead. All Sato had to do was leave part of his force behind to contain Kohima, strike off with the rest, seize Dimapur and cut the lifelines to Stilwell and China. Mutaguchi recognized the opportunity. He ordered Sato to send a force against Dimapur, and at the same time advised his own superior, General Masakazu Kawabe, commander of the Burma Area Army, of the plans to capture the vital railhead.

Kawabe, whose fiercely resplendent moustachio masked a rigid inflexibility, was not pleased. He may have been concerned that the aggressive Mutaguchi was in danger of overreaching himself. In any case, he replied that the seizure of Dimapur was "not within the strategic objectives of the 15th Army." Forced to relinquish the opportunity, Mutaguchi ordered Sato to recall his troops to Kohima. Many years after the war, he still believed that had Kawabe allowed him to press on to Dimapur, events in north Burma might have taken an entirely different turn.

Sato was confined to battering his division against Kohima, where the British garrison was putting up stubborn resistance. Slim, who was impressed by the bravery and tenacity of individual Japanese soldiers but who frequently felt that their commanders lacked imagination, was puzzled by Sato's performance. He wondered why the Japanese commander did not take advantage of the opportunity to march into Dimapur, instead of expending his troops in costly attacks against the defenses of Kohima. When a delegation of Royal Air Force officers paid the British general a visit to say that they were intending to bomb Sato's headquarters, Slim suggested, to their utter astonishment, that they forgo the raid. "I regarded their intended victim as one of my most helpful generals," he later explained.

En route to attack the British at Imphal-Kohima, elite Japanese cavalrymen, some of them on foot, make their way down a narrow mountain trail in early 1944. In the course of the grueling journey, the Emperor's horse soldiers lost almost two thirds of their mounts to the treacherous terrain.

Under Sato's urging, the Japanese at Kohima carried out attacks each night, sometimes shouting and blowing bugles, at other times silently infiltrating the perimeter. From the commanding heights they had captured, they poured devastating artillery fire into the thick canopy of trees shielding the garrison. Fighting from hastily prepared positions and open trenches, the defenders were exposed to deadly shrapnel when incoming rounds struck the trees. Later, after the forest had been all but destroyed by the blasts, Japanese snipers made daylight movement within the perimeter virtually impossible. As expected, the Japanese soon cut the garrison's water pipes and riddled the storage tanks, requiring the men to ration themselves to a pint of water a day—a terrible privation in the intense heat.

Under heavy pressure from the Japanese, the British were repeatedly compelled to contract their perimeter. Ultimately the garrison was pressed into a triangular area only 400 to 500 yards on a side. Doctors had to operate in dugouts with no overhead cover, and the sick and the wounded were left lying in the open or in slit trenches, where some were wounded all over again by flying shrapnel.

There were moments of extraordinary valor. A private named Williams, who had been a coal miner in civilian life, lost his rifle in hand-to-hand combat, then attacked a group of Japanese with a shovel. Sergeant-Major C. S. M. Haines, blinded by a head wound, refused to stay in the aid station; instead, tapping with a stick and guided by a young soldier, he returned to the forward position and exhorted his men to battle until he was finally killed by sniper fire. Lance-Corporal John Harman made a singlehanded attack on a Japanese machine-gun position on a hill with rifle and bayonet. He killed all five of the Japanese, then stood up and waved the machine gun triumphantly over his head as the British cheered. Although he was under heavy fire, he began to walk, not run, back toward the British lines. Halfway down the hill he was shot through the spine. Just before he died he said to his comrades: "I got the lot—it was worth it."

Some of the worst fighting at Kohima occurred in an unlikely setting, a once-elegant tennis court on a strategic rise above the bungalow of the British Deputy Commissioner. On the night of April 8, wave after wave of Japanese troops attempted to overrun the area. British troops were dug in at one end of the court, and the Japanese took up a position at the other end. Both sides lobbed grenades across mid-court where tennis balls had once soared. The battle surged back and forth through the next day, before the British pinned down the Japanese.

By the time the Kohima garrison had been under siege for a week, water, ammunition and medical supplies had all but run out. On April 13—a day that was remembered by the defenders as "Black 13th"—aircraft made an attempt to drop supplies by parachute. But the planes had no room for maneuver between the steep mountains, and were forced to run a gauntlet of fire from Japanese on the ridges. The garrison's perimeter had shrunk so much that it was a difficult target, and most of the parachutes landed inside Japanese lines. Urgently needed mortar ammunition was dropped to the 161st Brigade two and a half miles away, while the artillery shells required by the 161st for supporting fire were dropped inside the Kohima perimeter, where

With the aid of a head sling, a Gurkha soldier carries one of his wounded comrades out of the thick jungle of Arakan. During the bitter fighting in this coastal province of western Burma, the XV Corps lost more than 5,000 troops as the Japanese attempted to reduce the corps' effectiveness as a possible backup force for the IV Corps at Imphal, 300 miles to the north.

there were no artillery pieces. Some mortar ammunition landed among the Japanese, who quickly turned it against the garrison—using captured British guns. On that same day, Japanese artillery scored a direct hit on the Kohima aid station, killing two of the beleaguered garrison's three doctors, and killing or rewounding 40 patients.

On the 15th of April, after a bitter, seesaw struggle, the Japanese captured a critical ridge that lay to the southwest of the town, and on the following night they overran another hill overlooking Kohima. The defenders were now vulnerable to attacks on all three sides of their triangular-shaped perimeter.

Meanwhile on April 15, the 161st Brigade, supported by elements of the 2nd Division, newly arrived from southern India, had launched an attack toward Kohima from the northwest. The Japanese resisted furiously. But at daylight on April 18, as the Kohima defenders were preparing to make a final desperate stand, Punjabi troops of the 161st

Brigade broke through to them. The sick and wounded were evacuated, and two days later the garrison was relieved by men of the 2nd Division's 6th Brigade.

During the siege, the garrison had suffered 600 casualties. Members of the relieving force were horrified at the charnel house they found. "The ground everywhere was ploughed up with shell-fire," wrote Major John Nettlefield, a gunner, "and human remains lay rotting as the battle raged over them. Flies swarmed everywhere and multiplied with incredible speed. Men retched as they dug in. The stink hung in the air and permeated one's clothes and hair."

Within a matter of hours after the Punjabis had arrived at Kohima, firing broke out on the tennis court again. The new fighting marked the beginning of the second phase of the battle, which, in Slim's words, "was to be as hard fought as the first."

The Japanese were still dug in at strong points around the village, and the British struggled to oust them, first from a settlement to the north of Kohima, then from a commanding ridge to the south. It was not until reinforcements arrived from Arakan that the drive succeeded. Then came the blow that tipped the balance once and for all: British troops swung across the Japanese supply line to the southeast of Kohima and captured a vital communications center. They were aided by local Naga tribesmen, who guided columns, transported supplies, ambushed Japanese troops and brought in the wounded under heavy fire. In paying tribute to them, Slim later gratefully noted that "despite floggings, torture, execution and the burning of their villages, they refused to aid the Japanese in any way or to betray our troops."

By the beginning of June, Slim could report that the enemy in the Kohima area "was breaking and pulling out as best he could."

While the battle for Kohima was raging, the fighting around Imphal was mounting in fury. From the end of March, when the Japanese blocked the supply road to Kohima and Dimapur, Imphal's defenders were completely cut off—alarming almost everyone but the imperturbable Slim.

Early in April, Stilwell, fearful that his own line of communication would be severed, offered to slow down his drive along the Hukawng Valley and to send Slim relief in the

Launching their invasion of India in early March, 1944, the Japanese (red arrows) attacked British forces at Tiddim and in the Kabaw Valley. Under orders, the British withdrew (broken arrows) through the jungle to a defense perimeter on the Imphal Plain. To the north, on April 4, the British garrison at Kohima also came under attack and was besieged for two weeks. But the British 161st Brigade and elements of the 2nd Division (black arrows) arrived from Dimapur in late April and broke the siege. Two months later the 2nd Division advanced south to help relieve the troops at Imphal. On July 8 the Japanese began retreating into Burma.

form of the Chinese 38th Division under the command of General Sun. But Slim refused the offer; he did not want to see Stilwell relax the pressure in the Hukawng Valley and thereby free Mutaguchi's 18th Division for the fighting around Imphal. He told Stilwell to keep moving, and guaranteed him that if Stilwell's line of communication from Dimapur were cut, it would not be closed for more than 10 days. As it turned out, Dimapur was never taken, and the vital rail line to Ledo, on which Stilwell was depending, was not cut.

Imphal was like the hub of a great wheel with roads radiating from it in all directions. Over a period of four months the Japanese attacked along all of these routes. "There was always a Japanese thrust somewhere that had to be met and destroyed," Slim later wrote. "Yet the fighting did follow a pattern. The main encounters were on or near the spokes of the wheel, because it was only along these that guns, tanks and vehicles could move."

The most bitter fighting occurred southeast of the city around Tengnoupal, where Major General Tsunoru Yamamoto, under heavy pressure from his superiors, was desperately trying to break through to Imphal with tanks and artillery. Indian and Gurkha troops stubbornly resisted the Japanese attacks for six days and nights. The fighting went on until, as Slim put it, "both sides were so spent that neither could seriously revive the battle."

Around the wheel to the southeast, violent fighting erupted on the road to Tiddim. A Japanese unit inserted itself between the main body of the 49th Indian Brigade and its forward battalion, and fought until almost all of its men were wiped out. Blocked in their attempt to move along the Tiddim road, the Japanese now shifted their attack around to the west and attempted to break through along the Silchar-Bishenpur track.

In order to bar the flow of British reinforcements along this track, the Japanese decided to blow up a 300-foot suspension bridge spanning a deep gorge to the west. While a small-arms fight sputtered through the evening hours of April 14, three Japanese soldiers slipped past the engineers who were guarding the bridge and planted their explosive charges. It was a suicide mission: once there the men were cut off from all hope of retreat. One of them leaped to his death and the two others were blown up with the bridge.

Furious fighting flared at the village of Bishenpur on May 20 as the Japanese made an all-out attempt to break through to Imphal. The men of the Japanese 33rd Division were under do-or-die orders from their commander, Major General Nobuo Tanaka. "Regarding death as something lighter than a feather," he told them, "you must tackle the task of capturing Imphal. For that reason it must be expected that the division will be almost annihilated."

Japanese infantrymen commenced a series of suicidal charges, and artillerymen stuck to their guns until they were either shot at close range or bayoneted. Slim was deeply moved by the bravery of the Japanese troops. "Whatever one may think of the military wisdom of thus pursuing a hopeless object," he wrote later, "there can be no question of the supreme courage and hardihood of the Japanese soldiers who made the attempts. I know of no army that could have equalled them."

As the weeks passed with Imphal still cut off, the British Chiefs of Staff began criticizing Scoones for failing to break the Japanese siege. Mountbatten grew anxious, and senior officers urged Slim to relieve Imphal at all costs before it was too late. One staff officer suggested that Slim simply push an armored column and a truck convoy along the Imphal-Kohima road to break through to IV Corps headquarters. Slim responded that since the bridges were out, such a maneuver would be something like sending a convoy of destroyers and merchantmen down a canal whose banks were controlled by the enemy—and whose channel had stretches with no water at all.

Slim had devised his own solution to the supply problem at Imphal: he would have the IV Corps supplied by air—even during the monsoon season if necessary. To curtail requirements on the plain, nearly 30,000 noncombatants were flown out and the daily ration of the remaining 155,000 troops was reduced to 65 per cent of normal.

The process of airlifting supplies to an entire corps posed

Two British officers—one adjusting his helmet, the other wearing a beret—greet Indian soldiers 17 miles to the north of Imphal on the road to Kohima after the highway was cleared of Japanese blocks. The British 2nd Division broke through on June 22, 1944, from Kohima to link up with the 5th Indian Division, which had fought its way up from Imphal.

an enormous challenge, which was greatly complicated by a shortage of aircraft. The RAF used every available plane, including 79 that were borrowed from the Middle East Command. When it was time for the planes to be returned, Mountbatten decided to keep them until they could be replaced, and Churchill backed him to the full. "Let nothing go from the battle that you need for victory," he wired the Supreme Commander.

The Imphal airlift, appropriately code-named *Stamina*, was a monumental operation. Between April 18 and the end of June more than 12,000 reinforcements and almost 19,000 tons of supplies were flown into Imphal. Even prefabricated bridges were dropped by parachute, as well as live mules, sheep and goats. By the end of April the airlift was having its effect—the besieged troops were turning to the offensive on the Imphal Plain.

As in so much of the ground fighting in CBI, the battle of Imphal-Kohima pitted Asian against Asian. The British forces, with the exception of the 2nd Division, were made up largely of Indian troops. Rarely has an army been so diverse in religion, language and culture. Hindus, Moslems and Christians fought side by side, and spoke Tamil, Pashto, Punjabi, Gurkhali and Telugu. (To communicate with one another, the various groups resorted to Urdu, the common language of the Indian Army.)

There were tall Sikhs, who never cut their hair or beards, Semitic-looking Pathans from the northwest frontier, high-caste Rajputs and warlike Punjabi Moslems. There were Dogras, Marathas, Madrasis and fierce Naga head-hunters from the hills along the India-Burma border. And, of course, there were the famous Gurkhas. In almost nine decades of service in the Indian Army, these sturdy men from the Himalayan country of Nepal had earned themselves the reputation of being extraordinary infantrymen, tough, brave and cheerful. Although they were technically mercenaries, they were devoted to their British officers. And their officers—whose ranks had once included Slim—were in turn devoted to them.

Gurkhas seemed to specialize in singlehanded attacks on Japanese tanks, bunkers and machine-gun nests. In close combat a Gurkha usually turned from his rifle to his *kukri*, a kind of machete shaped like a boomerang with a razor-sharp edge on the inside of the blade. On one occasion at Imphal a British officer came upon a dead Japanese whose helmet, skull and body had been cleft by a *kukri* clear to the middle of the breastbone.

Tradition dictated that a Gurkha never unsheath his *kukri* without drawing blood—even if it meant that he had to spill some of his own. Admiring Western soldiers who asked to examine these splendid knives were fascinated to see the Gurkhas nick their fingers before they returned the blades to their scabbards.

The Gurkha and Indian troops possessed enormous physical and psychological endurance. British officers in the Indian Army considered their best units superior to those of the regular British service.

On the other side of the battle line, the Japanese were every bit as tough. Their valor was extraordinary. While the Japanese Army awarded medals for campaigns and long service, it gave none for bravery on the battlefield; such bravery was simply assumed. Although Japanese youths were presumably no more eager to die than anyone else, in their initial training they were subjected to three months of intensive indoctrination in *Bushido*, during which they were instructed to choose death over captivity. Japanese officers accepted the possibility of their own death so completely that they often had their funeral services performed before they left for the front. Soldiers' families were to do nothing, say nothing, that might make a son, husband or brother hesitate to give up his life.

In a desperate situation the Japanese soldier would save his last grenade or bullet for himself. If he was captured in spite of all his efforts, he would seek any means at hand for self-destruction. Accounts of the war in CBI are filled with stories of Japanese attempts at bizarre suicides—at Imphal one soldier even tried cutting his throat with the lid of a ration can.

In admiration of his foe, Slim wrote: "The strength of the Japanese army lay . . . in the spirit of the individual Japanese soldier. He fought and marched till he died. If five hundred Japanese were ordered to hold a position, we had to kill four hundred and ninety-five before it was ours—and then the last five killed themselves."

The special qualities of the Japanese fighting man were much in evidence as the Imphal-Kohima battle approached

THE BRIDGE-BUSTING TENTH AIR FORCE

While the Flying Tigers and the men who flew the Hump were gathering most of the headlines, the Tenth Air Force—which arrived in CBI in March 1942—went largely unheralded despite the devastating effect it too was having on the Japanese. From bases in India the Tenth launched hit-and-run bombings deep into Burma, disrupting rail traffic, blowing up airfields and crippling enemy shipping at Rangoon and other major ports. During one three-month stretch in 1944, the Tenth flew more than 8,500 sorties, dropping about 3.7 million pounds of bombs on the Japanese.

One of the Tenth's squadrons, the 490th, specialized in bridges, earning the nickname "Bridge Busters" by knocking out as many as eight in a single week. The 490th originated "hop-bombing"—releasing bombs from a shallow dive at an angle that ensured that the bombs would explode on impact and not ricochet. The precision attacks of the Tenth helped isolate the Japanese and starved them of supplies on the Imphal Plain; the attacks also caused a British engineer to complain, "Every time our forces come to a river they find the bridge bombed out."

A Tenth Air Force B-24 flies over three Burma bridges knocked out earlier in the day.

A storm of spray erupts around a stricken Japanese freighter at the port of Mergui, Burma, after bombing by a Tenth Air Force plane.

The rebuilt Mu River Bridge in Burma goes up in smoke during an attack by bombers. The Tenth first used hop-bombing here.

its climax. By mid-May, after the British achieved the initiative, the Japanese at Imphal and Kohima had begun suffering terrible privations. They had failed to capture the food and supplies they needed, and with the onset of the monsoon they could no longer count on their own lines of communication. Driven by hunger, they took to eating their mules. Many came down with beriberi as a result of an inadequate diet.

But their sufferings did not deter their commanders. With the inflexibility that Slim had noted as a characteristic of the Japanese military leaders, Mutaguchi refused to alter his plans. He sacked the commanders of the 15th and 33rd divisions and ordered their successors to continue the offensive. He backed up this directive with a grim order to his troops: "Continue in the task till all of your ammunition is expended. If your hands are broken, fight with your feet. If your hands and feet are broken, use your teeth. If there is no breath left in your body, fight with your spirit. Lack of weapons is no excuse for defeat."

Having dismissed two generals for lacking aggressiveness, Mutaguchi was soon faced with a problem of another kind—the insubordination of his third commander, General Sato, whose 31st Division was being badly mauled by superior British forces at Kohima.

Sato's casualties were approaching 3,000 dead and 4,000 wounded. On the 13th of May, he requested permission to fall back from Kohima to a place where he could receive aid. Mutaguchi refused. Sato asked again, and Mutaguchi again refused. Sato was furious. When he found out that Mutaguchi had relieved the other two division commanders, he ranted to his staff: "This is shameful. Mutaguchi should apologize for his own failure to the dead soldiers and the Japanese people. He should not try to put the blame on his subordinates."

Nevertheless, Sato did as he was told—for a while. Although their plight was by now clearly hopeless, his troops continued to fight as ferociously as ever at Kohima.

During the second half of May, Sato repeatedly asked Mutaguchi for permission to pull back and in return received stern orders to stay put. Sato sent an angry message to the commander of the Japanese Fifth Air Force requesting supplies: "Since leaving the Chindwin we have not received one bullet from you, nor a grain of rice." Sato waited, but the Japanese Air Force was stretched almost to the breaking point, and no planes arrived.

On May 30, Sato radioed Mutaguchi that he was going to withdraw from Kohima. Mutaguchi replied brusquely: "Retreat and I will court-martial you." Too angry to be tactful, Sato radioed back: "Do what you please. I will bring you down with me."

Sato fired off another bristling message to Japanese Army headquarters in Rangoon: "The tactical ability of the Fifteenth Army staff lies below that of cadets." Then, in a state of agitation and high emotion, he closed down his radio communications and gave the order for his division to withdraw. "I cannot see the enemy through my blinding tears," he wrote to his wife.

Mutaguchi, planning yet another assault against Imphal with the 31st Division, was furious. "He has lost the battle for me!" he raged. With radio contact broken, Mutaguchi sent his chief of staff, Major General Todai Kunomura, to find Sato in the jungle and order him back into the fight. Kunomura conveyed the message to Sato and reminded him of the consequences if he failed to obey Mutaguchi's order. In reply Sato shouted: "The Fifteenth Army has failed to send me supplies and ammunition since the operation began. This failure releases me from any obligation to obey the order—and in any case it would be impossible to comply." When Kunomura tried to warn him that he was taking a dangerous step, Sato replied that all he cared about was making Imperial Headquarters "realize how stupid Mutaguchi has been."

There was little Mutaguchi could do now in any case. His army was falling apart. One regiment had been reduced from 4,000 to 460 men, and only half of these were still capable of fighting. Food was in such short supply that some men survived on grass and large black slugs. And more bad news was in store.

On June 22, Lance-Corporal C. E. Canning, serving with an intelligence section of the 5th Indian Division, climbed a tree on the Kohima road north of Imphal and saw a startling sight through his binoculars. Hurriedly he climbed down from his observation post and reported to an officer: "Excuse me, sir! I've just seen some tanks coming down the road with infantry sitting on them." What he had seen was the 2nd Division moving south from Kohima. After almost three months of fighting at Imphal and Kohima, the British forces were united and Imphal was once again linked to the outside world. Wrote Slim: "The Imphal-Kohima battle, the first decisive battle of the Burma campaign, was not yet over, but it was won."

Even Mutaguchi understood that; by now he was waiting only for General Kawabe, the Burma Area Army commander, to order the retreat. Instead, Kawabe urged Mutaguchi to fight on. Taking personal command of his troops, Mutaguchi launched an attack on Palel, south of Imphal. It failed. Mutaguchi, now in almost exactly the same situation Sato had been in, asked Kawabe for permission to retreat, but was told instead to mount a four-pronged attack on Palel. It was not possible: Mutaguchi's army was too weak to take the offensive again. Distraught, Mutaguchi retired to a hillside and chanted a Shinto prayer in his hour of need. The next day he was told by Kawabe to fall back.

On July 8, four months from the start of the "March on Delhi," Mutaguchi's troops began their withdrawal across the Chindwin to Burma. It was a desperate retreat by exhausted and emaciated men through a country flooded by monsoon rains. Except in the elite 33rd Division, which remained a cohesive if much depleted unit, morale and organization had broken down. Food was scarce, for the rice supplies of villages along the way had already been raided during the Japanese advance.

A correspondent who took part in the retreat wrote: "In the end we had no ammunition, no clothes, no food, no guns. The men were barefoot and ragged, and threw away everything except canes to help them walk. Their eyes blazed in their lean bodies. All they had to keep them going was grass and water. And there were jungles, great mountains, and flooded rivers barring their way." When another correspondent came into contact with Mutaguchi and asked him for a statement, the general answered: "I have killed thousands of my men. I should not go back across the Chindwin alive."

British troops, following in the tracks of the fleeing Japanese, came upon unburied corpses by the hundreds, scores of wounded and diseased soldiers who were barely alive; they found field hospitals strewn with the bodies of men who had been shot by their comrades to spare them the disgrace of capture.

Mutaguchi was removed from command, and left Burma for Singapore in disgrace. Sato was also sacked. He was handed a sword by Colonel Shumei Kinoshita of Mutaguchi's staff and invited to commit hara-kiri, but he declined, insisting that the defeat had not been his doing. There was talk of a court-martial for Sato, but he was examined by doctors who were of the opinion that his mental health would not permit him to stand trial.

At Imphal and Kohima, the Japanese had suffered the greatest land defeat in their history. All together they had lost 30,000 men killed and 25,000 sick and wounded. In addition, much of their artillery, armor and transport had been destroyed or captured. The Fifteenth Army was no longer a fighting force. And the British, eager to exploit their victory, were planning to harry the retreating Japanese right through the monsoon season and retake Burma.

After the Japanese had fled from Imphal and Kohima, British troops occupying the village of Mao on the Imphal-Kohima road found a bit of graffiti scrawled on the wall: "British—Too many guns, tanks and troops. Japanese going, but back in six months."

The writer was wrong. The Japanese would never return.

STEP BY STEP TO MANDALAY

Shirtless in the sun, British soldiers pitch camp by a pagoda-roofed house near Mandalay. Their next assignment: to capture the city's stronghold, Fort Dufferin.

STORMING THE CITADEL OF THE ANCIENT CITY

In March 1945 the quiet streets of Mandalay erupted with the quick, sharp crack of bullets from Japanese snipers and the answering stutter of British Bren guns. Lieut. General William Slim led the assault, but before Mandalay was his, he would have to drive the Japanese from the ancient stronghold of Fort Dufferin in the heart of the city.

Blocking the way was what Slim referred to as the "great rock" of Pagoda Hill, which towered 774 feet over the fort. The hill was honeycombed with snipers holed up in its hundreds of pagodas. It took three days of fierce combat for a crack battalion of Gurkhas to take the hill, and even then the last holdouts had to be blown out of their bunkers by gasoline drums set off by gunfire.

From this hard-won vantage point Slim had a bird's-eye view of the fortress, a mile-square city within a city dominated by a great teak palace. Surrounding the fort were crenelated red brick walls 26 feet high and fully 30 feet thick at their base, backed up by an earth embankment 70 feet across. This massive barrier was in turn protected by a broad moat. "An immense edition of the toy fortress I used to play with as a boy," Slim thought as he examined the fantastic structure—and then, with characteristic British understatement: "a very formidable object to a lightly equipped army in a hurry."

Slim had bombers and close-range artillery brought in to break through the fort's walls. When 500-pound bombs proved insufficient, Slim tried skipping 2,000-pound bombs off the surface of the 225-foot-wide moat and into the walls. A week of thundering bombardment finally opened a few breaches. Now an assault team readied rafts and camouflage gear. Four times the force crossed the moat in late-night surprise attacks, only to be driven back by fire. Slim unleashed another day of bombardment. When six Burmese waving a white flag trooped out of the fort on March 20, Slim was surprised to learn that the surviving Japanese had escaped through drainpipes under the moat. At last the army in a hurry could move in and raise the Union Jack over the still-smoking citadel.

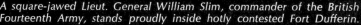

A square-jawed Lieut. General William Slim, commander of the British Fourteenth Army, stands proudly inside hotly contested Fort Dufferin.

A British mule train passes two of the thousands of brick pagodas in the scrub country near Mandalay. The water hole in the foreground is a buffalo wallow

A soldier driving a jeep pauses to peer up at the back of Pagoda Hill, Burma's Buddhist center. Visible on the crest is a great covered stairway that devout Buddhists and saffron-robed monks climbed every day in their devotions—before the holy hill became a bloody battleground.

From the balcony of one of the temples on Pagoda Hill, British soldiers cautiously look out over Mandalay and Fort Dufferin on the right. The smoke is from a bomb that had fallen outside the besieged fortress.

An Indian soldier atop Pagoda Hill directs the fire of two machine gunners. In front of them looms the tall spire of one of the hill's hundreds of pagodas.

British soldiers take time out for a quick cigarette at the base of one of Pagoda Hill's many gilded—and immensely valuable—figures of Gautama Buddha.

British troops (above) raise the Union Jack over a bomb-blasted tower at one of Fort Dufferin's gates shortly after taking the stronghold on March 20, 1945. At right, battle-weary soldiers stand at attention as the British flag is officially raised above the walls. Scars left by the recent bombing, which destroyed most of the fort, can be seen on the tree at left.

MASS EXODUS IN EAST CHINA

Draped with Chinese refugees from cities threatened by the advancing Japanese Army in 1944, a westbound train crawls through the province of Kwangsi.

A U.S. EVACUATION THAT INSPIRED PANIC

In 1943, Major General Claire L. Chennault's Fourteenth Air Force began operating out of east China air bases, striking at Japanese rail lines and shipping with increasing effectiveness. There were few ground forces to protect the advance bases, but Chennault felt that his planes were enough to ward off any enemy attack.

Stung to fury by the air strikes, the Japanese launched a massive retaliatory sweep south through Hankow in the spring of 1944, aimed at capturing the bases and the urban centers of east China. The Japanese advance pushed all opposition aside and spread before it a wave of terror. There were stories that civilians were being shot and their homes and businesses plundered. As rumor bred rumor, the citizens of Kweilin, Hengyang, Liuchow and other cities in the path of the Japanese became increasingly anxious about their plight. According to Graham Peck of the U.S. Office of War Information, who was in Kweilin, "A worse state of mind for resistance, or for an orderly, partial retreat and defeat, could not be imagined."

When the Fourteenth Air Force airmen and ground crews started blowing up their airfields and ammunition dumps to keep them from falling into the hands of the enemy, anxiety deepened to panic and people began fleeing—on trains, riverboats, on foot.

Boats and trains were burdened to the bursting point. Frantic families offered to pay almost anything just to get to the next city, and then—with the price paid and the journey under way—found that they would have to move on again as the Japanese continued their advance. Peck described the situation as one of "dog-eat-dog confusion, with the victims savaging each other in flight." When their money ran out, whole families committed suicide. The dead were stripped for clothing; exhausted mules and horses were killed and eaten.

Hundreds of thousands of Chinese died while attempting to escape, but millions succeeded in making their way into the countryside, there to wait out the war in relative safety and, in most cases, abject poverty.

Coolies plant a 1,000-pound bomb on a Kweilin airfield runway prior to detonating it as part of the U.S. plan to leave nothing useful behind.

Pocking the runway at Tanchuk are bomb craters made by planes of the Fourteenth Air Force after the Americans had evacuated and abandoned the airfield.

A soldier aims a flashlight so another can fire accurately into a gasoline drum stored inside a building at an air base in Kweilin. Before they departed, the Fourteenth Air Force set fire to every one of the 550 storage sheds and bunkhouses at the airfield. Some of the buildings had been used to house ammunition, which exploded when the flames reached it.

Deliberately started fires consume airfield buildings at Hengyang. Though they were surrounded by the Japanese in late June, 1944, the Chinese garrison at Hengyang held out until August. In the desperate hope that the city might be saved, many civilians did not try to leave until the garrison fell, creating sudden chaos along the roads and on the trains.

The railroad yard at Liuchow is the scene of a variety of domestic chores as refugees carry on with their daily lives while awaiting passage out by train.

Cushioned by a smattering of straw, a young refugee sleeps on the wheel frame of a railway car.

Children scoop hot ashes from under an engine to use for cooking—and to keep themselves warm.

DESPERATE BIDDING, AN EXCRUCIATING WAIT

As millions of Chinese refugees turned to the railroads to escape the onrushing Japanese, railway stations overflowed. Acres of men, women and children camped in rail yards, cooking, eating, sleeping and bathing in the open while waiting for transportation. All social restraints broke down. Prostitution became widespread and men gambled what little money they had in an effort to win enough for the journey. People begged, bribed or sneaked their way onto trains. Some train operators made a racket of extorting huge fares from their passengers, then forcing them off at gunpoint outside the city and returning for another load.

Those people who managed to escape considered themselves lucky, even when they had to ride on the roofs of trains, wheel frames or cowcatchers.

In despair after days of riding the rails, a woman gives way to tears.

A FRANTIC ESCAPE— TO NOWHERE

The train rides were a nightmare for the refugees. With their babies and belongings strapped to their backs, they fought for breathing space aboard cars packed wall to wall. Those who could not squeeze inside clung to the outside. Departures were endlessly delayed while conductors threw off all those unable to pay a bribe.

At Kweilin, hundreds were crushed to death when a hysterical train crew, faced with a mass of refugees struggling to get on board, plowed their locomotive into the crowd. Later, at Liuchow, seven people died in quick succession aboard one car of a freight train; three refugees on the roof were knocked off when the train entered a tunnel; two stowaways fell from the undercarriage to the tracks; in the cramped car, one man succumbed to a heart attack and a woman died in childbirth.

At each station, there were conflicting reports of the approach of the Japanese Army. In their confusion, some refugees simply gave up all hope of escape and went back to where they had started from.

A distraught mother cradles her son's head in her hands. The boy had just fallen from a precarious position aboard a packed train and badly injured himself.

6

At one of the low points in his career in CBI, Stilwell wrote in his diary: "There are times when I need a straight jacket. Ordinary straightforward shooting and killing would be a relief, and I prefer associating with soldiers and sleeping on the ground to this bickering and dickering I've gotten into."

Probably no theater in all of World War II asked so much of its commanders as CBI. They were called upon to wage war in an almost impossible setting. Merely to survive in the jungles and mountains of CBI and to surmount the terrible logistical problems that confronted them required a super-human effort. On top of all this, they were afflicted from the start by a basic disagreement as to how the war in CBI should be fought, and were forced to spend an inordinate amount of time, as Stilwell said, bickering and dickering and looking over their shoulders to make sure they were not stabbed in the back.

The disagreement encompassed Americans, British and Chinese, and it explained almost every action in this crazy-quilt arena. From the start, the Americans had been motivated by a simple purpose: to keep China in the War. Almost everything they had done was aimed at achieving that objective. The hazardous airlift of supplies over the Hump and the shoestring operations of Chennault's air force had been designed to buck up China. Stilwell's backbreaking drive down the valleys of the Hukawng and the Mogaung had stemmed from something much larger than a desire to avenge the bitter defeat of 1942. He was bent on seizing the airstrip and communications hub at Myitkyina and clearing the way for the Ledo-Burma Road so that more supplies could be routed into China. Once that was accomplished, he hoped to equip and train more Chinese troops so that the Japanese could be expelled from ports in south China and a new supply link established with the outer world. This in turn would enable U.S. planes to carry out heavy raids against the Japanese homeland while the Chinese launched a final drive against the Japanese.

The British had seen things quite differently. Believing that the Americans had greatly exaggerated the importance and the warmaking potential of Chiang Kai-shek, they were not interested in fighting in the jungles of north Burma and opening up the Ledo-Burma Road supply route to China.

What they were interested in was keeping the Japanese out of India and restoring their empire in Southeast Asia; in

AN UPSET IN COMMAND

their view, Singapore, as Churchill put it, was the "supreme British objective." But they had gone along with the Burma campaign under American pressure. Their resources were severely strained, and the defeat of Germany took priority in their planning over everything else. Initially they favored a limited effort in Burma featuring an amphibious assault against Rangoon. Ultimately, they coupled this assault with an overland drive to Mandalay and Rangoon, but that operation developed extemporaneously, as a result of their great success at Imphal, rather than as a part of any grand strategic design.

Chiang Kai-shek, on his part, had consistently viewed the war from a totally different perspective from the British and the Americans. What mainly interested him was surviving and keeping his armies intact for a resumption of the hostilities with his archenemies, the Communists. At Chungking, his wartime capital, he husbanded his strength and waited for the day when that conflict would be renewed.

The British managed to remain aloof from most of the wrangling in CBI, confining their arguments mainly to the highest of the war councils. But the fundamental disagreement about the prosecution of the war continued to poison relations between Stilwell on the one hand and Chiang and Chennault on the other.

As the war progressed, the bitterness festered and grew. Now, in 1944, when the Japanese were threatening to overrun all of China, the old argument erupted with a new virulence. And in one of the great ironies of that tormented theater, two of the men who had contributed most substantially to the ultimate defeat of the Japanese—Stilwell and Chennault—were to be brought down by their inability to agree over strategy.

The chain of events leading to this unhappy denouement originated in China. By late summer, 1944, the Allied situation was dramatically improving in India and Burma, but China was rapidly approaching catastrophe. The government's purse had been strained to the limit by the need to maintain an army of three million soldiers, and the population was subject to constant hardship. Manufactured goods were virtually impossible to obtain and hoarding was pushing prices out of range even for government bureaucrats. As inflation spiraled, paper money became all but worthless.

To make matters worse, China had suffered a series of devastating natural disasters. The countryside had always provided only a meager subsistence for the peasants who lived there. Now it was hit by recurrent droughts and floods that brought about famine, illness and death on a grand scale. In the spring of 1944 in the northern province of Honan, starving people resorted to eating anything to quell their hunger pangs—soil, tree bark, peanut husks, and even the dead, of whom there were perhaps three million. (All told, an estimated 15 million Chinese died in the war from military actions, natural calamities, epidemics and famine.)

On top of all these woes, military activity suddenly increased. In April 1944 the Japanese launched their first major offensive in China since the capture of Hankow in 1938. As part of an operation code-named *Ichigo*—meaning "Number One"—Japanese forces in north China were ordered southward to take the main north-south rail line and capture the Fourteenth Air Force's east China air bases. At the same time, other forces holding an enclave in the far south around Canton and Hong Kong were to drive to the west and clear a line to the French Indochina border. This separate action was designed to open a direct line of communication between the Japanese in China and those in Southeast Asia.

The prime targets for the Japanese drive fell into three categories: the north-south rail line, a series of key towns, and the air bases built in 1938 and 1939 by General Chennault for the Chinese Air Force and subsequently expanded to accommodate his Fourteenth Air Force.

To a certain extent, *Ichigo* was the fulfillment of a prediction by Stilwell. He had repeatedly said that the Japanese would move on Chennault's bases if provoked by American planes. And during the preceding year they had had plenty of reason to be provoked: the Fourteenth Air Force had incessantly attacked Japanese communications and transportation, striking hard at offshore shipping, severely disrupting enemy river traffic and leaving rail transport a shambles. The Japanese were concerned for another reason as well. It seemed only a matter of time before B-29s would be using the bases for raids against Japan itself.

Ichigo was executed by a powerful force of 15 divisions, plus five independent brigades, commanded by General Shunroku Hata. The very size of this force was enough to strike fear in the Chinese units opposing them. As the

Japanese advanced, a Chinese army of 300,000 men confronting them simply disintegrated. Enemy units consisting of 500 men routed thousands of Chinese. In the resulting chaos, Chinese officers commandeered most of the available trucks to escape with their families and possessions. It took just three weeks for the Japanese to realize their initial objectives between the Yellow and Yangtze rivers.

As resistance to the Japanese advance collapsed, Chennault became alarmed about the safety of his bases, and looked about for ways to defend them. He knew that the great American air base at Chengtu in west-central China was being prepared to receive B-29s of the Twentieth Air Force for raids against Japan's steel industry beginning in June. Chennault, supported by the Generalissimo, asked Stilwell to divert supplies from Chengtu to his Fourteenth Air Force. Stilwell refused.

"Chennault has assured the Generalissimo," wrote Stilwell in an angry analysis of the situation, "that air power is the answer. He has told him that if the Fourteenth AF is supported, he can effectively prevent a Jap invasion. Now he realizes it can't be done, and he is trying to prepare an

out for himself by claiming that with a *little more,* which we won't give him, he can still do it. He tries to duck the consequences of having sold the wrong bill of goods, and put the blame on those who pointed out the danger long ago and tried to apply the remedy."

The bitter feeling between the two commanders now boiled over. When Chennault submitted his own estimate of the situation to the Generalissimo, despite Stilwell's orders not to do so, Vinegar Joe regarded it as an intolerable act of insubordination. He attempted to have Chennault relieved of command, but the War Department feared the consequences of sacking a public hero and declined to act.

Chennault in turn blamed Stilwell for the predicament of the east China air bases. He insisted that he had always expected Chinese troops, adequately supplied with Lend-Lease equipment, to protect them. Though he got most of the supplies flown over the Hump, he felt he was not being given as much as he should have been by Stilwell. In his memoirs, Chennault expressed amazement "that Stilwell would bitterly oppose sending a single American bullet to any Chinese armies not under his direct supervision. . . . There is ample evidence to prove that my plans for air operations in China were based on coordinated action between Chinese ground troops and American air forces, with air power assuming the major burden of this joint effort."

In May 1944, after reaching the Yangtze River, the Japanese pushed on toward Chennault's bases. The first obstacle in their path was the city of Changsha. Its defense was the responsibility of General Hsueh Yueh, an officer who liked Americans and was generally liked by them. During the opening stages of the Sino-Japanese War, Hsueh had thrice repulsed attacks on Changsha; his Fourth Army had won itself the nickname "The Iron Army," and Hsueh had become known as "the Tiger of Changsha." But his tactics were of no avail this time in stopping the Japanese.

As the enemy marched south, Hsueh deployed his infantry in and about the city and massed his artillery on a nearby mountain. He was hoping to be able to suck the Japanese in, then hammer them with his guns and drive them off with his infantry.

But before the attack began, Hsueh moved his headquarters 100 miles to the south to prepare the defense of Heng-

Preparing for a shopping expedition, a Chinese loads his ricksha with a bag bulging with inflated currency he has just withdrawn from a bank in Kunming. By the end of the war, consumer prices in China ballooned to 2,500 times their prewar level, with a single egg costing as much as $50.

yang, where Chennault's northernmost bases were located. No one was now empowered to coordinate the defense of Changsha. When the artillery commander asked the infantry commander for men to protect his guns, he was refused. The advancing Japanese quickly silenced the unprotected artillery and then moved on the unsupported infantry—and the city fell. A few days later the Chinese army commander told U.S. liaison officers that he had been forced to withdraw because the Japanese were using gas in bombs and artillery shells. But an American sergeant who had been at Changsha told a different story. He simply awoke one morning to find the Chinese gone, he said; there had been no gas—and no significant fighting.

The next Japanese objective was Hengyang. Here, the Chinese Tenth Army under Hsueh put up a spirited defense. In Chungking the government announced that it was undertaking a huge counteroffensive to relieve Hengyang and drive away the Japanese. Theodore White, then a correspondent for TIME, went to Hengyang to see for himself, and found that the huge counteroffensive involved no more than two poorly equipped regiments.

Approaching the front, White ran into some of the troops on the march. "The men walked quietly, with the curious bitterness of Chinese soldiers who expect nothing but disaster at the end of a trip," he noted. "They were wiry and brown but thin; their guns were old, their yellow-and-brown uniforms threadbare. Each carried two grenades tucked in his belt; about the neck of each was a long blue stocking inflated like a roll of bologna with dry rice kernels, the Chinese soldier's only field rations. Their feet were broken and puffed above their straw sandals; their heads were covered with birds' nests of leaves woven together to give shade from the sun and supposedly to supply camouflage. The sweat rolled from them; dust rose about them; the heat clutched the entire country, and giddy, glistening waves rose from the rice paddies."

Upon reaching the front, the officers committed their troops to battle little by little. The infantry was supported by a pair of French 75s left over from the First World War, for which there were only 200 shells. "All that flesh and blood could do the Chinese soldiers were doing," White wrote. "They were walking up hills and dying in the sun, but they had no support, no directions. They were doomed."

In the meantime, Chennault's planes were desperately bombing and strafing Japanese supply convoys, attacking bridges and destroying roads—but still the enemy pressed on. Alarmed, Chennault offered to let the Chinese have some of the Fourteenth Air Force's own sorely needed supplies. But the Generalissimo barred this move. Rumors were rife that his commanders in this zone were plotting a coup against him—indeed, one group had approached U.S. Army Brigadier General Thomas S. Timberman, in charge of training Chinese troops in east China, and requested American support. Fearful that supplies would be turned against him, Chiang refused to allow arms and equipment to be sent to the Chinese troops fighting there.

Chennault now bypassed the Generalissimo and asked Stilwell to approve his request. But Stilwell believed the situation in east China to be all but hopeless. And given the politics of China, he, like Chiang, was not sure how the supplies might be used in the end. He too turned down Chennault, and wrote acidly in his diary: "Let them stew."

As he penned those words, Stilwell's own future was in jeopardy. A crisis of command had long been brewing, and it was intensified by Stilwell's formidable talent for making enemies. Mountbatten—who more than once had been

Stilwell's successors, Lieut. Generals Daniel I. Sultan (pointing) and Albert C. Wedemeyer (standing), pore over a map with Mountbatten (center). Observing the 1945 briefing in Burma is OSS Chief Major General William J. Donovan. Sultan commanded American, Chinese and British troops in northern Burma, while Wedemeyer headed up the U.S. forces in China.

offended by the undiplomatic American's behavior—felt that Stilwell had far too many conflicting responsibilities; he recommended that these be divided and that Stilwell's duties be restricted to China.

The opposition to Stilwell had been building for a long time, and had almost resulted in his removal even while he was slogging down the Hukawng Valley on the drive to Myitkyina. In June, Vice President Henry A. Wallace visited Chiang in Chungking and attempted to persuade him to allow American military observers to be stationed with Mao Tse-tung's Communist forces at Yenan in the far northern province of Shensi—with an eye to involving Mao's three million militiamen and army troops directly in the war. Chennault, always on the lookout for potential allies, assigned Joseph Alsop of his staff to Wallace as a guide and "air aide." Wallace spent several days in Chungking in the company of Alsop and the Generalissimo, but gave little time to Stilwell's representatives. Apparently a case was built up against the American commander. Stilwell, too involved in the drive for Myitkyina to go to Chungking, invited Wallace to visit him in Burma instead, but the Vice President declined.

Upon returning to Washington, Wallace recommended to Roosevelt that Stilwell be recalled because of his failure to grasp "political considerations." Wallace had initially considered Chennault as Stilwell's successor, but he was dissuaded by Alsop, who knew that the War Department would never approve the freewheeling airman as theater commander. Wallace now suggested to Roosevelt that a replacement for Stilwell might be Major General Albert C. Wedemeyer, a member of Mountbatten's SEAC staff and someone of whom the Generalissimo had spoken favorably.

Ironically, just as the pressures were mounting for Stilwell's recall, Roosevelt was beginning to give his beleaguered general some much-needed support. The President had been exposed to enough of Chiang's vacillations to have come around to Stilwell's point of view that only a *quid pro quo* approach would force the Generalissimo to take decisive military action. Roosevelt therefore determined to tie some strings to Lend-Lease aid. Furthermore, by this time Chennault's early promise that he could defeat the Japanese from the air had proved hollow, and the supplying of his Fourteenth Air Force had involved so many transport planes that crucial Allied operations in Europe had been hampered.

At this juncture, the War Department proposed that Roosevelt promote Stilwell to four-star general and ask Chiang to place him in command of all Chinese forces in the field—in China, as well as in Burma and India. In a lengthy

The final Allied drive down through Burma, commanded by British General Slim and American Lieut. General Daniel I. Sultan ended in victory. Starting out south of Myitkyina, troops of Sultan's X Force advanced in three prongs and made contact with the men of the Y Force along the Chinese border. Sultan's soldiers cleared the Japanese from the old Burma Road and drove south to Kyaukme. In the meantime, the XXXIII Corps and IV Corps of Slim's Fourteenth Army executed a pincer-style attack that resulted in the capture of Mandalay on March 20, 1945. To the west the Fourteenth Army's XV Corps, after pushing down into Arakan, mounted an amphibious and airborne assault against Rangoon and took that city on May 3, 1945. The Japanese forces tried to escape toward Thailand, but were caught by the British and slaughtered in great numbers.

memo advancing this suggestion to the President, the Joint Chiefs said: "We are fully aware of the Generalissimo's feeling regarding Stilwell . . . but the fact remains that he has proved his case or contentions on the field of battle in opposition to the highly negative attitudes of both the British and the Chinese authorities."

Roosevelt consented. He dispatched a message to the Generalissimo warning him that "the future of all Asia is at stake," advising him that Stilwell was being promoted to four-star rank and urging upon him the War Department recommendation that Stilwell now be placed in command of all Chinese, as well as American, forces in the theater.

It is unlikely that the Generalissimo ever seriously considered agreeing, for he knew that by elevating Stilwell to such a position he would be jeopardizing his own position as China's leader. He was worried by the opposition to him among Chinese officers in the eastern zone, and feared that Stilwell would weaken his grip on the government by obliging him to commit his own well-equipped, carefully hoarded reserves to the battle. He had no way of telling what might happen; it was conceivable that his men might even turn against him.

Still, Chiang could not easily refuse Roosevelt's request, for he desperately needed American support. The Generalissimo replied to Roosevelt that he agreed in principle that Stilwell should command all Chinese forces in the field— but only under two conditions. First, there would have to be a preparatory period, of unspecified length, during which the Chinese Army could become accustomed to the idea of serving under a foreigner. Second, Chiang asked Roosevelt to send to Chungking a high-level emissary who could "adjust the relations between me and General Stilwell." Upon reading Chiang's reply, Roosevelt was delighted. He thought that he had won his point with Chiang.

In fact, the struggle over Stilwell was rapidly approaching a showdown, and the events that would finally precipitate his downfall were taking place not in east China, but in the Salween River area along the China-Burma border.

In May 1944, after long urging by the United States, elements of the Chinese Y Force—the 198th Division, the 36th Division and the 346th Regiment of the 116th Division—had finally crossed the Salween with the intention of hooking up with Stilwell and clearing the Japanese from the old Burma Road.

After the crossing, the 36th Division surrounded Japanese outposts on the China side of the border. But the enemy vigorously attacked and forced the 36th back to the river. The Chinese then launched a counterattack and, with a prodigious expenditure of infantrymen, cleared a path through the enemy positions. (American liaison officers were aghast at the Chinese tactics—it was customary, for example, for a commander to send a single platoon in a stand-up assault against a strongly held Japanese position and then, when that platoon had been annihilated, to send in a second one.)

With support from the Fourteenth Air Force, the Chinese pushed on toward Burma. They gained control of a substantial stretch of the old Burma Road in the Tengchung area of western China and drove the Japanese into the hills. The Y Force—which had been built up by now to a strength of five divisions—took the walled city of Tengchung. Outside the city a group of approximately 100 infantrymen from the X Force, having marched for nine days from Myitkyina, made contact with the Y Force in the first direct linkup between the two units.

But the contact was not to last long. Late in August the Japanese, having abandoned their disastrous adventure at Imphal, decided to reinforce units opposing the Y Force in the Salween area and to regain control of the portion of the old Burma Road that had been lost to the Chinese. On the 26th of August, 6,000 Japanese counterattacked at Lungling, to the south of Tengchung, and the Y Force began to fall back.

Although the Japanese, as it turned out, had no intention of driving deeper into China, Chiang grew alarmed that they might push all the way to Kunming, the terminus of the Hump airlift, and cut his troops off from Allied aid. The Generalissimo asked Stilwell to rush his battle-weary Chinese divisions down from Myitkyina and attack the Japanese rear, thereby diverting the enemy from a drive on Kunming. To do so the divisions would have to make a 90-mile march through the jungle.

Stilwell refused; his men were too exhausted. He suggested instead that Chiang reinforce the Y Force troops now fighting at Lungling. In response to Stilwell's suggestion, the

At a leave center in Kandy, Ceylon, two work elephants absorb the attention of a group of officers.

For war-weary soldiers in CBI, leave centers located in India, Burma and Ceylon provided a welcome escape from the horror of the jungle war. Resort hotels and private residences were taken over by the British Army and various service organizations, and every effort was made to give the men a complete rest.

A BBC correspondent reported that the new arrivals at one center "were dusty and dirty, their faces were pretty grim. They sat at tables with white cloths and crockery and knives and forks; they were waited on by benign Indians in snow-white clothes and you could see incredulity amount-ing almost to suspicion on their faces."

Life in the centers was documented in pictures like these, and when people at home saw soldiers living in luxury, a storm of criticism erupted. But after British photographer Cecil Beaton defended the centers in a magazine article, the furor quickly subsided: "In the Burmese theatre of war, perhaps less known to the critics than any other, conditions are particularly hard. . . . The men who have lost many of their buddies, whose nerves had begun to be frayed, who have many times been 'frightened' . . . are now seen with their features relaxed, their eyes no longer strained."

Relaxing and soaking up the sun, furloughed troops and their dates enjoy a day on the beach at Mount Lavania, a popular resort site for civilians in Ceylor

Generalissimo threatened to withdraw the Y Force from the Salween River area altogether for the defense of Kunming. Stilwell was appalled, for such a move would free the Japanese to retake previously occupied sections of the old Burma Road—and would end any possibility that the Allies might soon open the overland supply route from India to China. "He will not listen to reason, merely repeating a lot of cock-eyed conceptions of his own invention," Stilwell angrily wrote to Marshall. "He imagines he can get behind the Salween and there wait in safety for the U.S. to finish the war."

Even before Stilwell sent his message to Marshall, the Japanese had been forced by tenacious Chinese resistance to call off their Burma Road counteroffensive, and the threat to Kunming had evaporated. But events had now acquired their own momentum. Upon learning of the Generalissimo's threat to withdraw the Y Force to Kunming, Roosevelt sent him a note that Stilwell was ordered to deliver to Chiang personally. The note—which even Stilwell described as "a hot firecracker"—was harsh and preemptory. It told Chiang that if he withdrew the Y Force he must "be prepared to accept the consequences and assume the personal responsibility" for the results. It went on to say that if Chiang did not quickly reinforce his armies across the Salween—and give Stilwell field command of the entire Chinese Army—China would face "catastrophic consequences." The note strongly implied that should Chiang fail to take such steps, American aid would end.

Stilwell hand-carried the note to the Generalissimo's residence in Chungking. Chiang was in conference with ranking Chinese officers and Major General Patrick J. Hurley, the special emissary Roosevelt had sent to CBI in response to Chiang's request for someone who could, in his word, "adjust" the relationship between Stilwell and the Generalissimo. Hurley had served as Secretary of War during the Hoover Administration, and Roosevelt often used him as a troubleshooter. Even as Stilwell appeared with the sizzling message from the President, Hurley was in the process of negotiating with Chiang over Stilwell's assumption of command of the Chinese forces in the field.

Stilwell had Hurley called from the conference room and showed him the note. With a politician's instinct, Hurley saw that the message meant trouble. He told Stilwell it was an ultimatum and suggested that he, himself, should read it to the Generalissimo, paraphrasing and tempering the language. But Stilwell did not want the language tempered; he had been ordered to deliver the note himself, and he would do just that. The two men then entered the room, and after the traditional rite of tea drinking had been observed, Stilwell gave the note to a translator to read to the Generalissimo. Because other Chinese officials were present in the room, Hurley realized that the reading of the note aloud would mean a serious embarrassment for Chiang. He quickly took the note from the translator and gave the Generalissimo a copy written in Chinese characters. After reading it the Generalissimo said quietly: "I understand."

Stilwell took great relish in the incident and wrote that he "handed this bundle of paprika to the Peanut and then sank back with a sigh. The harpoon hit the little bugger right in the solar plexus and went right through him."

But Stilwell was gloating too soon. The Generalissimo, who was furious, apparently concluded that Stilwell had engineered the note, and he reacted predictably. On September 24 he sent the President a message demanding that Stilwell be recalled instead of being assigned to field command of the Chinese Army. "General Stilwell is unfitted for the vast, complex and delicate duties which the new command will entail," he said.

Chiang meanwhile told the Central Executive Committee of the Nationalist government that he refused to appoint Stilwell to the overall command. This was an irrevocable step; once Chiang had made the announcement to the executive committee, he could not change his position without an intolerable loss of face. In effect, the matter was now closed. Roosevelt could no longer oppose Chiang except by challenging the Generalissimo's right to rule.

The President suggested a compromise under which Stilwell would retain command of Chinese forces in Burma. But Chiang was intractable. In a message given to Hurley for delivery to Roosevelt, he charged that Stilwell had shown complete indifference to the situation in east China and had caused "grave damage to the prestige and morale of the Chinese Army." He reasserted his demand for Stilwell's recall. "So long as I am Head of State and Supreme Commander in China," he said, "it seems to me that there can be no question as to my right to request the recall of an officer in whom I can no longer repose confidence." That was unarguable.

In a separate message to the President, Hurley—without commenting on Stilwell's military competence—endorsed Chiang's demand. Hurley maintained that personal relations had now so far deteriorated that the United States would have to choose between Chiang and Stilwell; given these circumstances, the choice could only be the Generalissimo.

On October 18, Roosevelt ordered Stilwell's immediate recall. Informed of the decision by Marshall, Stilwell wrote wryly in his diary: "THE AX FALLS."

Stilwell spent a week visiting various units, saying goodbye to old comrades and writing farewell messages—including a cordial one to Chennault complimenting him on his achievements. Chiang offered Stilwell the Special Grand Cordon of the Blue Sky and White Sun, China's highest decoration for a foreigner, but Stilwell declined it. He did accept an invitation to a final tea, however, at which Chiang was gracious and Stilwell said little. When the tea was over, Stilwell uttered the war motto of China: "Tsui hou sheng li"—"For the final victory." Then he left. The era of Vinegar Joe was over.

Stilwell was not the only victim of the CBI contretemps. Nine months later, Chennault was eased into retirement by General Marshall and the Chief of Staff of the Army Air Forces, General Henry "Hap" Arnold. Chennault would argue to the end that Stilwell, by his refusal to send supplies and troops to east China, was responsible for the debacle there. "He bled China white and squandered most of the resources available in the CBI theater," Chennault later wrote. He believed that Stilwell had been totally unsuited for the diplomatic-military post to which he had been assigned, and had been incapable of seeing the war from

U.S. Ambassador Patrick J. Hurley is flanked by Chou En-lai (left) and Mao Tse-tung at Communist headquarters in Yenan. On the right is the Nationalist envoy who participated in the unsuccessful attempt by Hurley to arrange a coalition between the Communists and the Nationalists in 1944. The building behind the men bears the name of an American Army officer who was stationed with the Communists and was killed by the Japanese.

anything but the foot soldier's point of view. "He was an even more violent partisan of the infantry than I was of air power," Chennault said.

With Stilwell's departure, the way was clear to divide CBI into two theaters—a move that had long seemed a sensible answer to the area's immensely complicated command problems. Stilwell's many responsibilities were now split up among three generals. Lieut. General Daniel I. Sultan, formerly Stilwell's deputy theater commander, became commanding general in India and Burma. Lieut. General Raymond A. Wheeler, who had been Stilwell's supply chief, became Mountbatten's deputy in SEAC. And General Wedemeyer, who had been serving as Mountbatten's deputy chief of staff, took over as the new chief of staff to the Generalissimo and commander of U.S. forces in China.

A tall man with aquiline features, Wedemeyer was regarded as a brilliant staff officer and planner. In contrast to Stilwell, he was an amiable, tactful man who, in his own words, made a practice of using "honey instead of vinegar" in his relations with the Generalissimo. As a start, he placed all papers pertaining to the Stilwell-Chiang feud in a special file, locked them away, and determined not to read them until after the war.

Wedemeyer soon established a cordial working relationship with the Generalissimo. It was based on real respect. The Generalissimo, Wedemeyer later wrote, was "a sincere patriot, pre-eminently concerned with the interest of his country and his people. He knew very little about modern military strategy, for he had been trained in guerrilla war concepts; but he knew a great deal about the political art of holding his people to the job at hand."

Like Stilwell before him, Wedemeyer—in his capacity as chief of staff and adviser to the Generalissimo—attempted to turn at least a part of the Chinese Army into an effective instrument for the long struggle that the Allies assumed still lay ahead. He set up a system of liaison between Chinese commanders and their American advisers, and worked on improving the diet of the Chinese soldier. The Chinese Army was half-starved, and Wedemeyer believed that malnutrition was at the root of most of the Army's problems.

But the number and quality of Chinese divisions at Wedemeyer's disposal were limited. Chiang, concerned as ever that the Communists might launch an attack against his forces from their base in the north, continued to use many of his best and most loyal troops to contain them. Wedemeyer could only look covetously at Chiang's "reserve"—and at Mao Tse-tung's own three-million-man force. Ever since Wallace's visit to Chungking in June, attempts had been made to bring the Communists into the war, and plans were being made to send them Lend-Lease aid. But the United States recognized Chiang's regime as the government of China, and it was not possible to assist the Communists without obtaining the Generalissimo's consent first. To get that consent, the United States had somehow to arrange a better relationship than the armed, uneasy truce that existed between the two factions. Toward that end Patrick Hurley was appointed ambassador to China.

Impressively tall, as well as handsome and wealthy, the high-spirited Hurley knew little of China and the Chinese. On arriving in Chungking he incorrectly referred to the Generalissimo by the last syllable of his name, calling him Mr. Shek instead of Chiang. (His humorous name for Mao Tse-tung was "Moose Dung.") A man who believed that problems could be overcome by charm and good spirits, Hurley was apt, at formal functions, to startle staid Chinese officials by loosing bloodcurdling Choctaw war whoops learned as a boy in his native Oklahoma.

Hurley began his negotiations in late 1944 and carried them on into the new year. Entering the discussions with enthusiasm and optimism, he shuttled back and forth between Chungking and Yenan, Mao's headquarters, and tried to bring the leaders to some sort of compromise. It was all to no avail. In retrospect his task seems to have been hopeless from the start. The Communists insisted upon significant representation in a coalition government, a demand to which the Generalissimo would not—and probably could not—agree.

In the meantime, China's situation was growing more desperate by the hour. The Fourteenth Air Force base at Lingling, 80 miles southwest of Hengyang, fell to the Japanese in September. When Wedemeyer took over from Stilwell late in October, the Japanese were threatening the city of Kweilin, the site of the largest of Chennault's bases. Wedemeyer was apprehensive about the situation, but the Generalissimo assured him "categorically" that the Chinese

Before getting down to business, a GI horse trader sips a cup of rice wine offered him by Tibetan tribesmen. Such formalities often took hours.

A BUNCH OF OLD-TIME HORSE TRADERS

In a theater with mountainous terrain and few roads, four legs very often counted for more than four wheels. Accordingly, a U.S. outfit—the Sino-American Horse Purchasing Bureau—was set up in the mountains of Tibet and China to provide the Chinese Army with pack animals.

Acquiring the animals was no easy task. Before the horse-rich Tibetans and Chinese Lolo tribesmen would bargain with them, Bureau agents often had to participate in lengthy eating and drinking ceremonies, and sometimes even had to prove themselves in shooting matches. When the deals were clinched, the mountain men insisted on payment in everything from silver bullion to felt hats. Finally, with horses in tow, the agents journeyed to Kunming—a month-and-a-half trip, often down icy trails and through stirrup-high snow.

A Bureau agent brands a new buy on the neck, while a buddy steadies the animal.

could hold the Kweilin area for at least two months. As it turned out, they were unable even to make a stand.

Kweilin was a beautiful place, and a lively one, with an active night life and plenty of bar girls who had fled there from Japanese-occupied areas. But now the city was in a panic. People crowded onto trains that were to leave no one knew when. Jammed on board, they lived in their own filth, afraid that if they left their places even to relieve themselves they might be unable to force their way back on. Chinese soldiers raided the abandoned restaurants and nightclubs for food and drink. "The last five soldiers I saw at the northern gate," wrote Theodore White, "had seventeen bottles of wine that they were finishing with great good cheer as they waited for the enemy."

In the end, the Japanese scarcely had to fight for the city at all; it fell to them on November 10. They then moved on and swiftly took Chennault's base at Liuchow, some 100 miles to the southwest. From there they pushed southward to take four bases around Nanning, then drove to the southwest for a linkup with their forces in French Indochina. The Japanese had now achieved their twin objectives: capturing the east China airfields and securing the main railway line to the south.

The army involved, the Eleventh, was heady with victory, and its commander, Lieut. General Isamu Yokoyama, entirely on his own, ordered his men to start moving northwest toward Kweiyang, where another airfield was located. The Chinese troops in the area put up little resistance; they were so short of weapons and supplies that they could not have held out long even if they had tried. Ironically, along the route of the Chinese retreat, an American demolition team operating just ahead of the Japanese discovered three Chinese ammunition dumps that held 50,000 tons of supplies, weapons and ammunition, hoarded for how long or what purpose no one ever learned.

By early December all that lay between the fast-moving Eleventh Army and the vital cities of Kunming and Chungking were Chennault's air force—which was now flying out of bases to the east of the *Ichigo* advance—and a few remnants of the Chinese Army. Chungking was China's wartime capital, of course, but it was the threat to Kunming that really disturbed Wedemeyer. China could continue to exist without Chungking, but if the Hump airlift terminus at Kunming were captured, it would spell the end of everything. At all costs that city had to be defended. A collapse of resistance in China, Wedemeyer estimated, would release 25 Japanese divisions to fight elsewhere; and if the Japanese possessed all of China, they might be able to hold out there for years after the home islands fell.

But how could they be stopped? Wedemeyer had discovered that most of the seasoned soldiers in the Chinese Army were too weak from undernourishment to fight, and that new conscripts "were ready for a General Hospital rather than the General Reserve." Moreover, in a comment reminiscent of Stilwell, he noted that "the disorganization and muddled planning of the Chinese is beyond comprehension."

To defend Kunming, Wedemeyer asked SEAC for two divisions of the X Force, now fighting in Burma. Mountbatten initially opposed the idea, but was overruled by the Combined Chiefs of Staff. The airlift of the 14th and 22nd divisions got under way on December 5, but when the divisions were assembled in China, they found that their presence was no longer needed. The swift-moving Japanese Eleventh Army had outrun its supply lines some 300 miles from Kunming, and pulled back slightly to go into garrison for the winter. The threat to Kunming, and to China, was over for the moment.

Meanwhile, in Burma the long and arduous struggle that had been going on since the Japanese invaded the country in early 1942 was now entering its final phase. In the middle of October 1944, Chinese, American and British forces under the newly appointed General Sultan had taken the offensive in a drive to wrench the Burma Road from Japanese control. With three Chinese divisions, spearheaded by the new U.S. Mars Force—successors to Merrill's badly mauled Marauders—Sultan pressed rapidly across northern Burma toward an effective linkup with the Y Force, near the Chinese frontier.

The linkup was almost a disaster. On January 27, one of Sultan's X Force regiments launched an attack against what the troops assumed was the last Japanese position barring their way up the Burma Road into China. An air observer reported blue-uniformed troops of the Y Force in the area. Artillery fire was canceled, but the word had not been

Amphibious troops of the British XV Corps bring their artillery ashore on the muddy banks of the Rangoon River in April 1945. After three years of bitter fighting in Burma, they landed unopposed, pushed northward to the vital port city of Rangoon and were welcomed by cheering throngs.

passed down the line and X Force soldiers opened fire with small arms. An American liaison officer, Brigadier General George W. Sliney, aware that the blue-uniformed troops were not Japanese but Chinese, rushed to the front and, marching up and down the line, managed to get the firing stopped. The overland route to China was at last open.

As Sultan's troops were linking up with the Y Force in the north, Slim's Fourteenth Army was carrying out its own offensive far to the south and setting the stage for the expulsion of the Japanese from Burma. Slim had hoped to fight a decisive battle on the Shwebo plain, a level area along the west bank of the Irrawaddy north of Mandalay. Such open country favored the British, with their superiority in aircraft, armor and artillery. But Slim was not to get the chance. General Kawabe, the commander of the Burma Area Army, had been replaced by Lieut. General Hoyotaro Kimura, a highly regarded artilleryman, fresh from Imperial

General Headquarters in Tokyo. Kimura was less predictable than his predecessor, and he shrewdly declined a battle on the Shwebo plain. Instead he withdrew behind the Irrawaddy, intending to make the river his defense line rather than fight with it at his back. This meant, of course, that any British attempt to cross the Irrawaddy would be heavily opposed.

Crossing a river under fire is one of the most difficult of warfare maneuvers. Slim concocted an elaborate plan to deceive the Japanese. The Fourteenth Army's XXXIII Corps— which had been fighting on the Dimapur-Kohima front and had since been heavily reinforced—would cross the river near Mandalay, openly and against opposition, in order to suggest to the Japanese that this was the main British attack. A dummy IV Corps headquarters, established to the north of XXXIII Corps, would send and receive fake messages, creating the illusion that the entire IV Corps was in the

vicinity. In reality, the IV Corps would be moving south under radio silence; it would cross the Irrawaddy well below Mandalay, building its own road through the jungle as it went, and attack the Japanese rear.

Slim's plan worked to perfection. Kimura denuded his commands, including those fighting Sultan in the north, and massed them to oppose the British on the Irrawaddy north and west of Mandalay. In the meantime, Slim's IV Corps not only had crossed the river to the south, but had done so with such stealth that Japanese patrols believed the few British troops they ran up against were no more than a small diversionary force. By the time Kimura realized that he had the entire British IV Corps behind him, XXXIII Corps was starting to break out of the bridgeheads it had established

across the Irrawaddy. The XXXIII Corps now came charging down on Mandalay from the north, meeting only crumbling resistance on the way.

Before Mandalay could be taken, Slim's troops had to storm the heights of Pagoda Hill, a religious center in the northeast quarter of the city, where hundreds of Buddhist shrines bristled with snipers. Then they had to lay siege to the ancient walled citadel of Fort Dufferin with artillery and bombers. After prolonged and heavy fighting *(pages 158-167)*, the surviving Japanese fled, and on March 20, 1945, Mandalay fell.

In early April, Slim made up his mind to continue his offensive and push south toward Rangoon. Even though the enemy was now on the run, the decision involved a gamble. Rangoon lay more than 300 miles away, and there were still large numbers of Japanese between Slim and his objective. Moreover, the monsoon was likely to strike within a month; if it did so before Slim captured the city and opened its port, the British Fourteenth Army, with only a long and tenuous line of communication to sustain it, would be in dire straits.

To reach Rangoon in time, Slim's men would have to move 10 miles a day, bypassing Japanese strong points and leaving large numbers of Japanese troops prowling about behind them. This thrust would entail moving armored spearheads down the railway and the Irrawaddy Valley—no mean accomplishment considering that the British tanks were obsolete and in drastic need of overhaul. Slim visited all of his armored units and exhorted his men to do everything possible to keep every tank—no matter how decrepit—operating until Rangoon. Upon securing Rangoon, Slim joked, they could push their tanks into the sea.

In order to reduce the considerable risk of failure, Mountbatten decided to strengthen the British hand by launching an airborne and amphibious attack on Rangoon in early May, thus giving the Japanese something more than the overland drive from the north to worry about. The amphibious operation would be carried out by troops of the XV Corps, which had captured Akyab in Arakan early in January and later had conducted a series of landings to seize key air bases along Burma's west coast.

Meanwhile, Slim started moving his other divisions overland toward Rangoon. They made rapid progress and were only 40 miles from their objective when the monsoon broke

At a ceremony in Delhi, the widow of a Punjabi soldier, one of thousands of Indians who fought in CBI, displays Britain's highest military honor, the Victoria Cross, awarded posthumously to her husband. Leading a bayonet charge at Kennedy Peak near Tiddim, Burma, in October 1944, he was hit by machine-gun fire, but still managed to kill four Japanese.

192

on May 1, two weeks early. The rains left the British mired behind rapidly rising rivers. But even as the landbound columns were struggling through the mud, the amphibious and airborne landings were taking place.

These actions were abetted to some degree by operations of the Japanese-trained Burmese Independence Army, which in an abrupt about-face had come over to the British side. The Burmese had marched out of Rangoon, ostensibly to join in its defense, but when well beyond the Japanese perimeter, they had turned around and marched back against Rangoon. Other Burmese units followed their example. After collaborating secretly with the British throughout most of the war, the Burmese Independence Army had finally come out openly on the British side. The Burmese "were regarded with considerable suspicion at first," wrote Slim, "but, almost without exception, obeyed orders well. They proved definitely useful in gaining information and dealing drastically with small parties of Japanese."

It was the British XV Corps, however, that captured the prize of Rangoon. Loaded onto six convoys at Akyab and Ramree Island to the south, the assault force sailed under an umbrella of RAF fighters and a protective screen of Royal Navy escort carriers. Paratroops of the 50th Indian Brigade landed south of the city on May 1, and troops of the XV Corps splashed ashore below Rangoon the following day. After heading north through waterlogged fields, they occupied Rangoon without opposition on May 3. The weakened Japanese had abandoned the city and joined the general Japanese retreat toward Thailand. Burmese villagers, who had welcomed the Japanese as liberators in 1942—but who had long since become disillusioned with them—now turned upon their recent masters as violently as they had turned against the British three years earlier.

The Japanese Twenty-eighth Army, which had been far to the west in Arakan and was responsible for the bloody slaughter of many of Slim's men during the first and second Arakan campaigns, now stood in danger of being left behind in the general retreat. The route eastward was barred by the British, who had sliced the country in half from north to south. The Twenty-eighth Army attempted to escape through British lines along a 150-mile front and cross the Sittang River into the safety of the mountains along the Thai border. But the British captured detailed plans of the break-

out routes and timetables. When the Japanese began their effort, the 17th Indian Division was waiting for them. Those who managed to reach the Sittang found it flooded by monsoon rains; any who were not shot attempting to cross the broad river drowned. A British outpost on the riverbank downstream from one of the main crossing points counted no fewer than 600 Japanese bodies floating by—clear evidence of the disaster that was beginning to unfold along the banks upstream.

The Japanese Twenty-eighth Army had started the breakout across the Sittang with more than 17,000 troops. Of these, fewer than 6,000 got across alive. Incredibly, only 95 British soldiers were killed in the action.

There was an almost uncanny significance to this disaster on the Sittang. When Japanese troops invaded Burma at the beginning of 1942, thousands of British, Gurkha and Indian troops were drowned or slain on the same river. Now the Japanese had been wiped out where they had achieved their first great victory in Burma.

The war in the Pacific was drawing to a close. In China, as in Burma, the situation had taken a dramatic turn for the better. The shift had begun in April when the Japanese started a drive into western China aimed at the city of Chihkiang. They were opposed vigorously by Chinese troops trained by Wedemeyer and supported by the Fourteenth Air Force—operating now out of "pocket" fields in areas that had not been overrun by the Japanese. The Chinese suffered heavy casualties, but they succeeded in beating off the Japanese and impressed the enemy with the improvement that they displayed in their air, infantry and artillery attacks.

Wedemeyer took heart from the victory. He had been planning an offensive down through China to open a port in the Canton-Hong Kong area and establish a sea link between China and the outer world. The offensive—the first major Allied one in China—was expected to get under way in July or August. The object, as Wedemeyer put it, was to "destroy the Japanese on the Asiatic mainland," and prevent them from redeploying their troops from China to protect Japan against American invasion.

The pendulum had swung; the Japanese were now on the defensive.

THE ROAD TO VICTORY

A U.S. Army supply truck hauling a 105mm howitzer intended as aid for China passes the junction of the Ledo and Burma roads at Mong Yu in Burma.

HACKING OUT A JUNGLE HIGHWAY

"An immense, laborious task, unlikely to be finished until the need for it had passed" was Winston Churchill's terse appraisal of the controversial Ledo-Burma Road project. Begun in 1942 by U.S. Army engineers, the project seemed an impossibility from the start. First, the stretch of the old, war-torn Burma Road leading east 600 miles from Mong Yu in north Burma to Kunming in China would have to be repaired and improved for all-weather travel. Then a new 500-mile road would have to be carved out of the wilderness from Ledo in Assam to Mong Yu. But if the two roads could be joined, they would provide a crucial overland supply route from India to China, as well as a pathway for a pipeline to fuel gasoline-thirsty bombers and fighters.

Heavy earth-moving machinery of the type needed for building the road was almost nonexistent in the perennially undersupplied China-Burma-India Theater. The engineers— mostly black Americans—were forced to rely on light D4 bulldozers, which would bravely push up against a great stand of bamboo, one engineer later recalled, "as a puppy dog might nip at the heels of a 500-pound boar." To make matters worse, 80 per cent of the region through which the engineers had to cut their way was—at least, theoretically— in enemy hands. As work on the road progressed, bulldozers frequently carried a man riding shotgun to guard against snipers; nevertheless, some 130 engineers were killed by the Japanese. Diseases, drownings, crashes of supply planes and construction accidents claimed the lives of hundreds more. It was said without exaggeration that the road was being built at the cost of "a man a mile."

All told, 28,000 engineers and 35,000 native workers labored for more than two years to complete the combined Ledo-Burma Road—known officially as the Stilwell Road. Churchill was not far wrong: by the time the $150-million highway was finished the war had only seven months to go. But the road's construction—along the edges of 8,500-foot defiles, down steep gorges and across raging rapids in some of the world's most impenetrable jungles—stands as one of the great engineering feats of World War II.

Major General Lewis A. Pick, director of the Ledo-Burma Road project, chats with a bulldozer crew. Workers dubbed the road "Pick's Pike."

Beyond the newly built Ledo-Burma Road, a U.S. Army convoy headed for supply-starved Chungking negotiates the notorious "21 curves" at Annan, China.

Working throughout the night by the light of buckets of burning diesel oil, a bulldozer crew clears away a landslide that has covered a portion of the Ledo Road.

American soldiers, protecting the Ledo Road construction crew, man a 40mm Bofors antiaircraft gun.

A Burmese Kachin tribeswoman hacks at a hillside with a hoe to make a shoulder for the Ledo Road.

DAY-AND-NIGHT STRUGGLE AGAINST MUD AND DISEASE

"The Ledo Road is going to be built—mud, rain and malaria be damned!" declared General Pick, director of the project, in a pep talk to his engineers in 1943. But mud, rain and malaria proved to be only a partial list of miseries. Workers were subject to the constant threat of attack by Japanese ground troops and planes, and they were plagued by dysentery, typhus, leeches and fevers. Many places were so inaccessible that supplies had to be sent in by mule train or dropped from planes. Nightwork was hampered by the lack of adequate lighting, and Pick was forced to improvise lanterns out of buckets of diesel oil with rope for wicks.

When the rains came, they were so torrential that road banks collapsed, gigantic teak trees toppled across newly cut sections—in one case crushing an engineer to death—and exposed earth in the unfinished roadbed turned into a yellow soup. Yet in spite of all the problems, the road was pushed forward a mile or more a day.

Led by motorcycles, the first convoy to China hits a rare level stretch 204 miles along the Ledo Road.

A troop truck in the convoy grinds its way up a section of the Burma Road cut out of a cliffside.

THE FIRST CONVOY RIDES TO TRIUMPH

On January 12, 1945, the first official convoy pulled out of Ledo for Kunming over the newly finished Ledo Road. Commanded by General Pick, the caravan comprised a total of 113 vehicles. Steep road grades—up to 17 per cent from the horizontal—frequently slowed the convoy to a crawl. At several rivers, ferries had to substitute for bridges that had not been completed.

When the convoy reached the Burma Road, it was held up for three days while Chinese soldiers cleared the area of lingering Japanese troops. Finally, after almost a month of hard travel over the 1,100-mile route, Pick's convoy rolled triumphantly into Kunming, where a silk banner proclaimed the new route "The Road to Victory." Before the war was over, more than 5,000 vehicles would make the trip, carrying 34,000 tons of vital supplies to China.

Near the China border, the convoy crosses a rebuilt suspension bridge over the treacherous Salween River gorge. More than 500 new bridges had to be built.

At the West Gate of Kunming, China, thousands turn out as Pick's convoy arrives on February 4, 1945. At ceremonies marking the event, Pick gave a proud reply to those who had insisted that the road could not be built. Pointing to his trucks, he declared, "There stands the proof!"

202

203

BIBLIOGRAPHY

Alexander, Field-Marshal The Earl of Tunis, *The Alexander Memoirs 1940-1945*. Cassell, 1962.

Anders, Leslie, *The Ledo Road*. University of Oklahoma Press, 1965.

Barker, A. J., *The March on Delhi*. Faber and Faber, 1963.

Belden, Jack, *Retreat with Stilwell*. Alfred A. Knopf, 1943.

Boorman, Howard L., and Richard C. Howard, editor, *Biographical Dictionary of Republican China*, Vol. I. Columbia University Press, 1967.

Brett-James, Antony:
   Ball of Fire. Gale & Polden Ltd., 1951.
   Imphal. Macmillan and Company, Ltd., 1962.

Bridgman, Leonard, editor, *Jane's All the World's Aircraft 1945/6*. David and Charles, Ltd., 1970.

Burchett, W. G., *Wingate Adventure*. F. W. Cheshire, 1944.

Burns, James MacGregor, *Roosevelt: The Soldier of Freedom*. Harcourt, Brace, Jovanovich, Inc., 1970.

Calvert, Michael, *Prisoners of Hope*. Jonathan Cape, 1952.

Calvocoressi, Peter, and Wint Guy, *Total War*. Pantheon Books, 1972.

The Campaign in Burma. Central Office of Information, Prepared for South-East Asia Command. His Majesty's Stationery Office, 1946.

Campbell, Arthur, *The Siege*. George Allen & Unwin, Ltd., 1956.

Carew, Tim, *The Longest Retreat*. Hamish Hamilton, 1969.

Chennault, Anna, *Chennault and the Flying Tigers*. Paul S. Eriksson, Inc., 1963.

Chennault, Claire Lee, *Way of a Fighter*. G. P. Putnam's Sons, 1949.

Churchill, Winston S., *The Second World War*, Vol. V: *Closing the Ring*. Bantam Books, 1962.

Clubb, O. Edmund, *20th Century China*. Columbia University Press, 1964.

Collier, Basil, *The War in the Far East 1941-1945*. William Morrow & Company, Inc., 1969.

Craven, Wesley Frank, and James Lea Cate, editors:
   The Army Air Forces in World War II. The University of Chicago Press, 1948-1958.
   Volume IV, *The Pacific: Guadalcanal to Saipan*.
   Volume V, *The Pacific: Matterhorn to Nagasaki*.
   Volume VII, *Services around the World*.

Crozier, Brian, *The Man Who Lost China: The First Full Biography of Chiang Kai-shek*. Charles Scribner's Sons, 1976.

Davies, John Paton, Jr., *Dragon by the Tail: American, British, Japanese and Russian Encounters with China and One Another*. W. W. Norton & Company, Inc., 1972.

Davis, Patrick, *A Child at Arms*. Hutchinson of London, 1970.

Dorn, Frank, *Walkout*. Thomas Y. Crowell Company, 1971.

Eldridge, Fred, *Wrath in Burma*. Doubleday & Company, Inc., 1946.

Elliott, James Gordon, *Unfading Honour: The Story of the Indian Army, 1939-1945*. A. S. Barnes and Company, 1965.

Esherick, Joseph W., editor, *Lost Chance in China: The World War II Dispatches of John S. Service*. Vintage Books, 1974.

Esposito, Colonel Vincent J., chief editor, *The West Point Atlas of American Wars*, Vol. II: *1900-1953*. Frederick A. Praeger, 1959.

Fergusson, Bernard, *Beyond the Chindwin*. Collins, 1945.

Griffith, Samuel B., II, *The Chinese People's Liberation Army*. McGraw-Hill Book Company, 1967.

Homer, Joy, *Dawn Watch in China*. Houghton Mifflin Company, 1941.

Hotz, Robert B., *With General Chennault: The Story of the Flying Tigers*. Coward-McCann, Inc., 1943.

Ho-yungchi, *The Big Circle*. The Exposition Press, 1948.

Hunter, Colonel Charles N. (U.S. Army, Retired), *Galahad*. The Naylor Company, 1963.

Irwin, Anthony, *Burmese Outpost*. Collins, 1946.

Kirby, Major-General S. Woodburn:
   The War against Japan. Her Majesty's Stationery Office.
   Volume II, *India's Most Dangerous Hour*, 1958.
   Volume III, *The Decisive Battles*, 1961.
   Volume IV, *The Reconquest of Burma*, 1965.
   Volume V, *The Surrender of Japan*, 1969.

La Farge, Oliver, *The Eagle in the Egg*. Houghton Mifflin Company, 1949.

McKelvie, Roy, *The War in Burma*. Methuen & Company, Ltd., 1948.

Masters, John, *The Road Past Mandalay*. Harper & Brothers, 1961.

Merrill's Marauders. United States of America War Office, Military Intelligence Division, U.S. War Department, 1944.

Moorad, George, *Lost Peace in China*. E. P. Dutton & Company, Inc., 1949.

Mosley, Leonard, *Gideon Goes to War*. Charles Scribner's Sons, 1955.

Mountbatten, Vice Admiral The Earl Mountbatten of Burma, *Report to the Combined Chiefs of Staff by the Supreme Allied Commander South-East Asia 1943-1945*. Philosophical Library, New York, 1951.

Ogburn, Charlton, Jr., *The Marauders*. Harper & Brothers, Publishers, 1956.

Payne, Robert, *Forever China*. Dodd, Mead and Company, 1945.

Peck, Graham, *Two Kinds of Time*. Houghton Mifflin Company, 1950.

Pogue, Forrest C., *George C. Marshall, Organizer of Victory*. The Viking Press, 1973.

Rolo, Charles J., *Wingate's Raiders*. The Viking Press, 1944.

Romanus, Charles F., and Riley Sunderland:
   U.S. Army in World War II. Office of the Chief of Military History, Department of the Army.
   Stilwell's Command Problems, 1956.
   Stilwell's Mission to China, 1953.
   Time Runs Out in CBI, 1959.

Scott, Robert Lee, Jr., *Flying Tiger: Chennault of China*. Doubleday and Company, Inc., 1959.

Seagrave, Gordon S.:
   Burma Surgeon. W. W. Norton & Company, Inc., 1943.
   Burma Surgeon Returns. W. W. Norton & Company, Inc., 1946.

Sevareid, Eric, *Not So Wild a Dream*. Alfred A. Knopf, 1946.

Sheridan, James E., *China in Disintegration*. The Free Press, 1975.

Slim, Field Marshal The Viscount, *Defeat into Victory*. David McKay Company, Inc., 1961.

Smith, R. Harris, *OSS: The Secret History of America's First Central Intelligence Agency*. Delta, 1972.

Stilwell, Joseph W., *The Stilwell Papers*. William Sloane Associates, Inc., 1948.

Swinson, Arthur:
   The Battle of Kohima. Stein and Day, 1967.
   Four Samurai. Hutchinson of London, 1968.

Sykes, Christopher, *Orde Wingate*. The World Publishing Company, 1959.

Taylor, Joe G., *Air Supply in the Burma Campaigns, USAF Historical Studies: No. 75*. USAF Historical Division, 1957.

Thorne, Bliss K., *The Hump*. J. B. Lippincott Company, 1965.

Toland, John, *The Flying Tigers*. Random House, 1963.

Tuchman, Barbara W., *Stilwell and the American Experience in China 1911-1945*. Bantam Books, 1972.

Wedemeyer, General Albert C., *Wedemeyer Reports!* Henry Holt & Company, 1958.

Whelan, Russell, *The Flying Tigers*. The Viking Press, 1942.

White, Theodore H., and Annalee Jacoby, *Thunder Out of China*. William Sloane Associates, Inc., 1946.

Yeats-Brown, Francis, *Martial India*. Eyre and Spottiswoode, 1945.

PICTURE CREDITS

Credits from left to right are separated by semicolons, from top to bottom by dashes.

COVER and page 1: Wide World.

A TORRENT OF BOMBS: 6, 7, 8, 9—Carl Mydans for LIFE. 10, 11—Carl Mydans for LIFE; Wide World. 12, 13—Central News Agency, Taiwan. 14, 15—Carl Mydans for LIFE.

"A HELL OF A BEATING": 18, 19—Map by Elie Sabban. 20—*Mainichi Shimbun,* Japan. 23—Carl Mydans for LIFE. 25—Map by Elie Sabban. 26—UPI. 28—George Rodger from Magnum for LIFE. 30, 32—Wide World.

THE MAN CALLED VINEGAR JOE: 34, 35—U.S. Army. 36—The George C. Marshall Research Library, Lexington, Virginia. 37—George Rodger from Magnum. 38, 39—George Rodger from Magnum for LIFE. 40, 41—George Rodger from Magnum for LIFE; U.S. Army (2). 42, 43—U.S. Army. 44, 45—U.S. Army.

CHINA'S GENERALISSIMO: 46, 47—UPI. 48—*The New York Times.* 49—From *Chiang Kai-shek* by Hollington K. Tong. 50, 51—LIFE Picture Collection; UPI (2). 52—Robert Capa from Magnum for LIFE—Wide World. 53—Harris & Ewing. 54, 55—China Film/Guillumette; UPI.

STILWELL VS. CHENNAULT: 58—Illustrations by John Batchelor. 60—Map by Elie Sabban. 65—UPI.

THE FLAMBOYANT TIGERS: 68, 69—Illustration by John Batchelor. 70—Copied by Charlie Brown, courtesy The National Air and Space Museum, The Smithsonian Institution. 71—UPI. 72—Wide World. 73—George Rodger from Magnum. 74—Colonel David L. "Tex" Hill. 75, 76, 77—U.S. Air Force.

VAULTING THE HIMALAYAS: 78, 79, 80—U.S. Air Force. 81 through 87—William Vandivert for LIFE. 88—William Vandivert for LIFE; U.S. Air Force—U.S. Air Force (2)—William Vandivert for LIFE (2). 89—U.S. Air Force, except center, William Vandivert for LIFE (2). 90, 91—William Vandivert for LIFE.

HIGH STAKES AND HEAVY ODDS: 94, 96—Wide World. 97—Library of Congress. 98—Map by Elie Sabban. 100—William Vandivert for LIFE. 101—U.S. Army.

THE JUNGLE FIGHTERS: 104, 105—U.S. Air Force. 106—Imperial War Museum, London, Crown Copyright. 107—Popperfoto, London. 108—William Vandivert for LIFE. 109—UPI. 110, 111, 112, 113—U.S. Air Force. 114, 115—Imperial War Museum, London. 116, 117—U.S. Air Force.

THE DRIVE TO "MITCH": 121—UPI. 122—U.S. Army. 125—Kyodo, Japan. 127—Map by Elie Sabban. 128, 131—U.S. Army. 132—Wide World.

BURMA'S CRUEL TORMENTS: 134, 135—U.S. Army. 136, 137—Imperial War Museum, London. 138, 139, 140—U.S. Army. 141—U.S. Army—Imperial War Museum, London. 142—UPI. 143—Imperial War Museum, London. 144, 145—U.S. Army.

THE JAPANESE LOSE FACE: 148—Kyodo, Japan. 149—William Vandivert for LIFE. 150—*Mainichi Shimbun,* Japan. 151—Imperial War Museum, London. 152—Map by Elie Sabban. 153—Wide World. 155—U.S. Air Force.

STEP BY STEP TO MANDALAY: 158 through 167—Popperfoto, London.

MASS EXODUS IN EAST CHINA: 168, 169—UPI. 170, 171—U.S. Air Force. 172, 173—U.S. Air Force; Wide World. 174, 175—U.S. Army; Wide World (2). 176, 177—King Features Syndicate, Inc.; UPI.

AN UPSET IN COMMAND: 180—Jack Wilkes for LIFE. 181—U.S. Army. 182—Map by Elie Sabban. 184, 185—Popperfoto, London. 187—Ed Souders for LIFE. 189—U.S. Army. 191—Popperfoto, London. 192—*London Illustrated* from Black Star.

THE ROAD TO VICTORY: 194, 195—U.S. Army. 196—Bernard Hoffman for LIFE. 197—U.S. Army. 198, 199—Bernard Hoffman for LIFE, except bottom right, U.S. Army. 200, 201—U.S. Army. 202, 203—Jack Wilkes for LIFE.

ACKNOWLEDGMENTS

The index for this book was prepared by Mel Ingber. For help given in the preparation of this book the editors wish to express their gratitude to Dana Bell, U.S. Air Force Still Photo Depository, Pentagon, Washington, D.C.; Leroy Bellamy, Prints and Photographs Division, Library of Congress, Washington, D.C.; Carole Boutte, Senior Researcher, U.S. Army Audio-Visual Activity, Pentagon, Washington, D.C.; Lieut. Colonel James W. Boyce, Austin, Texas; John Callf, Worcestershire, England; Phyllis Cassler, Reference and Interlibrary Loan Librarian, Carlisle Barracks, U.S. Army Office of Military History, Carlisle, Pennsylvania; Walter Cate, U.S. Air Force Still Photo Depository, Pentagon, Washington, D.C.; George Challou, Supervisory Archivist, General Archives Division, Washington National Records Center, Suitland, Maryland; Moreau Chambers, Staff Historian, Army Center of Military History, Washington, D.C.; T. C. Charman, Imperial War Museum, London; Peter Coats, London; Major-General David Cowan, CB, CBE, DSO, Hampshire, England; Danny Crawford, Research Historian, U.S. Marine Corps Historical Center, Washington Navy Yard, Washington, D.C.; Patrick Dempsey, Geography and Map Division, Library of Congress, Alexandria, Virginia; Lieut. General Sir Reginald Denning, KCVO, KBE, Kent, England; V. M. Destefano, Chief, Reference Library, U.S. Army Audio-Visual Activity, Pentagon, Washington, D.C.; Captain Rick DuCharme, Deputy Chief, Magazine and Book Branch, Air Force Information Office, Pentagon, Washington, D.C.; Gary Fitzpatrick, Reference Library, Geography and Map Division, Library of Congress, Alexandria, Virginia; Al Hardin, The Army Library, Pentagon, Washington, D.C.; Lieut. Colonel Jasper J. Harrington, USAF (Ret.), Montgomery, Alabama; Mary Haynes, Staff Historian, Army Center of Military History, Washington, D.C.; Major Peter Heffler, Chief, Magazine and Book Branch, Air Force Information Office, Pentagon, Washington, D.C.; Jack Jacoby, Chinese Section, East Asian Library, Columbia University, New York, New York; Captain Theodore Jessup, U.S. Air Force Still Photo Depository, Pentagon, Washington, D.C.; Amy Kahagin, Assistant Archivist, General Archives Division, Washington National Records Center, Suitland, Maryland; Jerry Kearns, Prints and Photographs Division, Library of Congress, Washington, D.C.; Dr. Lewis Kolodny, Baltimore, Maryland; Gene Kubal, The Army Library, Pentagon, Washington, D.C.; Edward M. Law-Yone, Durham, North Carolina; William H. Leary, National Archives and Records Service, Audio-Visual Division, Washington, D.C.; Ronald Lewin, Surrey, England; Donald S. Lopez, Assistant Director of Aeronautics, The National Air and Space Museum, The Smithsonian Institution, Washington, D.C.; Ernest R. McDowell, Chicago, Illinois; Neil L. Maurer, Editor, *Ex-CBI Roundup,* Laurens, Iowa; The Dowager Viscountess Monckton of Brenchley, CGE, London; Lieut. Colonel Brian Montgomery, London; Earl Mountbatten of Burma, KG, PC, GCB, DSO, FRS, Hampshire, England; Lynn Murphy, Public Information Officer, The National Air and Space Museum, The Smithsonian Institution, Washington, D.C.; Charlton Ogburn Jr., Oakton, Virginia; Thomas Oglesby, National Archives and Records Service, Audio-Visual Division, Washington, D.C.; Caroline Reed, Imperial War Museum, London; Dick Rossi, President, Flying Tigers Association, Fallbrook, California; James A. Shields, Assistant Archivist, Canadian Pacific Ltd., Montreal, Quebec; The Dowager Viscountess Slim, London; Brigadier The Rt. Hon. Sir John Smyth, BT, VC, MC, London; Glenn Sweeting, Assistant Curator of Aeronautics, The National Air and Space Museum, The Smithsonian Institution, Washington, D.C.; Joseph Thomas, National Archives and Records Service, Audio-Visual Division, Washington, D.C.; Lieut. General William H. Tunner, USAF (Ret.), Ware Neck, Virginia; Patricia Turner, Historian, Air Force Museum/RD, Wright Patterson Air Force Base, Ohio; Dr. George M. Watson, Office of History, Air Force Systems Command, Washington, D.C.; William Joe Webb, Staff Historian, Army Center of Military History, Washington, D.C.; Paul White, National Archives and Records Service, Audio-Visual Division, Washington, D.C.; Marie Yates, U.S. Army Audio-Visual Activity, Pentagon, Washington, D.C.

INDEX

Printed in U.S.A.